T0199140

FALLEN JUSTICE

A Mystery of Truth, Faith, and Reason

LEE WALLACE, AUTHOR
DR. PAM PRYFOGLE, EDD, CO-AUTHOR/EDITOR

WESTBOW
P R E S S®
A DIVISION OF THOMAS NELSON
& ZONDERVAN

WestBow Press books may be ordered through booksellers or by contacting:

WestBow Press
A Division of Thomas Nelson & Zondervan
1663 Liberty Drive
Bloomington, IN 47403
www.westbowpress.com
1 (866) 928-1240

ISBN: 978-1-9736-3856-8 (sc)
ISBN: 978-1-9736-3855-1 (hc)
ISBN: 978-1-9736-3857-5 (e)

Library of Congress Control Number: 2018910374

Print information available on the last page.

WestBow Press rev. date: 10/10/2018

Contents

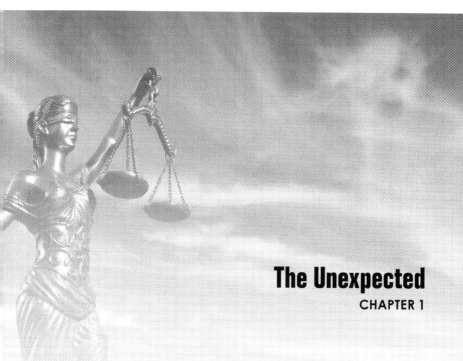

The Unexpected
CHAPTER 1

My life changed forever in unimaginable ways one busy morning with a phone call from my eldest daughter. From the tone of Lori's first words, I sensed that something was wrong, so I listened carefully as an earth-shattering story unfolded. She explained that the previous afternoon paramedics rushed Angie, a toddler attending her newly established daycare, to the hospital after she could not be awakened from a nap and was not expected to survive. Her words soccer-punched me in the stomach, made my heart skip several beats and left me breathless.

Lori gave me a quick summary of what happened but did not understand how a simple fall could have been so dangerous. Her two-year-old son and Angie were watching a video when they began jumping back and forth from the couch to the oak coffee table. Before going into the next room to care for her infant daughter, she sat them down again to enjoy the video but shortly she could hear that the children had resumed their frolicking. Suddenly, she heard a thud and Angie crying out, so she quickly returned to the living room to find the toddler lying on her back in front of the coffee table. Lori picked her up off the floor, hugged her, and checked for injuries or a bump on her head but found none and assumed Angie's groggy demeanor was from being overly tired. So, she prepared a bottle and laid her down for the scheduled afternoon nap.

Later that afternoon, she was unable to awaken Angie and noticed she was having trouble breathing and not responding to her voice and light shaking. Her immediate response was to give CPR and call 911 for help. A few minutes later, paramedics arrived and transported the unconscious child to the emergency room at the hospital. Mysteriously, neither Lori, paramedics, police, or emergency room doctors could see any signs of physical trauma or a head injury, although they were told about the short-distance fall.

Shortly after paramedics arrived, an army of police officers and detectives from the city police and county sheriff office showed up. As usually happens when there is an unexplained injury, police investigators asked Lori many questions and repeated them several times before audio recording only a part of the entire interview. Meanwhile, detectives asked her to compose a handwritten statement detailing the events of that afternoon. Without hesitation, she began doing as they instructed but had difficulty writing the events in their proper chronological order while answering their many questions and was concerned because police detectives would not allow her to rewrite the statement as she desperately needed to do.

During the phone call to me, my daughter asked me why the police photographer would ask her to take Angie's bottle out of the refrigerator and put it back in the playpen where Angie had been sleeping and take photos of it. I replied that was not proper protocol and it raised a red flag about his motives. He also snapped many photographs of the entire house as well as contents of the refrigerator and the outside of it where a scripture was posted that mentions patience as a fruit of the Holy Spirit. Lori was further puzzled as to why police questioned her about why she used the herbs, teas, and supplements in her kitchen.

She mentioned that due to the nature of their questioning, she was afraid they thought she might have done something to harm Angie. I agreed with her and recommended that she not say anything more to the police until she talked to an attorney. She replied that a friend from church already referred her to Attorney Wilson who was believed to be the best criminal attorney in town, and she and her husband had an appointment with him for the next morning. Without Lori asking for help, that same friend paid the $5,000 first deposit of the retainer to the attorney on her behalf.

After police left that evening, Lori phoned Angie's mother who told her that the doctors believed the prognosis was very bleak and Angie might not survive although the doctors had performed emergency brain surgery to relieve pressure on the brain caused by a skull fracture, severe swelling, and blood clots. Lori phoned her pastor at once to ask for special prayer for the toddler and her family and he agreed to put the request on the church prayer chain. He later also visited the grieving parents at the hospital to offer prayers and consolation.

Lori promised to call me if anything changed and I told her that I would be there as soon as possible, but first it would be necessary to find a paralegal to take over my one-girl law office while I was gone.

Resolving not to panic and make a scene at work, I retreated into an emotionless cocoon of shock for a couple of hours before informing my boss about the tragedy. He was very gracious and told me to call a temp agency and take off as long as needed since he realized it was a life-threatening event and the worst could happen.

The next morning my son-in-law called to tell me that when he and Lori were leaving the attorney's office, police arrested her on charges of child abuse. Thankfully, the police officers allowed him to drive away with their three small children before putting her in handcuffs and taking her to the county jail for booking.

After arranging to take time off work and finding a seasoned paralegal to temporarily do my job, I prepared for my trip to Reno. My son-in-law would need help caring for their children; a six-week-old infant daughter, a two-year-old son, and a six-year-old daughter. And I wanted to be an emotional support for them and get first-hand knowledge about what was happening.

Before daybreak the next morning, I began the long drive from Fresno, California to Reno, Nevada. The pain in my soul and the urgency of the unfolding calamity blurred the posted speed limit signs and my odometer. Fortunately, about an hour into the drive, a California Highway Patrol officer interrupted the daze I was in and stopped me for speeding.

He asked me, *"Do you know how fast you were going?"*

I replied, *"No, I don't."*

Then he told me, *"You were going ninety-five miles per hour."*

I replied tearfully, *"I am so sorry, but I am in a hurry to get to Reno because my daughter was arrested for child abuse and I need to get there right away to find out what happened and take care of her three children."*

He replied, *"Well, if you don't slow down you won't get there at all. If I issue a ticket based on your actual speed, it would require that you make a personal appearance in court, but since the court is far from your home, I will put a lower speed, so you won't have to appear before a judge personally."*

I thanked him profusely and promised to slow down and drive more carefully.

On that journey, there was plenty of time to think about what was happening and try to make sense of it. Confusion, questions, and prayers shot through my mind, piercing my heart and soul like laser beams trying to shed light on the unfolding tragedy. My conversation with God went something like this; *"Why is this taking place? What is the purpose of all this? Is this real or is it a bad dream? You say that all things work out for good to those who love you, so what good can come from my daughter being charged with child abuse?"* But, no answers came. I mumbled to myself, *"Surely, it must be a big mistake, and once police complete the investigation Lori will be released."* Although disturbed and confused by all that was happening, I knew we could endure any uncertain days ahead by faithfully relying on a loving and compassionate God. He promised to not allow us to suffer more than we can bear, since he would give strength and courage to overcome or walk-through any challenges ahead.

Recently Lori had been optimistic about the future because she had realized her dream of running her own licensed daycare business after more than a year of hard work and planning, getting the licenses, and buying business liability insurance. More importantly, only six weeks before she had given birth to a beautiful baby girl and was rejoicing because of all the good things that were happening.

The Sunday evening before the tragedy I had called her once again to ask how my new granddaughter was doing after being hospitalized for several days with a life-threatening lung infection. Lori had taken the baby to church that morning just as I suggested and seemed refreshed and energized to start a new week. She did not mention any extra stress that could have caused a lack of control on her part. Besides, I knew it was not her instinct to express her frustrations by becoming physically aggressive. Instead she expressed her emotions verbally, and if she had accidentally or impulsively hurt Angie in any way, she would have been unable to keep quiet about it.

I recalled my visit two weeks before (Presidents' Day weekend) to see my newborn granddaughter for the first time while she was in the hospital. That Saturday morning, I agreed to stay home and take care of the two older children while Lori went to deliver her breast milk for the nurses to feed her baby daughter and to spend time nurturing her.

While she was gone, a woman by the name of Colleen Rison telephoned to check out the possibility of using the daycare center starting in two days, Monday. To screen the phone caller, I asked Colleen if she had references from prior daycare providers that Lori could check out. She replied that she had none because several friends and relatives had watched her daughter on an as needed basis, but she had now taken a full-time job and needed a regular sitter. I told her that Lori would return her call when she returned from the hospital.

During the next week I phoned Lori a few times to see how my new granddaughter, Bella, was doing, how the advertisements for new children were working, if she had hired an assistant, and whether Colleen had enrolled her child. Lori told me that she and Colleen met Sunday afternoon to discuss childcare. They had made an agreement that included a discounted childcare rate due to Colleen's financial limitations and Angie started attending daycare the very next day which was a legal holiday.

During one of our phone calls that week, Lori told me that on the first day at childcare Angie had a severe diaper rash with painful raw sores. To correct the problems, Lori tested the absorbency of her diapers, and found they failed the test. So, she used diapers from her children's supplies and instructed Colleen to take care of the problem by buying better diapers and using ointment to help with healing. Also, Lori said that Angie had a bruise on the hollow part of her cheek on the first day at childcare but decided it must have resulted from falling, as toddlers often do, and decided not to make a big deal about it.

Several times during that week, Lori joyfully described Angie as the cutest little thing with big blue eyes and blondish hair who meshed very nicely with everyone in the family and played enthusiastically with her two-year-old son. She told me that she hoped and prayed that all the new daycare children would be just like Angie because she was a perfect fit.

Lori planned to run the daycare business until all three of her children were full-time students and then perhaps she would sell the business or set up a franchise company to duplicate her systems so that other mothers could be more financially secure. Common sense told me that it was implausible that she would carelessly do any impetuous or dangerous act that would jeopardize her goals of successfully running her newly established business which she had worked so hard to set up.

Regardless, some people live a double life, and I wondered if she was one of those people. No matter what the evidence should turn out to be, I vowed to keep an open mind and always seek the truth. While on my way, I prayed that all the questions about the tragedy would be answered by my arrival and that authorities would release Lori to go home and take care of her children. Besides, I could think of nothing that pointed to anything in her personality or character that would cause her to abuse a child and concluded that the charges against her must have been a terrible mistake of gigantic proportions.

Shortly after arriving in Reno, Lori's husband called from work telling me that despite what the doctors tried to do, they were not able to save Angie's life. A bitter cold whirlwind of shock, grief, devastation, confusion, and disbelief engulfed me all at once, immobilizing me. After hanging up the phone, I sat frozen on the couch for what seemed like an eternity; my head was spinning while trying to process what was happening and wondering what I should do next.

While sitting there, many other questions came to mind, such as: Why had God allowed this child to die? Why had God allowed this to happen to my daughter? How would it all end? I had no answers. I prayed that God would comfort the family of the deceased child and reveal the truth. This tragedy surely was not happening! It felt like the devil was a roaring lion, taking charge of this world, and winning in his quest to devour lives and destroy families. I remembered the scripture in I Peter 5:8 [AKJV] that says:

> Be sober, be vigilant; because your adversary the devil, as a roaring lion, walketh about, seeking whom he may devour.

Dark clouds of grief and anxiety overwhelmed me when I realized that most certainly the police would upgrade the criminal charges to murder unless authorities quickly discovered another reason for the child's head injuries and death. The indescribable anguish was more gut-wrenching and heart-piercing than anything I ever had experienced. Like an earthquake, it violently shook Lori, her husband, and me to the very core of our being and made us wonder if we would overcome this or if we would crumble into a thousand pieces and be unable to function.

I was encouraged when I remembered that many prior disappointments and difficulties had been survived by leaning on God's grace and mercy, and I hoped this would be no different. I recalled my childhood of being hungry, unloved, unwanted, and being sexually violated. As an adult I had survived divorces, broken relationships, miscarriage of a child, periods of unemployment, life-threatening lung disease, foreclosure on my home, seriously ill children, single-parenting four children, a heart attack, and deaths of several family members. All those difficulties made me more resilient and aware that God would enable us to also endure and overcome this calamity. I believed He would give us the strength to fight whatever battles were ahead and not collapse.

My immediate and extended families were unaware of what was

happening but now it was time to let them know that the police had arrested Lori on charges of murder by child abuse. Since she had never given anyone a single day of trouble or concern, I hoped they would react sympathetically to her plight. The first phone call was to my elderly bed-ridden mother to tell her and ask her to let the rest of the family know what was happening. She was sympathetic and non-judgmental and agreed to quickly spread the word to my sisters, brothers, and other family members. One by one, each of my seven sisters and two brothers called to offer help. My family was amazingly supportive and became an integral part of the journey ahead.

I asked myself how did we arrive at this critical moment in our lives that contradicted everything known about Lori and what she believed? The roads we traveled had been paved with good intentions, prayer, preparation, and sometimes careful planning but despite all that, all plans were now on hold because of circumstances beyond our control. What lessons would we learn from this tragedy? Where and how did it all start? Did it begin with Lori's family needing more income to buy necessities? Or, was it all part of His providential plan with a more significant purpose and goal?

An unforeseen complication arose because of Lori's incarceration at the county jail. Her pediatrician had instructed that breast milk was critical for her new-born daughter's recovery from the lung infection. During the first two days of incarceration, the jailers were kind enough to let her to pump the breast milk and allow her husband to deliver it to the infant's caretaker, but after the second day they no longer allowed it. As an alternative, she asked for permission to pump her breast milk and discard it, but the jailers refused. Instead, they tightly bound her breasts with visibly dirty and unsanitary towels to stop the leaking. Lori's breasts became painfully engorged, and during a collect call to me a few days later, she complained that her breasts were not only extremely sore, but that she had a fever, felt ill, and was unable to sleep. This news made me extremely concerned as I had heard of mastitis and sepsis developing from blockage of milk ducts.

The overall conditions at the county jail were very scary, depressing, and unsanitary. The showers were moldy, and the toilets, floors, and walls were strikingly dirty. The food was barely edible, and the water was undrinkable. Also, the deputies were very hostile, and, on several occasions, she saw them taking their frustrations out on inmates without provocation, making her fearful for her own personal well-being.

Lori's bedding consisted of a hard four-inch mat, only one blanket, and no pillow. Since arrival, she had been cold and could not stop shivering and shaking. There was no detectable heating source in the jail, even though daytime outdoor temperatures during March averaged in the forties and fifties.

Lori was placed in 24-hour solitary confinement to protect her from inmates who may have seen the massive news coverage and might try to harm her. Jailers told her that she would have twenty minutes out of her cell each day to take a shower and make a phone call, but some days the jailers neglected or forgot to arrange time for it. After learning of her extreme grief and despair, her attorney asked that she be placed on suicide watch. The jail followed his request and always stationed an attendant outside the cell to watch her.

The jail allowed us to visit her on the fifth day of incarceration at a designated time but only through a thick glass window with a phone intercom. Lori said the 24-hour solitary confinement was almost unbearable and she feared it could make her lose her mind. She had little to do except read and listen to the painful groaning and crying out of other inmates and she was too depressed to exercise in the small cell. Upon arrival, a jailer had told her that no reading material was allowed but several days later she was informed that a soft-covered Bible would be okay. So, she asked me to bring one to her. Before I could do that, a kind jailer brought her one, and she said reading it during her very long days and nights brought her clarity, comfort, and strength. Also, she mentioned that humming praise songs lifted her spirits and brought relief from her inexplicable misery.

During one visit, Lori explained to me that an astonishing thing had happened the previous night. She had been bone-chillingly cold since arrival and felt as if she was experiencing hypothermia and would surely die, but the jailers denied her request for an added blanket. In deep despair, Lori cried out to God for help. Miraculously, the Holy Spirit enveloped her body and mind and brought such comfort and warmth that she could sleep for the first time since arrival. She beamed as she told me she was at peace while experiencing God's love in a real and personal way and was thankful for the gift.

Of course, the natural human questions were; Why would God only wink at her and bless her in this smaller way, but not resolve the criminal charges against her and get her out of this miserable place? Why did God only answer this one prayer in a straightforward and personal way? Mysterious for sure!! The miracle gave me reassurance that God was listening and reminded me of a familiar scripture:

Isaiah 55:8-9 (KJV) For my thoughts are not your thoughts, neither are your ways my ways, saith the LORD. For as the heavens are higher than the earth, so are my ways higher than your ways, and my thoughts than your thoughts.

Lori talked to me about interesting things she experienced at the jail. Such as, the female guard assigned to her suicide watch who would sit outside her cell every day reading the Bible and talking about spiritual things but then a few minutes later would be extremely cruel, disrespectful, and rude to her and the other inmates. She wondered how the deputy could reconcile the conflicting behaviors, but this was not the first or last of such hypocrisies Lori experienced on her journey.

In the beginning, Lori feared her children would be further traumatized by seeing her behind bars and decided they should not visit her. But after a few days, she changed her mind because she was missing them so very much and we brought her two older children who were two and six years old to visit her. But they were too young to understand what was happening. The children were emotionally disturbed and confused by her absence and often cried themselves to sleep at night. When I visited, I prayed with them and gently rubbed their backs until they fell asleep. While trying to answer their many questions, I would tell them that their mom loved them dearly, but she had a problem with the court and the judge said she had to stay there for now but that she would be home as soon as she could. Although not an answer they could fully understand or accept, it was all I could think to say.

Since the day of her arrest, news reporters with their vehicles and TV cameras camped out on the streets in front of Lori's residence hoping for an interview with family members. There was an immediate explosion of TV and newspaper coverage about her arrest for murdering Angie. "Breaking News" often interrupted regularly scheduled TV shows, with the slightest turn of events, usually with a police mugshot of Lori, depicting her as a child abuser and killer. The stories continued to dominate the local TV and newspaper media with many pictures of her, the deceased child, and describing a horrible crime against a helpless toddler by a violent daycare provider.

During all this chaos and uncertainty, we were trying to figure out what was happening and how to resolve it. We would rely on Lori's attorney to give us answers about what to expect.

Miracles of Mercy and Grace

Shortly before Lori's first court appearance, one of my sisters and her husband, and my son-in-law (Lori's husband) and I met with Attorney Wilson who had already been paid a $5,000 retainer by a church friend of Lori. While discussing the case, he explained the Nevada criminal process and gave us a better understanding of what we could expect to happen in the days ahead.

It was a shock to learn that he needed a non-refundable flat fee retainer of $100,000, plus investigative and court costs to defend Lori through the trial phase. After I explained that we did not have that much money but would try to raise it by asking friends and family for donations, he agreed to accept payment in three installments. On that basis, one of Lori's aunts quickly volunteered to withdraw money from her retirement account to pay the first payment. Encouraged by this first step, I felt compelled to sign the *"Non-Refundable Flat Fee Retainer Agreement"* promising to do something that I knew only God could make happen. I was uncertain as to whether my extended family and friends could come up with the remaining money needed, especially on such short notice. That was an enormous amount even for our entire extended family and seemed like an impossible mountain to climb. We would need a miracle.

Also, at that first meeting with Lori's attorney, we discussed the issue of bail, and he informed us he would ask the judge to release her on her own recognizance with no bail. But he thought bail might be set between $100,000 and $200,000, based on the weakness of the state's case, Lori's lack of any criminal record, and her strong ties to local family and friends. Then he referred us to a local bail bondsperson that he had worked with and trusted, to start the required paperwork for posting bail.

I knew that sometimes a miracle can only happen when we act in faith to do our part, so I swallowed my pride and started asking people for contributions. It was our prayer that God would burden the hearts and minds of family members and friends who knew Lori and compel them to give generously to pay her attorney fees plus bail premiums of up to $20,000.

If attorney fees were not collected, our only alternative would be to ask the court to appoint a public defender. But we were told that it would be a "kiss of death," as they were usually assigned at random with no regard for their prior experience or ability to defend against murder by child abuse charges.

A few days after our meeting we learned there would be an autopsy of the deceased child, and I informed Attorney Wilson that we needed to hire an Independent Medical Examiner (IME) to attend and observe the autopsy. I also asked that he not allow harvesting of the child's organs since they might have crucial forensic evidence needed for Lori's defense. Those recommendations came from an attorney friend of mine who was a retired prosecutor for the US Justice Department. But for unknown reasons, Attorney Wilson refused to act on either recommendation and seemed annoyed that I had discussed the case with my attorney friend.

Arraignment and Bail Hearing Results

Lori's first arraignment on charges of child abuse was on calendar in the County Justice Court for Thursday, March 14, 1996. Several of Lori's friends, family members and I packed the courtroom to show our support and learn what was next. At the hearing, prosecutors said that since the injured toddler had died after they filed the child abuse complaint, they were cancelling the arraignment and referring the case to a grand jury seeking an indictment for "murder by child abuse."

At that hearing, Attorney Wilson asked the judge to release Lori on her own recognizance. The judge did not agree to that request but set bail at $100,000, over the strenuous objections of the prosecuting attorney who demanded that it be $1,000,000.00. The bail amount was meager considering the serious charges filed against Lori. However, the judge said he made his decision based upon the weak evidence in the case, the fact that Lori had no prior arrests or convictions and was a low flight risk because of strong ties to family and the community. We believed the low bail was a miracle and made her release more likely. Understandably, the judge ordered that a condition of her release on bail was that she could have no physical contact with any children, including her own until further order of the court.

As soon as the hearing was over, I called friends and family with a more exact estimate of funds needed for posting bail at once so that Lori could be released by the weekend. The bail bondsperson had given us a quick overview of the bail-posting process. In addition to the premiums needed, it would also be necessary to pledge $100,000 worth of assets as security, either in the form of a guaranteed bank account or a pledge of equity in real estate. Fortunately, one of my sisters and her husband had enough equity in their residence in Reno and willingly pledged that house as security. It was my duty to collect donations of $12,000 for the premiums and associated cost and to take a cashier check to the title insurance company by close of business the next day, Friday.

The bail bondsperson explained the dynamics of the county jail and how to make sure all went smoothly to facilitate Lori's safe release and trip home. He instructed us not to say anything to Lori by phone or in person about when bail is posted or the expected timing of her release. Based on his experience, he knew the info would leak to news reporters and be announced on local TV instantly as breaking news and that would create more hysteria. Demonstrators outside the jail and courthouse who were picketing against her release would increase in number and try to assault her. The grandmother of the deceased child organized the demonstrations that were promoted by local TV and newspaper media.

The bondsperson explained that the various news venues had their stooges in the jail system who habitually leaked information to the media about prisoner releases in high-profile cases such as this one. Since various news outlets were competing for the latest scoop of events in the case, it was more likely to happen. He also informed us that it usually takes from twenty-four to forty-eight hours after posting bail for jailers to release an inmate. He promised to do his best to speed up the process because of the extenuating circumstances and the danger it would present to Lori's safety if the information was known by the media and public before her release.

Our goal was to get my extremely distressed daughter safely released from jail by the weekend which looked like an impossibility without God's intervention. Our bank accounts were empty, and we had less than two days to collect funds from family members and friends who promised to send money by electronic wire, bank transfers or overnight mail. The deadline for depositing of all premiums and costs for processing bail was 5 p.m. on Friday with the title insurance company. We spent most of two days rushing around, either meeting with the bail bondsperson, doing paperwork, or going from one place to another collecting Western Union funds or overnight deliveries of cashier checks from family and friends.

In fact, an unexpected and troublesome delay occurred that Friday afternoon when, after receiving a phone confirmation, we went to pick up the last contribution which was $2000 wired from my brother in Michigan. When trying to obtain the funds, the Western Union cashier noticed that my driver license had expired a few weeks before. Since I had no acceptable identification, she would not allow me to receive the cash. Stunned by this news, I asked her to make an exception this one time and explained the reason why. After understanding the urgency of our plight, the cashier whispered that she could not help us, but the Western Union found in the Washoe Inn and Casino a few blocks away would cash anything, and there should be no problem getting the cash from them.

After thanking her profusely, we ran quickly on foot to the Washoe casino which was unforgettable. It seemed we had stepped into a time machine and were visiting a century-old wild west casino that was ideal for pictures and an expose in the National Geographic Magazine. The dirty, antiquated, smoke-filled casino was packed with crusty, wrinkled, and unhappy faces of an assortment of men and women who were being held hostage by their gambling disease.

True to her reputation, the Western Union clerk at the Washoe did not even ask for an ID and paid me the funds with only the wire confirmation number. It was after 4 p.m. when we collected that last sum, so we jogged several blocks back to the car and rushed to the bank to get a certified check for the entire amount. If not done on by 5 p.m., Lori would not be released by the weekend. And it would be Monday before bail could be posted which could mean she would spend another four or five days behind bars.

The Friday afternoon traffic was moving very slow, so I phoned the title company and asked the legal officer, Jennifer, to wait for us since we were on our way. We arrived at precisely 5:05 p.m. and could not get into the building as the doors were locked. When an employee exited the front door, she agreed to find Jennifer for us.

Upon receipt of the cashier check and signatures on the property lien, Jennifer informed the New York bonding company and instructed them to ship the bail bond via Fed-Ex marked for early Saturday morning delivery to the local bail bondsperson. Otherwise, if the package did not arrive before 10 a.m. on Saturday morning, there would be little chance of Lori getting released that weekend. We all prayed that God would smooth the way so that Lori could be released by the next morning.

Later that evening, I visited Lori and informed her that we had not been able to complete business by 5 p.m. and it would be Monday or Tuesday before bail could be posted. This miss-information or half-truth was made so she would not be disappointed if the bond did not arrive promptly on Saturday morning. But it was also intended to mislead the jailers to prevent them from inevitably leaking the timing of her expected release to the TV news media. During our visit, Lori was physically ill due to the infection in her engorged breast and the stress of all that was happening. I encouraged her to hang on and not despair because it was just a matter of time (Monday or Tuesday) until she would be free.

As mentioned, secrecy was vital to prevent the TV media and newspapers from stirring up more public outrage and hysteria. Public demonstrations were already taking place at the jail because of her expected release and the low bail set for a "monster" who they believed had killed an innocent toddler.

Although he could not guarantee the bond would be posted with the jail before 10 a.m. on Saturday, he assured us he would do his best and agreed to telephone Lori's husband as soon as it happened. In anticipation of it, he said we should be up early and be ready when he called to go to the jail and get Lori before the news could be revealed to the public via the media stooges at the jail.

The next morning a few minutes after 9 a.m., the bondsperson called to say his job was done and we should go pick her up. Lori's husband, one of my sisters and I rushed to the jail. While on our way, we were surprised by a phone call from Lori saying she was already out and would be hiding behind one of the massive concrete columns in front of the jail, hoping that no one in the jailhouse crowd would recognize her.

Upon arriving at the jail, my son-in-law parked at the curb directly in front of the building and my sister and I ran as fast as we could up the stairs and noticed her hiding behind a large concrete column. By the time we reached her, several people in the crowd had already found her and started feverishly yelling obscenities at her, including remarks like: *"Baby killer." "Murderer." "I'm going to kill you."* and *"You deserve to die."* Getting even closer to our faces, they were ready to attack. We did not respond in any manner to the hysteria of the crowd except to shield and protect her from them. My sister and I each grabbed one of her arms and helped her walk swiftly to the car.

As soon as Lori sat down in the front seat, we reclined the back of it, so the public and news people would not recognize her and try to follow us. From the stress of it all, she blacked out as soon as we drove away. When she became conscious, she asked for water because the putrid jailhouse water was not drinkable, and she was very thirsty, so we promptly found a market and bought cold bottled water for her. The entire disturbing event was surreal and a nightmare that I never imagined any of my children would ever experience.

We had arranged for Lori to stay at her aunt and uncle's house in another part of town hoping that TV cameras and newspaper reporters camped out at her residence (ten days after the tragedy) could not find her. This home proved to be a haven where she could have peace while recuperating from the traumas she had endured without the demanding news reporters.

As soon as Lori arrived home, she wanted and needed a bath. After being in jail for ten days with no shower or clean clothes with leaky breast milk and secretion of normal afterbirth bodily fluids, her body reeked of a putrid deathly smell that is hard to describe. A very weak, mentally exhausted, and emotionally distraught Lori sank into the bubble bath and scrubbed off the scum and dead cells that encrusted her body.

During her bath, she was trembling, sobbing and at times talking incessantly and incoherently while trying to wrap her head around all that was happening to her. In my motherly way, I wanted to console her by letting her know that all who knew her, believed in her innocence, and with God's help she and I would get through this nightmare. When Lori finished bathing, she enjoyed putting on new pajamas that her aunt bought her, and then tried to relax with a clean body for the first time in ten days.

During all of this, realizing that Lori had a significant and worrisome fever, extremely sore, red-streaked, swollen, and infected breasts, it was necessary to phone her OB/GYN doctor to ask for help. The doctor knew about the situation and did not hesitate to conduct a phone conference with Lori and prescribe a strong antibiotic for the infection, as well as an anti-anxiety medicine to help her get through the PTSD that had engulfed her like an unrelenting and overpowering thunderstorm. The doctor mentioned that the breast infection was causing the fever and further delay in treatment would have caused her to become more gravely ill, especially if Sepsis should develop.

While trying to decompress from her earth-shattering experiences, Lori needed someone to listen to her pent-up frustrations and anxieties. The right words were hard to find, but I tried to console her by letting her know that we believed in her innocence and were praying for a successful outcome. I reminded her that God promised that some good would come from the hurt and pain she was going through and would give her strength to go through whatever the future brought. However, I was not confident that she could process what I was saying because of her highly emotional and exhausted condition and that she needed me to just listen.

Seeing my daughter in this broken state brought soul-piercing and gut-wrenching emotional pain. Lori had had always tried to live an exemplary life and habitually did her best by taking the moral high ground at whatever she tried to do. Nothing about this made any sense, and I continually asked God why it was happening. In a few moments of dark despair, I had a spiritual epiphany when I realized that the anguish that permeated every cell of our bodies was in a very small way like what Christ and His mother must have felt when He was unjustly accused and then crucified. Everyone, including the public and ruling classes, except for his mother and a few others, believed he was the worst criminal and wanted Him dead. Similarly, we were also fighting against the seemingly unlimited power of the ruling authorities and the public who were intent on prosecuting Lori for murder.

Although we had worked diligently to get Lori released from jail by Saturday morning, we considered it a miracle that this was done since it was not under our human control. We were feeling incredibly blessed and grateful for our extended family, close Christian friends, and new acquaintances who voluntarily prayed, sent money, and helped in various ways to get the bail bond posted quickly. Despite my confusion over why God had allowed this entire tragedy to happen, I realized Lori's release from jail and her ability to obtain prompt medical treatment was a miracle from God. It was as if we were standing at the edge of an ocean too vast and stormy to think about controlling or crossing to the other side without God's help, and He had not forgotten us.

After resting for several weeks and taking her medication, Lori felt much better physically. But emotionally she was suffering not only because of the tragic death of Angie, her anguish was magnified by being criminally charged with murder and the excessive TV and newspaper articles about the tragedy. The news depicted her as a cold-hearted murderer and created public outrage and hysteria that threatened Lori's emotional well-being and personal safety. It also diminished the chances of finding an unbiased jury pool and having a fair trial.

One condition of her release on bail by the criminal court was that she could have no contact with her three children without supervision until completion of the CPS investigation and approval of the criminal and family law courts. The hospitality offered by her aunt and uncle to stay at their home at no cost was a huge blessing and made compliance with the court order possible without added expense.

In the meantime, trouble was brewing at the courthouse as the public and family of the deceased were enraged that Lori had been released on bail. These events prompted Prosecutors Bird and Snuffelpaw to file a *"Motion to Increase Bail,"* to $500,000. A hearing on the motion was scheduled for three weeks away.

To our shock and horror, the bail hearing began by state Prosecutor Snuffelpaw announcing that the Reno Metro Police were investigating a second case against Lori for child abuse of her eldest child and it was his understanding that charges would be filed soon. This rhetoric proved to be a hyperbolic stretch of his imagination and a distortion of facts to sway the court to increase the bail. Prosecutors also argued that the original judge who set the low bail was uninformed and did not know all the facts of the case.

Fortunately, Attorney Wilson was at the hearing to defend Lori and replied that the state was trying to use the bail as punishment and that was not its purpose. He also informed the judge that the Washoe Family Court had stepped in and the children were out of the home and not living with Lori and someone else had been appointed guardian over the children. He also argued that if another case is filed, that bail hearing would be set for another day and the only issue to be discussed was whether Lori was a flight risk or danger to the community.

Lori's supporters in the courtroom were caught off guard by the new allegation that most of us knew was untrue. But, it seemed as if prosecutors were in an alternate universe and were trying to obliterate the one where truth and justice lived. Why?

Finally, the judge ruled that the existing $100,000 bail was enough and denied the state's motion. However, he reminded Lori not to have any personal contact with any minor children (under 18 years old) unless agreed to by Child Protective Services (CPS) and not to be involved in childcare in any way. The refusal of the judge to increase bail was truly a miracle considering the public outrage and hysteria caused by excessive news coverage with the specific intent of putting pressure on the judicial system and prosecutors to do something about Lori's low bail amount.

We breathed a huge sigh of relief and thanked God, as the court's ruling meant that Lori would not have to go back to jail while waiting for the outcome of the trial. That was an enormous accomplishment as it would have been humanly impossible for us to pledge security of $500,000 since the property that was available was only worth about $175,000 and there were no other available assets in Nevada. Additionally, we did not have the 10% cash ($50,000) that would have been needed to pay the new bond premium.

As previously mentioned, when our extended families and friends who lived in other areas and states heard of Lori's need for financial support, they voluntarily agreed to contribute what they could, and we started getting contributions in small increments from seven different states. Regardless, we still did not have quite enough to finish paying attorney fees. Our efforts were successful as we raised enough funds to pay the final installment owed to the attorney. It was encouraging that many friends and extended families were willing to go the extra mile to extend their compassion and love.

Grand Jury Hearing
CHAPTER 2

The circumstantial events of the tragedy, emergency room doctor statements, the coroner's autopsy, along with media and public outrage caused the district attorney (prosecutors) to conduct a grand jury investigation looking for an "Indictment for Open Murder" which could include 1st or 2nd Degree Murder, Voluntary or Involuntary Manslaughter. [The grand jury hearing is designed to investigate whether there is enough evidence to go forward to trial.] The circumstantial evidence against Lori consisted primarily of the fact that she was the caretaker of Angie the afternoon of the tragedy and had no supporting witness to confirm the short-distance fall and what did or did not happen. Evidence against her primarily consisted of assumptions and opinions of emergency room doctors and the coroner who swore the injuries were non-accidental.

Perplexed by why there was a referral to a grand jury in this case, I consulted with several attorneys including a former prosecutor at the US Department of Justice. He explained that a grand jury hearing is a tool used primarily in circumstantial cases when prosecutors think a judge might not be inclined to find there is enough legal grounds to prosecute someone for murder. Instead, a grand jury has the power of subpoenaing anyone and everyone they feel necessary, and it is common knowledge that a grand jury will "indict a ham sandwich" when instructed to do so by the prosecutor. He explained that this phenomenon is well known among the legal community and the process is nothing more than a rubber stamp for whatever charges the prosecutor's office requests. And, he explained that we should not expect anything different unless Lori's defense attorneys could find a way to persuade state prosecutors to do further forensic investigations before the hearing. His opinion was that Lori should testify at the grand jury hearing to give her account of what happened since she was the only person who knew precisely what occurred that afternoon, and it was the only chance of her not getting an indictment. These recommendations were given to Lori's defense attorney, but for some unknown reason, he decided she should not testify at the hearing and saw no need to conduct or ask for any further forensic investigation.

In hindsight, it is obvious that the prosecutors knew that if a *"Preliminary Hearing"* was held instead of a grand jury hearing, a more legally savvy judge could refuse to prosecute without them presenting evidence of malice aforethought on the part of Lori. Consequently, to assure that murder charges would be filed and avoid further public hysteria and outrage, they chose to refer the case to a grand jury. Although such manipulative games by prosecutors may be considered legal, the question remains as to whether they advance the pursuit of justice.

From reading the transcript, it was also clear that the prosecuting attorney presiding over the grand jury hearing had only one goal in mind and that was to obtain an indictment against Lori. His questioning of various people, including first responders, police investigators, the mother, and father of the deceased, and two of the attending physicians at the emergency room, produced no specific concrete evidence or testimony (except for opinions of doctors and coroner) of what caused the child's injuries and death.

The Indictment

Based on a majority vote of twelve to fifteen after hearing only circumstantial evidence and speculation by medical doctors, the grand jury issued an indictment that included all possible scenarios when they declared:

> The Defendant(s) above named, LORI WATSON, accused by the Washoe County Grand Jury of the crimes of MURDER [OPEN MURDER, a Felony – NRS 200.010, 200.030, 200.508], committed at and within the County of Washoe, State of Nevada, on or between March 4, 1996, and March 6, 1996, as follows:

> Defendant did, on or about March 4, 1996, then and there willfully, feloniously, without authority of law, and with malice aforethought, kill Angie Rison, a human being; the Defendant being responsible under the following theories of criminal liability, to wit: (1) premeditation and deliberation, and/or (2) by the Defendant subjecting Angie Rison, a minor child being approximately 14 months of age, to acts of child abuse, including violent shaking of the body of Angie Rison and/or throwing the body of Angie Rison against a hard surface and/or the striking of the body of Angie Rison with an object and/or by other manner or means unknown, which resulted in the death of Angie Rison on or about March 6, 1996.

As the above alludes to, police investigators had no specific evidence showing how the alleged crime was committed. So, prosecutors made multiple alternative allegations in the indictment as to how the child's head injuries (violent shaking and/or throwing and/or striking, and/or unknown means) and later death happened. Therefore, the indictment held two theories of criminal liability, either (1) murder with malice aforethought, premeditation and deliberation, or (2) murder by child abuse (Felony Murder). The prosecuting attorneys used this comprehensive no-fail multi-faceted strategy to make sure there was an indictment. Consequently, the overly broad allegations made room for evidence they might discover later to support a conviction of murder. They were merely guessing that Lori had murdered by child abuse because she was the only adult at the scene on the afternoon of the tragedy. This speculation combined with the opinions of non-forensic emergency room doctors and the coroner autopsy report resulted in the indictment. In keeping with the common practice of many prosecutors; were they intentionally charging Lori with Open Murder and hoping that the ambiguity of the charges would pressure her to plead guilty to a lesser degree of murder and avoid a trial?

It felt as if my thoughts were being fed through a paper shredder and the pieces were blown away by the wind. Nothing made any logical sense. In my deep despair and confusion, there were profound questions that needed to be answered, such as: Why would God allow this to happen when Lori's children needed her so very much during their formative years? Was there anything that I was blind to in my daughter's character that hinted she was capable of child abuse and murder? How is it possible that a crime of such horrific magnitude could be committed by someone who was a practicing Christian with a generous and upright moral character? How had God allowed this entire tragedy to happen in the first place?

Although God did not give me answers to my many questions, I knew I could rely on Him. His Holy Spirit gave Lori and me strength, comfort, and courage enough to endure the earth-shattering events and wait for the answers. In quiet moments of reflection and during stormy days, it was comforting and encouraging to remember the instructions in Philippians 4:6-7, (NIV):

> Be anxious for nothing, but in everything, by prayer and supplication with gratitude, make your requests known to God. And the peace of God, which surpasses all understanding, will protect your hearts and minds through Christ Jesus.

We were experiencing the reality that life on this earth is not always fair and bad things sometimes happen to good people. Even after the grand jury indictment, Lori, I, and many others continued praying that God would intervene and clear Lori of any wrongdoing. In my human way of thinking, I reasoned that God would want that to happen. Why would he not?

Multiple Overlapping Investigations
CHAPTER 3

There were several simultaneous, overlapping, and distinct police investigations into different events being conducted by CPS and the local police department under the auspices of the district attorney and family court. The CPS investigations were happening only because of the ongoing criminal case and extenuating circumstances, such as Lori having three very young children of her own. But they reported their findings to the district attorney's office and the family court.

Additionally, Defense Attorney Wilson tried to find out what happened by hiring private investigators to prove Lori did not commit child abuse. This strategy was necessary because, in these highly emotional cases, the scales of justice tip in favor of the prosecution which forces a defendant to disprove the allegations against him. After the defense investigator talked to every parent for whom Lori had ever babysat, he found no report of possible or suspected abuse, except the child Lori had mentioned to them who had fallen from the highchair several weeks previously.

When investigating the living conditions of the deceased and the possible causes of her injuries, the defense investigator found that potential witnesses who knew Angie Rison's family were sympathetic to the family's tragic loss and unwilling to talk. Although the defense attorney interviewed a couple of medical experts, neither were hired to conduct a thorough examination of any forensic medical issues and legal evidence.

The first police investigation began the afternoon of the tragedy when detectives specializing in investigating child abuse cases were sent to the alleged crime scene. On their way to Lori's house they learned about two three-year-old unsubstantiated phone calls made to CPS reporting suspected abuse by Lori. Although they also knew that CPS filed no criminal abuse charges and no follow up visits were necessary, the phone calls were red flags that made them conclude they were dealing with an open and shut case of child abuse.

Investigators found nothing out of order, broken or upset at the crime scene, so they did not see the need to search for DNA residue or fingerprints on any surfaces, such as the coffee table. The only item of evidence mysteriously confiscated was a newborn milk bottle having six ounces of milk (erroneously thought to be Angie's bottle). Additionally, the police detectives, paramedics, and doctors found no physical marks, hand prints, other broken bones or injuries on Angie that would show she had been hit, thrown, or slammed against anything.

Overriding all circumstantial evidence were the hasty statements made by the attending emergency room who said that the injuries were too severe to have happened accidentally and were equivalent to falling from a two-story [approx. 20 feet) building onto concrete. They said that some form of intentional child abuse caused the injuries and police considered the two doctors' words as gospel even though neither doctor was board certified, trained or experienced as a forensic medical examiner, biomechanical engineer, accident reconstructions/analyst, pediatric neurologist, or pediatric forensic examiner.

The police detectives in charge of investigating the alleged crime later testified that they completed their investigation by 11:00 p.m. the evening of the tragedy and concluded that a violent crime had occurred although they found nothing at the scene or visible on the body of Angie to show that had happened.

The primary goal of the prosecution continuing their investigation after 11 pm on the day of tragedy was to find instances of child abuse by Lori against other children. If found, that would bolster and solidify the state's case by proving that Lori was a habitual child abuser with a malignant and depraved heart and a callous indifference to human life. With that goal in mind, detectives interviewed parents of every child for whom Lori had ever given childcare, looking for evidence of abuse in her history. Confident she had nothing to hide, she had provided them with a list of their names and contact information.

We waited impatiently thinking that all criminal charges against Lori would be dismissed once the various investigations were completed. I often thought of the scripture in John 8:32 (NKJV) that says, *"And you will know the truth, and the truth shall make you free."* Although that scripture refers to freedom that regeneration through faith in Christ brings a person, a broader interpretation could also apply to Lori's tragic dilemma.

Without first asking whether an interview could be arranged legally and voluntarily under a more proper environment, two police detectives went to Reno Christian School and illegally interrogated Lori's six-year-old daughter, Tanasha. They asked questions about her mother's treatment of her. Fortunately, Tanasha asked the teacher to stay with her during the questioning, and the teacher was able to accurately convey what Tanasha said to the detectives. The teacher disputed an essential word in the written report made by the detectives wherein they had altered Tanasha's statement from, *"My mommy used to spank me but not anymore,"* to *"My mommy used to beat me but not anymore."* It was peculiar that the detectives did not record an audio of their conversation with Tanasha as they usually did when questioning someone.

More importantly, since the detectives had illegally gathered the so-called evidence by questioning a minor without permission, it was *"fruit from a poisonous tree,"* and any statements made by the six-year old to the detectives could not be legally used or quoted during any later court hearings. [*Silverthorne Lumber Co., Inc. v. United States*, 251 U.S. 385 (1920).] Regardless, state prosecutors recited the investigators' perverted version of Tanasha's words to influence the judge during many future court hearings.

Equally disturbing was that police investigators did not read Angie's hospital medical records given to them and the prosecutors' office. If they had, they would have seen a possibly exculpatory (favorable to defendant) pathology report issued by the hospital pathologist department concerning microscopic examination of the two tissue masses removed from her cerebellum during emergency brain surgery. The pathology report described the two tissue specimens, as follows:

> One container labeled "posterior fossa subdural hematoma" has within two portions of friable grayish-brown tissue measuring 1.2 cm and 1.4 cm in greatest dimension, respectively. Each are entirely submitted.

Under diagnosis it read;

> "Posterior Fossa, Oligodendroglioma and Hematoma."

Police negligently or intentionally overlooked the first pathology report which said the specimens not only held blood clots but also what appeared to be an Oligodendroglioma tumor (cancer) near the exact spot of the fracture. Additionally, the pathology report had a cancer screening sheet attached to it. At the very least, prudent, and unbiased investigators would have read the original hospital pathology report and recommended further medical forensic testing before going ahead to a grand jury hearing. However, since they had already decided Lori had committed a crime, there was no need to go down that road and be publicly embarrassed and lose credibility in the eyes of the public by not being able to indict Lori.

All the while, police investigators did not find it necessary to consider the dynamics of the deceased child's family. No one examined whether she had a genetic or pathological condition; whether some toxic chemical had damaged her health; or whether something traumatic happened to her while in the parent's care or under someone else's supervision.

Initially, police did interview the mother and father but did not scrutinize their troublesome answers. Several of their responses were inadequate, ambiguous, and conflicted with each other. An example was when police detectives asked the mother about the child's falls during the last week, she gave this strange answer: *"No, not in the last week...other than bumps or bruises, where she trips over her own feet...Catches herself, but nothing severe."*

Further, in response to a question whether she had seen anything that you would make her think would cause a head injury, she stammered for a minute, then said, *"I mean, No. Nothing at all."*

A similar question was posed to the father about whether in the past forty-eight hours he had seen anything happen to his daughter that would cause a head injury, he strangely said, *"No, I have not. Not in my sight."* Appropriate follow-up questions should have included, *"Okay, then in whose sight was it?"* But that question was never asked.

When responding to questions from police and the grand jury, neither the mother or father mentioned the accidental fall that Angie's mother previously told Lori about that happened shortly before enrolling her daughter in daycare. Perhaps because of fear of implicating herself, she may have been afraid to admit to the police that Angie fell from the kitchen countertop while in her baby carrier. Or she may have considered the fall not relevant, especially after hearing emergency room doctors saying that all her head injuries happened that afternoon and could not have been accidental.

During questioning by police, Angie's mother, Colleen, did not know how to pronounce or spell Lori's first or last name, while in the next breath claimed she checked with the county licensing before using Lori's daycare center. There was no follow-up question to see how this was possible since all county offices are closed on weekends and legal holidays, including that Monday when she first brought Angie to daycare.

Also, her parents and roommates gave conflicting information about whether it was Saturday or Sunday that the toddler recovered from the allergic reaction to immunizations, and precisely who cared for Angie and how many hours they cared for her on the prior weekend. Strangely, police made no effort to delve into their conflicting statements or to visit their apartment or investigate their environment and lifestyle which could have proven to be very troublesome and unsafe for a young child.

Lori had already told police and defense investigators that a few months before this tragedy, an eight-month-old baby, in her care, accidentally fell out of the highchair and fell face down on the floor hitting her head and her lip. She had been giving part-time childcare for the baby on an as-needed basis, usually two days per week for several months. When this accident happened, Lori informed the parents and kept watch for any dangerous symptoms. She also went to the trouble of having her pediatrician look at the child (during an appointment for her own child). The pediatrician saw nothing that looked worrisome and did not recommend a CT scan. However, this was the standard recommendation at the time as pediatricians would recommend to parents that such short-distance falls did not need a CT scan unless certain obvious symptoms were present.

Conversely, when the child's parents learned of the tragedy involving Angie and the child abuse allegations, they took their child to her doctor and insisted that a CT scan be done on her head. It revealed a hairline fracture along the cranial midline sutures. Medical specialists who reviewed the CT scan concluded the injury was consistent with the reported fall from a highchair. Also, the parents of the eight-month-old later refused to cooperate with the police investigation, and since no evidence implicating Lori could be found, police were not able to file new criminal charges. Regardless, the real facts and lack of cooperation from the parents did not stop prosecutors from using this event to their advantage whenever they felt it would help their arguments and influence the judge to rule in their favor.

Police investigators and prosecutors were working overtime trying to find another case of child abuse by Lori, including (among other things) talking to all parents for whom Lori had given childcare, and thoroughly examining her young children. But they were unable to find any abuse whatsoever.

During the first week of Lori's arrest, Attorney Wilson received a call from a lady who said that she had seen Angie falling from her stroller on the prior Saturday. She said Angie fell from a standing position in the stroller onto the hard marble floor onto her head which made a deafening noise, but she was not sure which part of the child's head struck first. She had seen Angie's picture on the TV that convinced her it was Angie accompanied by two women, one who appeared to be in her forties and the other a younger woman. Attorney Wilson said he shared this information with the District Attorney's office for investigation. Much later we learned they never followed up on the phone call. The district attorney (prosecutors) assumed the case against Lori was rock-solid and they did not need further evidence. Neither did Attorney Wilson conduct a thorough investigation into the phone call or take it very seriously at that time. It was not until years later that a defense investigator (hired by a new defense attorney) made a personal visit to the lady to confirm the identity of the child whom she had seen fall. However, five years had passed since the tragedy she was now unsure she could identify the two women from the pictures shown to her. Thus, the accident and its relevance could not be proven.

Additionally, around that same time (five years later) when defense attorneys served a subpoena on the shopping mall that demanded they produce a copy of any video and/or an accident report. it appeared to be asking for accident reports or records involving Lori Watson and the mall reported they had no such records. Instead, the subpoena was supposed to demand any video and accident reports of any fall of anyone in the mall on that weekend. In retrospect, it appears the defense team dropped the ball by not issuing a new subpoena specific enough for mall security to have responded to correctly.

During our frantic search for direction and information, several local defense attorneys told us that the criminal justice system in the county consisted of a "good old boys club" who were known for patting each other on the back with favors and showing little regard for promoting justice. Several sources, including a deputy sheriff and a local police officer (not connected to the case), informed us that unless Lori's defense attorney happened to also be in that club, Lori would be found guilty.

Furthermore, a family friend who was an active police officer reported that the department was in turmoil and divided into two camps. In one camp were the dedicated police officers who obeyed the rules, were trustworthy, and were honest. In the other camp were officers who were more concerned with playing political games and had little regard for truth and justice or doing their job correctly. As a result, there was continual strife, and power plays between the two factions. How this dysfunction adversely affected the investigation of Lori's case will never be known, but it indeed was not helpful. Additionally, an acquaintance informed me that his uncle resolved a severe criminal matter in the area by paying off the "right party" and suggested that we do the same if Lori expected to win. Even if that was true, it was not our nature to seriously entertain such thoughts. All the above stories and conversations were very disturbing, and the hope that Lori would get the charges dismissed against her were fading quickly.

We soon realized that modern forensic science and police investigating techniques were light years apart and functioned on two different tracks-scientifically modern and the other outdated. Emergency room and other doctors not educated, trained, or experienced in the specialties of forensic pathology, biomedical or biomechanical engineering, histopathology, cytopathology, nor hematopathology, habitually make unscientific, unprofessional, and damaging statements to police investigators.

Later, it came to light that although these same emergency room doctors involved in Lori's case were genuinely unqualified and untrained to diagnose the cause of a toddler's death, skull fractures and severe intracranial injuries, their words had previously resulted in the conviction of a dozen other child abuse defendants in this county alone. Ironically, they used the identical "two-story fall" and "SBS" theories in those cases. It was as if these theories were auto-filled into their minds and reports by a coded transcription machine and used when brain injuries or skull fractures in children could not be quickly or easily explained.

CPS & Family Court Investigations

As customary in this type of criminal case, police authorities registered a complaint with CPS, prompting the county family court to make Lori's three children wards of the court until a completion of a court-supervised investigation could determine whether they were safe with her. That investigation would take several months and then the family court judge would decide about custody of her children based on their findings.

The uncharted waters of CPS rules and regulations are very

overwhelming and threatening to inexperienced and non-legally trained individuals. Therefore, an attorney who was the wife of Defense Attorney Wilson represented Lori in the family court matter. She was very experienced with CPS, knew all the rules, and helped us navigate safely through many months of investigations and court hearings. Without her ability, our family's journey through the maze of criminal and family law courts procedures would have become a lot more complicated and ominous.

The court-supervised CPS investigation into Lori's background proved to be very comprehensive and involved interviewing her children, many friends, mothers of daycare children, casual acquaintances, and family members. Additionally, to make sure they did not miss any evidence, CPS required that all three children have skeletal surveys taken at Sunny Side Hospital. That consisted of having twenty-five x-rays taken from every angle to see if there were any past or present broken bones or scars that might show prior abuse. This was a very threatening situation as many children have invisible scar tissue or undiagnosed healed fractures from unknown sources or accidents. Regardless, their father and I took the three children to have all the required exams completed. The results were that the children had no evidence of healed bones, unexplained injuries, or psychological indications that they were victims of abuse at any time.

After completion of the physical and psychological exams the investigative reports were provided to the family court and they changed their order to allow Lori supervised visitation for few hours each day with her children. As usual, each change in the Washoe Family Law Court order was issued at a court hearing after reviewing the most recent report from CPS with their recommendations. Both courts were extra cautious because of the high-profile criminal court case that alleged Lori had committed murder by child abuse. On a personal level, living under the court restrictions was an emotionally unsettling process for Lori and her children as they had always very close on a 24/7 basis.

When we were suddenly faced with both the family and criminal court restrictions on Lori, we were uncertain about what would happen to her three small children since I was not physically or financially able to take care of them full time, and their dad could not quit his full-time day job. Since there were no relatives living close by, two close Christian friends of Lori's, Lanny, and Bill, who lived down the street came to the rescue. They volunteered to care for all three children including the seven-week old infant in their home until the crises blew over or better arrangements could be made.

With consent of the children's father and mother, the family law court granted legal guardianship to Lanny and Bill so they could handle all duties of caring for them, including schooling, emergencies, and healthcare issues. While hoping that Lori would return home and resume her duties shortly, they lovingly gave full time care for more than a year for the two younger children and afterschool care for the six-year-old with very little financial help. When Lori's absence became longer than expected, other Christian friends voluntarily cared for the infant at different times, including a woman who gave childcare on a reduced fee basis.

Lanny and Bill were "God sends" because without their help all three children would have been placed in the Nevada foster parenting system arranged by CPS. That would have been necessary because there was no money in our personal budgets to pay the extra cost of full-time infant care, nor cost of after school care for the two older children while we worked. We were grateful for the CPS social workers who were very professional, non-assuming, honest, compassionate, and helpful in making the guardianship arrangements possible.

As previously mentioned, police had immediate access to reports of two phone calls made to CPS more than three years prior to the tragedy at hand. Both phone calls involved Lori's oldest daughter when she was three years old and concerned the same incidents. The first CPS call was from Lori's marriage counselor from what appeared to have been a misunderstanding when she asked him for help in handling discipline problems and building a better relationship with her three-year-old daughter, Tanasha. She also needed guidance about how to better manage the issues of children, family, financial, and her marriage successfully. It is obvious there was significant miscommunication between Lori and her counselor. I was the one who encouraged her to seek guidance from him about how to develop more effective discipline methods since her discipline methods consisted of yelling and threatening punishment but never following through. It was obvious that Lori's firstborn was a "mini-me" of herself with the same body build, coloring, and type-A personality. They both had a built-in desire to be the leader that caused conflicts that could mostly be avoided with improved parenting skills. Even though Lori was having marital and extreme financial stress at the time, I never saw nor heard of any abusive behavior by Lori. The biggest discipline problem was that the three-year-old was becoming more and more demanding because Lori did not follow through with her verbal warnings. If Lori did not put action to her words, I feared the two of them might end up having a perpetually confrontational and unhealthy relationship and that my granddaughter would not get the guidance and emotional security she needed.

The first incident the counselor mentioned in that same phone call to CPS was one that I personally saw that involved inappropriate and ineffective discipline, but it did not involve physical abuse. It happened one day when Lori was driving the car and I was in the front passenger seat. My three-year-old granddaughter, Tanasha, was in her car seat in the back seat directly behind Lori. She was crying and yelling because she wanted to get out of her seat while Lori was driving. This disruption went on for what seemed like an extensive amount of time while Lori was repeatedly yelling at her to be quiet, but the child only became louder. Finally, trying to get her attention and startle her, Lori flung her right arm around behind her to hit the side of the infant car seat. I chastised Lori for doing that, because she could have accidentally hit her daughter's face or eyes instead of the car seat. That was the sum of what happened on that occasion, nothing more. However, the marriage counselor included an altered version of the incident in his CPS phone call.

The second incident mentioned to her counselor was one that Lori had already told me about. It happened when her three-year old, Tanasha, unexpectedly came into Lori's bedroom crying loudly and awakened her in the middle of the night when she was very tired and in a deep sleep lying with her back to the door. The noise and loud crying startled her mom who thought there was an emergency, or something was wrong, she quickly sat up and flung her arms out while trying to get out from under the covers and out of bed. Not realizing that the three-year-old was that close, she accidentally hit her in the chest but caused no injury except for startling her and causing her to cry louder. Lori mentioned that she was horrified that in her tired stupor she could have hurt her child. Her tiredness stemmed from working three-part time jobs and taking care of a sick baby as well as managing household chores at the same time.

Ironically, many years later Tanasha verified Lori's account of what happened in detail when I asked her what she remembered. She clearly recalled going into her mom's room during the middle of the night crying loudly from a bad dream while her mom was sleeping with her back to the door. It startled her when her mom tried to get out of bed quickly, flung out her arm to remove the covers and not realizing Tanasha was so close, hit her in the chest. Although she remembered how it startled her and running from the room crying, she remembered it as a spontaneous event and that her mom did nothing intentionally to harm her.

Strangely, Lori's defense attorneys never insisted on questioning the child about this event, and Tanasha said I was the first and only person who ever asked her if she remembered that night. Evidently, everyone thought she, as a six or seven-year-old, would not remember the incident since she was only three years old when it happened.

Questions about why her marriage counselor made this phone report to CPS can be answered by reading the Nevada Revised Statutes that demands the reporting by counselors of situations that a reasonable person believes could lead to abuse in the future. Also, his decision to make that report to CPS was during a period when public and media hysteria and hype was full blown because of many child abuse cases being broadcast excessively and repeatedly by the national and local media.

Unbelievably, Nevada and many other states laws demand that anyone who has "reasonable" cause to suspect child abuse may have happened or may happen in the future, must report it to CPS for investigation. As a result, many professionals decide to make a CPS report (more often than they would otherwise) to protect themselves and their careers against a potential misdemeanor and losing their professional licenses if something later goes wrong with the child.

In response to the counselor's advice concerning child rearing, and recommendation of a close friend, Lori and her husband completed an extensive eighteen-week parenting class called *"Raising Kids Gods Way."* Also, upon recommendation from her marriage counselor, Lori arranged with a close friend (a stay-at-home-mom) who lived within walking distance to temporarily care for the three-year-old until she was financially able to quit one of her three jobs and her infant son was no longer ill. The two women became very supportive of each other by trading childcare on an as needed basis for many years.

The second phone call to CPS was from an aunt who lived in California and heard about Lori's problems. At the time, she did not have a close relationship with Lori, had not seen her for more than a year, and could not have personally known or been a witness to any abuse and was repeating hearsay information incorrectly to CPS. When questioned later about why she made this phone call, she said it was not to report abuse but was to offer an alternative place for the toddler to stay. According to CPS records, that call was an abuse report because of unwise statements she made to them that comported with the comprehensive mandated reporting laws of Nevada. I know the aunt was only repeating third party information incorrectly because she learned it during a phone conversation with me.

By the time the phone call was made, Lori had already asked for parenting guidance from her marriage counselor and Tanasha was already staying at her friend's house temporarily. During our phone conversation, the aunt said she was going to call CPS and I told her not to do that since it would serve no useful purpose. She ignored my instructions for some unknown reason and made the call anyway.

CPS promptly did an investigation into both phone calls and found no facts or evidence of child abuse by Lori. As a result, CPS never filed a child abuse "complaint" with the Court, nor supervised Lori's activities. The phone calls to CPS were completely without merit and no follow up visits were necessary.

Regardless of the facts, prosecuting attorneys, and the news media continually implied that prior criminal "complaints" of child abuse had previously been filed against Lori. They chose to ignore the results of the investigation which found there was no basis for allegations of child abuse and no need for further action. This was another prime example of where the Prosecutors Bird and Snuffelpaw carefully selected only portions of the records or reports they knew would bolster their claims in front of the judge and jury, while disregarding all other more significant or contradictory evidence.

Without a doubt, knowledge of those three-year-old CPS phone calls caused the police and prosecuting attorneys to only focus on Lori and fueled their quick jump to judgment of her guilt. The dull lens of moral relativism and emotional hyperbole caused them to focus on those old phone calls, instead of diligently considering and pursuing all evidence.

In connection with the subject criminal case, it took more than one year for CPS, police, and district attorney to complete their investigations into Lori's history and family dynamics and file a "final report" with the family court showing they found no evidence of child abuse by Lori at any time. Certainly, if investigators had found any abuse, they would have filed a new criminal case with other charges of child abuse. Although prosecutors knew (based on their own investigations) there was no evidence to support their claims of other child abuse, they made no attempt to correct or change their accusatory public statements or drop their false allegations but continued to repeat them for years in many court hearings and motions they filed.

Although the criminal case had not yet gone to trial, CPS eventually recommended to the county family court to order that Lori could be with her children 24/7 with the condition that there was always an approved supervisor or her husband present.

What Happened That Tragic Day?

Knowing what really happened at Lori's daycare on that fateful day and the week before goes a long way in helping to understand the real events and issues involved with the criminal case.

To avoid confusing the reader, I do not include or try to explain the many statements made by first responders, emergency personnel, witnesses, prosecuting attorneys, and police investigators during their trial testimony that contradicted each other. Instead, vital information is assembled here from Lori's handwritten and recorded statements to police, other investigative reports, medical reports and records, transcripts, documentation in my files, and from my conversations with Lori before and after the tragedy.

On March 4, 1996, Angie arrived at daycare around 7:30 a.m. Although she did not have an appetite for breakfast, she appeared to be feeling better and was more active than the week before when she was suffering from severe adverse reactions to her immunizations. After breakfast, Lori took the children to Food for Kids to give them her first report for the daycare center. She had a double stroller, which allowed her six-week old baby and Angie to ride and her two-year-old son walked alongside her. Afterward they went to a drive-through drycleaner, picked up dry cleaning, and returned home. Then she fed the children a lunch of macaroni and cheese and starting a video playing for the two older children to watch. However, they started roughhousing by bouncing up and down on the sofa and jumping back and forth to and from the coffee table. She sat them down a second time to watch the video, before stepping into the bedroom a few feet away to tend to her newborn. While in the bedroom, Lori could hear that the children had resumed roughhousing. Suddenly she heard a thump and Angie crying as if she was hurt, so she quickly returned to the living room to check out the problem. She found the child laying on her back on the floor, away from the coffee table and it appeared that she had tried to jump onto the heavy oak coffee table and fell off. Lori picked Angie up from the floor, checked her for injuries and bumps on her head. Finding none, she assumed the child was okay. While comforting Angie, she noticed that she seemed groggy and since it was now 2:00 p.m. and time for her afternoon nap, Lori thought it was just because she was tired and sleepy. So, she gave her a bottle of milk and put her down for a nap in the portable crib in the front bedroom.

About a half hour later, (roughly 2:30 p.m.) Lori checked on Angie and discovered that she had not drank any milk, so she removed the bottle and put it in the refrigerator. She noticed Angie was lying on her stomach and making funny little whimpering sounds like children make when trying to stop crying so the sounds did not alarm her.

At 2:45 p.m. a lady named Shelly arrived for a meeting to discuss childcare possibilities for her own children and stayed until about 3:35 p.m. Shelly testified that all the daycare children were napping, that she did not notice anything abnormal in the environment and that Lori did not seem stressed. After discussing the daycare routines and requirements she left a few minutes before the six-year-old arrived home from kindergarten. A friend whose child attended the same school drove her home but did not come inside.

Next, Lori had scheduled a 4:15 p.m. appointment to meet with a woman by the name of Jenny to interview her for a position as a part-time helper at the childcare center and it was important to see how Jenny interacted with the children. With that goal in mind, at a minute or two before 4 p.m. (one and one-half hours after she last checked on Angie) Lori went to awaken her but found her unresponsive. Her skin was very pale and bluish, and she was having difficulty breathing. No doubt something was dreadfully wrong, and her first thought was that she missed something important earlier when checking the child's condition after she fell from the coffee table or couch.

At about the same time, Jenny and her boyfriend rang the doorbell who were fifteen minutes early to discuss possible part-time work. Lori answered the door with a limp non-responsive Angie in her arms. After giving her CPR, Angie had a pulse but was struggling to breathe. Lori turned the CPR over to Jenny and phoned 911 for help and told the operator that Angie was unresponsive after a nap but had fallen and hit her head earlier.

When paramedics arrived at her residence a few minutes later, Lori met them outside the front door with the limp toddler in her arms. They told her to go back inside and she told them about the earlier fall and not being able to wake her up. After paramedics examined Angie and gave her breathing aid, they placed a collar on her to stabilize her head (because of the reported fall) before transporting her to the hospital.

Lori asked Jenny to call Angie's mother, Colleen, and let her know about the emergency and inform her that paramedics were already taking her child to the closest trauma center a few miles away. In response, Angie's mother instructed Jenny to direct the paramedics to turn around and take her across town to a more distant hospital, presumably because Colleen's mother worked there as a nurse. Paramedics delivered the unconscious child to that hospital about thirty minutes later.

Considering that Angie was unconscious and in severe respiratory distress with a reported head injury, it was shocking to find that it took two hours after arrival at the emergency room for a radiologist and neurosurgeon to review CT scans of her head and perform an examination to decide that immediate surgery was necessary. The anesthesia for emergency surgery began three hours after arrival (around 7:30 p.m.) and lasted a little more than two hours. This slow intervention was because this facility was not a trauma center equipped to handle urgent life or death issues promptly. Strangely, despite their slow intervention to save her life, upon arrival the emergency room doctors decided this was a child abuse case and injuries were equivalent to falling from a two-story building.

During surgery, the operating surgeon drilled a hole in Angie's skull to release pressure and removed fragments of the fractured skull bone, two grayish brown tissue masses, and blood clots from near the fracture site. The surgeon sent the two tissue masses to their pathology department for diagnosis but did not preserve any part of the removed fractured skull bone for forensic analysis and/or aging.

Although police thoroughly searched Lori's home that evening and knew about the child abuse diagnosis from emergency room doctors, they did not read her the *"Miranda Rights"* or ask her to sign a "Consent to Search" form. [An investigator later testified in court there were at least nineteen people (not counting Lori and her family) in and out of the residence that evening, asking questions, taking pictures, and trying to figure out what happened, and that they left the house around 10:30 p.m.]

Lori described the atmosphere as totally chaotic and terrifying. Police were asking dozens of questions while at the same time instructing her to write a statement about what happened that day. But they would often interrupt and instruct her to write down what she had just said. At the same time, multiple police officers were asking her to do many things simultaneously and kept repeating the same questions in different words, obviously trying to get her to contradict herself. During all this bedlam, her three-page statement of events was not written in proper chronological order. However, detectives would not allow her to re-write it.

[Note: Later, during court proceedings, a two (1st and last) page version of Lori's statement was used by prosecutors and attached to the police information report they provided to the grand jury seeking an indictment for Open Murder. That version was also attached as an exhibit in support of several motions by prosecutors. After diligently searching for the missing page two of her original statement, I found it attached to the original police report for child abuse given to Attorney Wilson.]

Additionally, police were taking photographs of everything, including Lori, her kids, and their house. When her husband put their six-week-old baby on the couch with pillows propped around her, they took photos of the baby. They also took a photo of a card posted on the refrigerator that quoted Galatians 4:22-23 (NJKV) that named patience and self-control as being fruits of the Spirit.

Investigators asked her about everything imaginable, like why she drank coffee and why there was herb tea on the stove, and about all the spices and herbs in her kitchen cabinets and why she used them. Based on their strange questioning, it appeared to her as if they thought she might have poisoned the child or something. The interview consisted of asking Lori the same questions about five times before recording her answers. By that time, she said her brain felt like scrambled eggs and she was exhausted.

Desperate to find incriminating evidence and cast doubt on Lori's truthfulness, police instructed her to take the toddler's bottle out of the refrigerator and put it back in the portable crib where she had been sleeping and then took pictures of it. However, while pandemonium swirled around her, she inadvertently grabbed one of her six-week-old infant's newborn nipple bottles and laid it in the crib for the officer to photograph. It was not until several months later when her attorneys showed her the photograph, that she realized what had happened. For sanitary and other obvious reasons, she never would have given a fifteen-month-old a bottle with a "newborn nipple" and breast milk in it.

In many later court hearings, the prosecutors made lite of Lori's claim, saying she fabricated the tampering allegations. However, a simple test of the contents would have proven it was breast milk in an infant's bottle and not the formula or same bottle she was feeding Angie.

As expected, Lori was truly shaken by the tragic events, police tactics and the commotion surrounding her. As a result, some of her verbal statements were misunderstood and taken out of context, especially to do with timing of that day's events. While police investigators were negligent and incompetent in many arenas, they excelled in questioning techniques designed to put more stress on Lori to cause her to say or write something self-incriminating. An unbiased careful reading of the police recordings and written statement by her proves that did not happen. While shock and indescribable terror consumed her heart, soul, and mind, the behavior of the experienced and trained police investigators further upset Lori.

The investigators could find no evidence of anything broken, damaged, or disrupted to show a violent act had occurred and the "crime scene" was not preserved for further forensic investigation. During their search one detective removed some papers from Lori's daycare records and put them in his folder. But the police report did not list any of those items as items confiscated at the crime scene; the only item listed was the baby bottle taken from the refrigerator.

Although Lori told emergency paramedics and police investigators about Angie's fall, they made no effort to confirm or refute Lori's account of the child falling by swabbing for any residue or DNA of Angie on the solid oak coffee table by her bare feet and her head. Instead, concluded that same evening that Lori had committed child abuse.

Regrettable, neither did defense investigators test for Angie's DNA on the coffee table, question Lori's children, or hire a biomechanical/biomedical engineer or forensic medical examiner to evaluate the evidence and scenarios to explain the reason for Angie's catastrophic head injuries.

Also, it is unfortunate that police investigators did not ask Lori's two-year-old, who could speak and was very friendly to strangers, about what happened. They also ignored Lori's six-year old daughter, who was not considered a witness because she was either at school or playing in the back yard during most of the time in question.

Later that evening after police left, Lori phoned Angie's parents to find out how she was doing. After learning that Angie might not survive, she called a pastor at Calvary Chapel and asked for special prayer for Angie and her family. One of the pastors went to the hospital and visited the parents to offer spiritual and emotional support and prayers.

Without knowing what was really happening, a local TV news anchor criticized Lori because she did not go to the hospital that evening with Angie or visit her, implying she was a callous and cold-hearted killer. This began a circus of false rumors and narratives by the TV news media and newspapers that we had no opportunity to dispute.

When Angie died, her parents agreed that the Calvary Chapel pastor would conduct the funeral service as they had no pastor or church. Sadly, the grandmother of Angie objected, and the plans were cancelled because Lori had referred him, and her family had come to believe that Lori had murdered their child and wanted no association with her.

Coroner's Investigation and Autopsy

A few days after Angie's death, Attorney Wilson informed us that the Washoe County Chief Medical Examiner would do an autopsy on her. At that point, I informed him that it was critical that we hire an Independent Medical Examiner (IME) to attend and critique the post-mortem examination process to verify it was done properly and that the coroner kept all available medical evidence. Since this was a speculative case against Lori based on circumstantial evidence, other attorneys (that I worked with) believed this step was extremely crucial. Being less experienced, Lori's attorney insisted this was unnecessary and believed it would be a waste of time and resources, so he refused the request. Attorney Wilson was under the naïve impression that the Washoe County Chief Medical Examiner was impartial and a highly trained medical examiner.

Much too late, we all realized that not having an IME attend the autopsy was a huge mistake because the postmortem examination was performed very unprofessionally and had the primary goal of substantiating what the police and the hospital emergency room doctors and police had already decided. The coroner simply incorporated the emergency room doctors' remarks into his autopsy report saying that the death was a homicide and non-accidental without doing a thorough review of available hospital and pediatric records.

Ironically, the coroner later admitted during testimony at a family court hearing that he had received no specific training on how to perform autopsies of small children, nor training on how to analyze brain injuries in them. This fact, plus his admission that he could not read x-rays and CT scans, raised more suspicion about the validity of his autopsy report. Despite his lack of specific training, he admitted to having performed many autopsies on children during his career. He testified that he had not attended any seminars in the prior four years to update his knowledge of how to best perform postmortem exams. As expected, when the defense hired their own medical examiner/pathologist ten months later, serious questions and concerns about the coroner's activities and report were discovered.

Although this writing is not a scientific analyze of the autopsy report, I have applied common sense and logic based on a simple review of all trial testimony, medical records, reports and feedback from medical specialists, and my own experience as a paralegal. Since there are some obvious discrepancies and flaws in the autopsy report that a paralegal could spot, a conclusion can be drawn that the report would be equally or more defective on more technical and scientific matters.

When comparing the coroner's report with available evidence and medical records, the following incongruencies were found:

1. He evaluated the growth and development of Angie based on a fourteen-month-old child, when three days later she would have been fifteen months old. Her growth and development should have been evaluated on that basis, since this is a period of rapid growth for small children.

2. He did not notice or mention that Angie had several physical anomalies, such as being unusually short, underweight, and having a large head compared to her small size. Instead of analyzing these issues, the coroner's autopsy report incorrectly said:

    > The body is that of a normally developed ......a well-nourished white female infant whose general appearance is consistent with the reported age of 14 months.

    The child's medical records contradicted his statements because they show that at the time of death, her height was at the 25% mark and her weight of nineteen pounds at autopsy was between the 5th and 10% mark on the chart used by pediatricians to professionally measure children's growth and development. Also, her pediatric records showed that Angie's last well baby check was conducted at seven months when her height was between the 25th and 50% mark and her weight was between the 10th and 25% mark and was not within the normal range.

3. Another anomaly, not mentioned in the autopsy report, was that Angie's pediatric records show her head circumference at birth was a

little above the 95% mark, which was very large in comparison to her low weight and short height mentioned above.

> [Note: Before the tragedy happened, Lori mentioned that Angie's head was larger than most children her age and it was funny and odd shaped; and she was very short and small for her age. She also mentioned that the toddler's skin was not soft and smooth like baby skin, instead it felt thicker and rubberier than it should be. Similarly, photographs show her eyes were wide-set apart. *Recent medical science and research has discovered that those symptoms (especially Macrocephaly, rubbery skin, and wide set eyes) indicate the presence of one or more cranial and/or congenital collagen defects or metabolic conditions.*

4. Another strange and incongruent statement in the autopsy report read as follows;

> EVIDENCE OF RECENT INJURY: There is a faint bluish discoloration of the entire occipital section of the scalp from the hair-line upward. It is very diffuse and has no distinct margins.

Regarding the referenced bruising, it should be noted that a competent medical examiner would have known that a contusion is red the first day, then in two to four days appears blue and then turns blue/black before fading away and disappearing. Since her mother saw the faint bruising at once when she came to visit her child in the emergency room, obviously, she knew of the prior injury and bruising. It would have happened a few days, otherwise it would not have appeared as a fading out bruise, but it would have still been red. Also, because it was underneath the toddler's light brown/blond hair on the back of her head, it was only visible to the mother who knew it was there. Keep in mind that none of the paramedics, medical doctors or surgeons noticed any bruising during their examinations and preparation for surgery.

Obviously, the "faint bluish" fading out bruising to the back of her head under her hair should have been a signal to the coroner that further forensic investigation was needed. Although this bruising was mentioned in the autopsy report, the photographs taken during autopsy did not show any faint bluish bruising.

[Question: Would defense attorneys question the mother during the trial about her ability to see this bruise and ask when and how the bruising happened? Or would they continue under the common belief that they should handle the parents of a deceased child with "kid gloves" and should not pressure them for direct answers in fear of alienating jurors.]

5. Contrary to the coroner's report, several other medical specialists consulted agreed that an earlier primary impact could have weakened or fractured her skull, causing bleeding, swelling and hydrocephalus, which would have been further worsened by a minor secondary fall such as falling onto the hard-oak table, or a short distance of about four feet onto the floor, or a combination of both.

6. In addition to all the above issues, instead of trying to substantiate the preconceived notions of the emergency room doctors and the suspicions of police investigators, it was the coroner and chief medical examiner's duty to be unbiased, ask questions, and to rule out other possible causes of and/or contributing factors to the deadly intracranial injuries. Since that was not done, the following questions and many others are still unanswered:

 o Was the child deficient in nutrients such as Calcium, Vitamin D and/or Vitamin K, or other nutrients, which cause brittle or weakened bones, fractures and/or can make bleeding more likely?

 o Why did the coroner not initially prepare and examine tissue specimens from the (1) Dura (lining of the brain) and (2) the exact site of impact (left cerebellum) (3) the bone adjoining the linear fracture for scientific examination and diagnosis? Medical experts have said that if a proper forensic examination had been done it could have provided the state and defense with conclusive evidence of whether there was a prior skull fracture, prior intracranial injuries, and a rebleed of a prior hemorrhage.

o   Why did the coroner not take a tissue sample of the very faint bluish area of her scalp and/or the underlying tissue to forensically determine more precisely how old the "fading out" bruise was? This could have verified a much older injury in addition to the short distance fall on the day of the incident.

o   Why did he not explore the possibility that the child may have been suffering from some undiagnosed pathological condition, cranial deformity, metabolic disease, or environmental contamination (smoking or chemicals) causing a birth defect? Medical science and research show that either of those could have caused hydrocephalus, edema, bleeding, and blood clots that build up intracranial pressures making Angie more susceptible to injury and a skull fracture possible from the short distance fall onto the table or floor.

o   Why did he not investigate the impact the many simultaneous immunizations given to her the previous Tuesday, (Diphtheria, Tetanus, Pertussis, Haemophilus Influenzas-Type b, and her very first Measles, Mumps and Rubella) that sometimes causes edema (tissue swelling) and hydrocephalus (water accumulation), intracranial bleeding or vascular problems, may have had on her brain?

7.   Although Dr. Gray, the Washoe County Chief Medical Examiner later admitted during a related family court hearing that he could not read CT scans, he described the skull fractures as follows:

> Anyway, we have got a clear impact point toward a little bit of the left midline back of the head, one fracture going up, another fracture going forward to or toward the ear, and the third heading down here to the, oh, where the spinal cord meets the brain.

8.   The autopsy report also described the natural suture lines in the skull as separating and found one as intersecting with a fracture line but did not describe it as a diastatic fracture, so exactly what he meant is in question. Regardless, his incomplete description of the skull fracture

contradicted the radiology report of the CT scan taken of Angie's brain before surgery that described a linear (straight simple) fracture. In any case, the coroner's description of the fracture comported with the CT scans taken after surgery. His description of the skull fracture gave state prosecutors and their medical experts a license to exaggerate the fracture and thus, the force needed to cause the skull fracture and intracranial injuries.

Also, since he could not read x-rays, and was not trained in doing autopsies on children, he could have confused the naturally occurring Lambdoid Sutures (the lines of union between the occipital and pariental sections of the skull) as being part of a complex fracture system. Medical journals have written about this mistake by other less-skilled radiologists.

An explanation for the conflicting radiological findings may be found in the operating surgeon's report about the brittle bones he found, which he described as sharp and splintering, tearing his gloves. Based on that testimony, it is reasonable to assume that if Angie's bones were that brittle, drilling into the fragile skull to relieve intracranial pressure could have caused the existing linear fracture to become a complex one.

As a longtime member of the *"Good Old Boys Club"* of the county criminal justice system, the coroner believed his job was to rubber stamp the previously determined theory of non-accidental injury diagnosed by the emergency room doctors and police investigators, whom he later testified in court hearings *"pointed him in the right direction,"* during the autopsy.

Because the defense attorney relied solely on the county coroner and did not hire an Independent Medical Examiner (IME) to attend the autopsy forensic examination process, to ask pertinent questions and explore all possible causes of the toddler's skull and brain injuries, the answers to the above and many other questions may never be known. Alternatively, if authorities did not allow an IME to attend the official autopsy, the defense attorney could have demanded the court intervene and enforce the defendant's inherent right to see all evidence and conduct its own forensic examination before burial.

Since the justice system considers the coroner's autopsy report to be the final word about the cause of death, it is rarely corrected or amended even in the face of contradictory evidence.

Evidence Ignored by Investigators

There are many salient facts known by only a few people, including important events Lori told me about during several phone calls between us prior to the tragedy, and others she mentioned later that would have illuminated the investigative process,

Investigators never knew that Angie was a child Lori adored and was extremely happy to have attending her home daycare center. Several times before the tragedy, she gushed to me how Angie was a "perfect fit" for her daycare and family. Lori told me she was the sweetest little toddler with blond hair and big blue eyes, who tried to speak with a cute little jibber-jabber that could not be understood. She prayed that all her new children would be just like Angie. The toddler quickly became very attached to Lori and seemed to crave her attention because she would cry or make a little fuss when she could not see Lori's face. Also, Angie played beautifully with her young son, whom she continually followed around and would run to the front door for a hug and kiss when she heard Lori's husband arriving home from work. Obviously, she was an ideal fit with their family dynamics.

Prior to the tragedy, Lori told me that when Angie's arrived the first day of childcare she had a bruise on her face in the fatty (hollow) part of the left cheek and asked me if this was anything she should be concerned about. At that time, we thought it might have happened during a simple fall as her mother said she often fell over her own feet and it was no big deal. Lori also mentioned this concern to a couple of other women friends at the time, but she did not ask Angie's mother or dad about what caused it.

Also, Colleen (Angie's mom) informed Lori during her first week at daycare, that Angie had recently fallen off the kitchen counter top (typically 32 inches high) while sitting in her baby carrier. She said the baby flipped off onto the floor and hit her head very hard and it really scared her. Lori assumed the accident happened within the recent past. Otherwise, why would Colleen have thought to mention it? Could she have been trying to explain the reason for the child's bruise on her cheek that was obvious the first day at childcare? Unfortunately, Lori never asked the child's mother or father exactly when that accident happened and if it was the reason for the bruise on her cheek.

On the first day of childcare, Angie also had a severe and obviously painful diaper rash with open sores that concerned Lori. Colleen told Lori that the condition had been a continual problem. Immediately, Lori resolved the problem by cleaning and treating her bottom often with medication and using a better-quality diaper to allow healing. She also gave Angie's mother instructions and a homeopathic remedy to help with yeast infections that contribute to diaper rash. Lori explained that Angie was always clean except for that issue but said the parents appeared to be struggling financially and had been buying cheap diapers.

Prior to the tragedy, during one of our phone calls Lori mentioned to me that Angie's head was unusually large and odd shaped, and that her skin was very pale, rubbery, and thicker than normally found in children of her age. Additionally, she mentioned that Angie was extremely short and small for a fifteen-month-old. She could not pronounce any words yet but had a cute jibber-jabber when trying to say something.

After the tragedy and the ongoing criminal case, I was compelled to review Angie's pediatric and medical records and discovered confirmation of most of Lori's observations. Further, I discovered that neither the emergency hospital personnel nor coroner's office took a complete inventory of physical attributes, such as her small size, height, and head circumference as a pediatric exam would have included. Photographs show that her head and face appeared unusually round and that her eyes were wide-set apart.

The week before the tragedy, Lori informed Angie's mother, Coleen, that her immunizations were several months past due and she could not take care of her any longer until brought up to date and in compliance with state laws. In response, her mother promised that Angie's father would be there around four that same afternoon to get it done.

After he did not show up by 6 p.m., Lori called Coleen, to ask who was picking up the toddler. Coleen came to get Angie and was very angry with her husband because he did not do what he had promised. She cussed and called him names saying she would really let him "have it" when she got home. Without a doubt, there was some family conflict and tension in the home that evening.

The next morning, Angie's father took her to get her immunizations and around 10:30 a.m. they met up at the speech clinic where Lori had taken her two-year-old son for speech therapy. Upon arrival, Angie was very upset, crying inconsolably and obviously unhappy with her father who could not console her. Since Lori had her own two small children with her, another lady in the waiting room volunteered to hold Angie and quickly consoled her after her dad left. This struck Lori as being very unusual that a stranger could console when her father could not.

This happened six days before the tragedy. Angie was given multiple immunizations simultaneously. They included the DTAP (Diphtheria, Tetanus, Pertussin -whopping cough), HIB (Haemophilus Influenzae-Type B), and her very first MMR (Measles, Mumps, and Rubella) vaccinations.

Around midnight that same evening, Angie started vomiting profusely and had a slight fever, so the parents took her to the emergency room. The mother testified that the examining doctor only glanced at her but did not give her a thorough examination. He diagnosed that she had an extremely rare severe reaction to one or more of the multiple immunization shots she received earlier that day. The doctor's diagnosis was;

"1. Gastroenteritis, 2. Possible local reaction to immunizations."

The next morning, Lori was told that the doctor said Angie was suffering from a rare adverse reaction (1 in 1700) to the immunizations and gave a doctor's written release to allow her to go back to daycare. She was prescribed Tylenol for fever and Pedialyte to help with vomiting and given instructions to return to the doctor if her symptoms worsened.

Lori kept the parents informed that Angie was ill for the rest of that week and had several troublesome symptoms including not eating and being unable to stand up for more than a few seconds and being unable to walk at all. When she tried, she would stumble, loose her balance, and fall or sit down. She had hand tremors and refused to eat solid food but would infrequently drink from her bottle of milk or Pedialyte. She slept most of the time until Friday and would only lay on the right side of her head. When Lori laid her on her left side, she would instantly roll over to the right side. Also, she could not jibber-jabber like before but would whimper or cry when uncomfortable or when she needed something.

Police Investigators overlooked and were not interested in these symptoms although Lori told them and had mentioned to several people that Angie had a mysterious hand tremor and a severe reaction to immunizations she received. Ironically, medical specialists know those symptoms are consistent with receiving immunizations when there is either an intracranial injury, rare neurological genetic defect, and/or other medical conditions. In Angie's case, none of those pre-existing conditions had yet been explored or diagnosed.

Although Lori was taught (in one of her childcare start-up training classes) that she should not take care of children when they were ill, she knew that Angie's parents were on a tight budget, they had a doctor's release, and could not afford to stay off work to take care of their baby, so she continued to give childcare that entire week. In retrospect, she realized this was a big mistake on her part. Regardless, her motives were good as she was trying to help them, and she needed the income as well.

What Kind of Person Would Do That?

Most parents of an adult child in these circumstances would search the recesses of their mind for any clue that could help them discover the truth. However, many of my friends and relatives would never consider their child could do anything wrong. Instead, I prayed for courage to view my daughter's behavior and attitudes objectively. I examined everything I knew about Lori's habits, character, personality, and goals. Was there something about her character that no one knew? Was she who I thought she was? Was there a secret side to her personality and character? Her biggest character flaw was that she spontaneously spoke her mind about what was bothering her or what a person was doing or saying without much regard for the emotional impact it would have on those around her. When she was a child, I usually listened to her unfiltered opinions without criticizing, choosing not to stifle her desire to be open and honest with me. Also, Lori had a quick mind with strong leadership abilities that sometimes caused her siblings distress. They would complain that she was telling them what to do or how to do something. Many times, I would have to tell her to back off or mediate the differences between them.

Nothing I recalled showed that Lori had violent tendencies. In fact, several memorable events in her life as a young child, teenager, and adult showed the opposite was true with strong evidence of her admirable character, love of children, and respect for all life. The scripture found in Matthew 7:16 (NLT) says, "*You can identify them by their fruit, that is, by the way they act. Can you pick grapes from thorn bushes, or figs from thistles?*" Had I failed as a fruit inspector?

During my long drive to Reno, significant life-events flooded my mind like white water rapids that were impossible to stop. The first event that came to mind was of Lori as a five-year-old who became upset at me for smashing a grasshopper. It happened one day when I came home from work during lunch to check on the sitter and the children. She was sitting at the breakfast bar with her nose only a few inches away from the grasshopper. I quickly grabbed a napkin and smashed the insect and threw it in the trash before it could do any harm to her. This surprised and upset Lori and she loudly chastised me for killing her friend. In tears, she exclaimed that I did not have to kill it, but instead I could have just caught it and put it outside where it could live. Wiser and smarter than most kids her age, Lori chided me, "Everyone has a right to live. That was not right!" For years afterward, I felt a pang of guilt each time I saw a similar insect and remembered Lori's chastisement. In fact, for quite a while when an insect or fly was in our presence, she would remind me not to kill it. How could this child have grown up to become a child abuser? I certainly hoped that was not possible.

As an elementary school student, Lori attended public schools, a private Christian School, and Sunday School. During her very early years, she asked Christ into her heart, and as a teenager was baptized in the Pacific Ocean. There is no doubt in my mind that she made diligent efforts to please her Lord by living out the Judeo-Christian principles that were imprinted on her heart and mind.

Another poignant memory that quickly came to mind was of teenage Lori saving the life of her ten-month-old brother, Willie. After finding him missing from his crib, Lori searched for him and found him bobbing up and down in the backyard swimming pool where he had fallen. She pulled him out of the water, turned him upside down, pumped the water from of his lungs and gave him mouth to mouth resuscitation. If she had not taken such swift action, there is no doubt that Willie would have died or suffered brain damage from the lack of oxygen. She was like his second mother and enjoyed entertaining him, dressing him up for holidays, and taking him on trips to the park or beach. When she left home to attend Embry Riddle University, there was a void in Willie's life that no one else could fill.

Teenager Lori took part in the "March for Life," held by the Christian community supporting the right of unborn children to live. She firmly believed that all unborn children were sacred and should be protected. I knew this because we openly discussed the issues of unwanted pregnancies and alternatives to abortion.

After we moved the family to a new neighborhood, Lori found it difficult to adjust to the social environment at high school and decided she wanted to quit school. She told me she felt pressured to compromise her personal standards and did not fit into the school social scene as her peers were into partying and drinking. At first, I disagreed with her quitting school but later agreed that she could if she could find an alternative way to continue her education. A high school counselor informed Lori that she could attend the local junior college after passing an entrance exam and could get an AA degree without first having a high school diploma. If she kept her grades high and earned her AA degree she would qualify to attend a university.

Lori enrolled in a junior college at once, and at the same time found a job at the grocery store across the street from campus to earn her own spending money. She never went through a rebellious stage, excelled academically, and graduated with honors and an AA degree. Lori then attended USA Aeronautical University where she excelled in Calculus, Physics, and Trigonometry. Even with a heavy curriculum that involved many hours of homework, she worked part time as a server at a cafe to support herself. Unfortunately, after completing all academic requirements, she still needed more funds to pay for the remaining flight training since school loans could not be funded for that purpose. Additionally, deteriorating eye-sight became an obstacle (at that time glasses were not allowed by the industry) and she was unable to achieve her goals of graduating with a BA in Aeronautical Science and becoming licensed as a commercial airline pilot.

Another event came to my mind that proved Lori's compassion, tenderness, and affection toward children. It involved a life-threatening situation that occurred when she and James were newly married. While becoming more intimately acquainted with his young son by his first wife, Lori noticed that the seven-year-old was unusually uncoordinated, clumsy, and that his eyes did not look right. Also, he was having difficulty learning and doing his homework. Realizing that something was wrong, Lori insisted his parents take him to a pediatrician for a physical examination.

Medical specialists discovered that the boy was suffering from a birth defect (Congenital Hydrocephalus) that was preventing proper drainage of his cerebral fluids and causing fluid retention and swelling of brain tissue. These were conditions that would have eventually resulted in extensive brain damage or death. Emergency surgery was necessary to install a shunt to allow drainage and prevent further decline in his mental and physical health. Several follow up surgeries were necessary, and Lori helped his recovery by keeping a close eye on him when he was in their home. Without Lori's care and concern, the young boy would not have received proper medical intervention and could have been severely injured or died within a very short time. The condition had already caused minor brain damage, but it would have been a lot worse if Lori had not intervened.

As a young wife, Lori took drastic and painful steps to overcome a serious reproductive disease called Endometriosis to fulfill her desire to have children of her own. Her doctor recommended that since her condition was so dire, if she ever wanted to have a child she needed to have corrective procedures done right away to halt or cure her decline in health and try to conceive as soon as possible. After receiving this advice, she underwent several painful procedures before she could conceive and give birth to her first child. Afterward she had more surgical procedures to keep the Endometriosis from advancing.

Eventually Lori gave birth to three beautiful children. For this young mother, life was not easy or simple as it was necessary for her to become employed outside the home to help with buying necessities for her young children. At times, she worked as many as three part-time jobs to supplement her husband's income by working hours that he was not working, during evening, weekends and/or nighttime. It was an exhausting schedule with no time to spare, but it revealed her love and dedication to her children.

After considering everything I knew about Lori, there was nothing I remembered that gave me a clue that she was the type of person who would intentionally abuse a child. Some people have been known to live a secretive double life and I wondered if she was one of those people. Regardless, as her mother, I would always be there whenever she needed me with unconditional love no matter what the truth should turn out to be.

The idea of running a childcare business began with Lori looking for an efficient way to meet family financial needs, and at the same time be present to nurture and train her own her children on a full-time basis. She decided those goals could happen if she took her part-time babysitting seriously and set up a licensed childcare business in her home. This motivated her to carefully plan and work diligently for more than a year to set up a legally licensed and insured childcare facility. To pass inspections and complete the licensing process, it was necessary to move the family to a larger more suitable rental home that had a separate playroom and sleeping area for all the children. Lori bought second hand kid-size furniture and toys that she cleaned and painted as needed. She went to great lengths to make sure the daycare was a clean, fun, and safe environment.

It was mandatory that she attend and complete state and county licensing courses, complete a background check, and pay various county and state fees to obtain her county daycare business license and buy business liability insurance to protect the business and her new property owner. Since Lori was expecting her third child, all of this was no small undertaking. Additionally, she asked a friend and me for loans to pay the various costs associated with setting up her business. After completing all the training, investigations and inspections, the county issued her daycare license about one month before the tragic events of March 4th.

Before the tragedy, she was feeling optimistic and excited about the challenges and opportunities ahead and the promise of a better financial future and family life.

After surveying Lori's life and character, I realized that she aimed for the highest moral standing and put her heart and soul into every task she tried; setting up the daycare center was no different. Her lifestyle was guided by instructions from King Solomon in Ecclesiastes 9:10 (NAS) *"Whatever your hands find to do, do it with all your might."*

Challenges on Every Side

CHAPTER 4

To the average citizen, there is no reason to believe that a grand jury can issue an illegal criminal indictment, but to legal defense attorneys this is a common concern. From the very beginning, Lori's attorney was concerned about the validity of the indictment, but he let the established legal deadline pass that would allow the filing of proper petition papers to challenge it. To correct the situation, he obtained an agreement with prosecutors and the court to extend the deadline to file a *"Petition for Writ of Habeas Corpus"* to attack the legality of the indictment. Without Lori's knowledge or consent, her attorney out-sourced the preparation of the petition to another attorney and left for an extended vacation in the Caribbean with his family.

The petition challenged the indictment by bringing the court's attention to many Nevada statutes that state prosecutors did not adhere to. The petition argued that the arrest, incarceration, and restraint of Lori was unlawful and illegal on three grounds. The first was because it (a) violated her right to due process (the 5th and 14th Amendment to the US Constitution) and did not put her on notice as to what specific act she was expected to defend against; and (b) the prosecutor made remarks improperly instructing the grand jurors that they were not required to decide whether to indict on first degree, second degree of murder or a lesser offense, and (c) there was insufficient evidence to establish what criminal agency (i.e., by who, what activity and how) caused the death.

Additionally, the petition asked the court to consider that enough probable cause was not presented to the jurors (1) to substantiate that a crime had been committed, and (2) that the person charged committed any crime. While it was clear that a child had died without explanation, there was no evidence of exactly what mechanism caused her death presented to the grand jury except for the "opinions" of the coroner and emergency room doctors whose testimony contradicted each other in some respects. Their testimonies were accepted by the prosecutors and grand jurors as evidence (although neither the doctors nor the coroner were skilled or certified in the required specialties but were merely giving their opinions as non-experts) even though existing Nevada statutes specifically said that "opinions" were not to be presented as testimony in a grand jury hearing.

The petition also claimed that prosecuting attorney erroneously informed the grand jurors that the trial jurors would decide what degree of murder was applicable and thus, it was not necessary for them to consider indicting on a less serious charge. The petition pointed out that his instruction was also contrary to written Nevada statutes which mandates that the grand jury decide what specific offense is proper and whether enough evidence is presented to indict on that crime.

Further, the defense's *"Petition for Writ of Habeas Corpus"* pointed out that prosecutors ignored and violated Nevada Revised Statute 173.075(1) which says;

> The indictment or the information must be a plain, concise, and definite written statement of the essential facts constituting the offense charged.

Most people and first-year law students would recognize that the wording of the indictment was unclear and convoluted because it suggested several ideas as to how the alleged crime of murder happened, and did not give the defendant a plain, concise, and definite written statement of the essential facts constituting the offense charged. Alleging several different methods of criminal activity created an avenue to prosecute for any evidence found later.

The county district attorney assigned Prosecutors Bird and Snuffelpaw, two very experienced attorneys, the job of prosecuting the case for the state and county. Prosecutor Bird was a tall domineering woman with yellow frizzy hair, very adept at feigning passion, outrage, and disgust whenever she spoke. Her courtroom performance had been rehearsed and perfected during more than twenty-five years of prosecuting child abuse and child murder cases. Prosecutor Snuffelpaw was her male counter-part who seemed to work primarily under her control and direction.

Naturally, they strongly opposed the *"Petition for Writ of Habeas Corpus"* and filed their *"Return"* to it citing legal authorities they felt applied. Prosecuting and defense attorneys filed hundreds of pages of sophisticated legal wrangling and arguments claiming their arguments and legal citations were more applicable than the opposing position, and why the judge should rule in each respective favor.

The prosecution response documents filed with the court having their legal writings and hyperbole proved they were only interested in laws and procedures that would enhance their chances of winning (just as they had done during the grand jury hearing to get an indictment) and ignored others that were more significantly relevant and germane. This habit of manipulation strongly suggested that prosecutors functioned on the "moral relativism" principle-that if they achieved a greater good, any unprincipled methods used to get those results were permissible.

Two months after filing the *Petition for Writ of Habeas Corpus*, the defense and prosecuting attorneys presented oral arguments to the court. After returning from his vacation, during oral arguments on the petition, Defense Attorney Wilson argued for dismissal of the grand jury indictment because of the defects and insufficiencies mentioned above. The prosecuting attorneys decried that they had done nothing wrong and their statements to the grand jury were proper and met all legal requirements.

Sadly, the judge agreed with prosecutors and decided that the indictment was proper and ruled in their favor so that the case would continue uninterrupted. We were informed that the judge was experienced in civil litigation but not well versed in criminal law and seemed to be unaware of the stark differences.

Lori's attorney thought he would be successful in getting the indictment dismissed or amended and at that time did not need to conduct legal forensic discovery or hire medical experts in preparation for the trial that was scheduled to begin in one month. Regardless, once Lori and I realized that he had not prepared for trial (or asked for an extension of it) nor had he explored the medical issues, we were extremely disturbed and disillusioned. Our anxiety increased with each non-response to our many phone calls. The lack of communication and action on his part undermined our confidence in his ability to give her the best legal defense possible.

Financial and Family Challenges

The extra expenses imposed by the criminal case and family law court ordering Lori to have no contact with her children presented several problems, including financial and schooling issues. This caused family members and Christian friends to voluntarily help where they could. For many years, they provided essential food, clothing, childcare, and moral support, along with much prayer, love, and concern. Their many gifts were true blessings and examples of love in action.

Eventually, conditions had changed enough to allow my son-in-law to resume taking care of his children during non-working hours, evenings, and weekends. Multi-tasking to the extent needed to work a full-time job, manage a busy household, and take care of young children was a huge challenge. Further, he was suffering from severe Asthma that drained his stamina and exhausted him, and he had little energy or motivation to do much else after dinner but fall asleep on the couch. Also, he made several trips to the emergency room to get help with breathing. It was clear that the strain of what he and his family were going through had contributed to his ill health.

Although my son-in-law was emotionally drained and traumatized, and many times wanted to escape the chaos, he was faithful and diligent in working a full-time job in the construction industry to support his family.

During all of this, it was not possible for me to offer fulltime childcare for my three grandchildren since it was necessary for me to continue my full-time paralegal job to earn my son's and my essential living expenses. Fortunately, my attorney boss was very understanding and allowed me to work overtime and use the extra hours to take time off to attend the various court hearings and help take care of my grandchildren. As such, I did not lose any income, but there were extra expenses involved with supporting my daughter during incarceration, my traveling, and helping financially with my three grandchildren's needs.

Juggling my many responsibilities during those difficult years was not easy. I learned to deliberately compartmentalize my emotions and thoughts (turning them off when needed), so I would not be too distracted from my stressful paralegal duties while at work, my home responsibilities and keeping up with the criminal case. Otherwise, my whole world would have fallen apart, and I would have sunk deeper into despair. Frequently, my thoughts and emotions seemed to have a life of their own requiring me to take short breaks to recuperate and refocus on the task at hand. When swirling clouds of panic surrounded me, I found peace in knowing that some good would come from this experience and God would give us the strength and courage to endure whatever we faced.

Words are inadequate to describe the mental, emotional, and spiritual agony caused by the false charges against my daughter. Her suffering and the anguish of her husband and children caused me to keep a constant attitude of prayer, seeking God's wisdom, mercy, and grace. Knowing the outcome was in God's hands, not mine or the court systems, brought confidence that we would eventually survive any evil thrown at us.

Having close Christian friends and family who responded to our anxiety and confusion over each turn of events was a tremendous source of strength and encouragement compelling us to continue the fight on a day-to-day basis. Their continual outpouring of care and concern was immeasurably helpful as they spoke encouraging words without the slightest finger-pointing or ugly remarks. However, a friend of Lori's made an astounding comment one day while we were waiting in line to go in the church. She said to me, *"I don't understand. If God is working through Lori for some divine plan, I do not know why God would choose her. She is not a spiritual giant. Surely he would pick someone who is more gifted and equipped."* That statement haunted me for a long time. But since then, I have grown in my understanding of the character of God and I know that He chooses whomever he pleases. He does not think as we do, nor does He make decisions like we do, as mentioned in Isaiah 55:8, [NKJV] which says:

> For My thoughts are not your thoughts, nor are your ways My ways," says the Lord. "For as the heavens are higher than the earth, so are My ways higher than your ways, and My thoughts than your thoughts.

Also, I learned that many times God uses the weak and simple things as written in I Corinthians 1:27b [NKJV] which says, *"...and God has chosen the weak things of the world to put to shame the things which are mighty..."* I diligently prayed that this would happen sooner than later.

Another friend reminded me of several characters in the Bible who had to wait for many years before the plans God had for their lives became obvious. Those heroes and prophets suffered through what appeared to be desperate and impossible circumstances. She reminded me of Moses, Abraham, Isaac, and specifically of Joseph who was sold into slavery and then imprisoned for no valid reason. Approximately twenty years later Joseph became the second most powerful leader in Egypt and he was able to save many of his family and fellow citizens of Israel from starvation and extinction.

As mentioned previously, taking care of the three children during the absence of their mother was a life-altering challenge and needed coordination of several family members and dedicated friends. In that regard, one of the most gut-wrenching experiences I endured during those early years happened one day when I was driving my youngest granddaughter (by then over one year old) to the new babysitter's house after my weekend visit. Within several blocks of the sitter's house, she recognized where we were going and started crying and saying "No, no." Indicating that she did not want to be left there and upon entering the home, she began crying hysterically and clinging to me. After spending a considerable time trying to console and settle her down with no success, I tore myself away and left with much trepidation and sadness to begin my drive back home.

Very quickly, my tears, blurry vision, a severe headache, nausea, and dizziness forced me to pull off the road and try to recuperate from my low-blood sugar and anxiety. I was extremely distraught at having to leave my baby granddaughter who was suffering emotionally because of being suddenly taken from her mother at six and one-half weeks old. Undoubtedly, she felt secure with me but otherwise was confused and insecure, although several ladies from Lori's circle of friends had taken good care of her during the previous eighteen months. I prayed that a guardian angel would minister to this helpless child, protect, and comfort her mind and spirit, as promised in Psalms 91:11-12 [NKJV];

> For He shall give His angels charge over you, to keep you in all your ways. In their hands, they shall bear you up. Lest you dash your foot against a stone.

My grandchildren were continually in my heart and my prayers. I prayed that they would not grow angry and bitter because of their mother's absence. Several other Christian friends and family members also continually prayed for their physical, emotional, and spiritual healing, and wellbeing.

As previously mentioned, Lori's six-year-old daughter was already attending Calvary Christian School when the case began. Later, after Lori's two-year-old son was potty-trained, we found it necessary also to enroll him at the same school. But the decision presented another problem because there was no room in the family's budget for added tuition. Because of the children's urgent needs, the school graciously allowed both children to attend on a reduced tuition basis, and one of my dear sisters agreed to pay the tuition and invested her time and energy making sure the children had proper clothing and school supplies.

Increasingly as time passed, our families became more financially devastated by the extra expenses imposed by the criminal and family law cases. It was necessary for me to cash out my retirement account and life insurance policy to help with the financial needs. Several of Lori's friends and other extended family members were faithful in supplementing the family budget with monetary gifts. Usually on a weekly basis, different women from the local church would deliver bags of groceries and second hand or new clothing for the growing children. Without their help, it is hard to imagine how the family could have survived.

When this tragedy happened, Lori was driving a very old automobile prone to break down and leave her stranded. This situation was no longer tolerable because of her need to attend court hearings on time, sometimes with only a few moments' notice. Although my budget was very tight, I leased a new Toyota that was economical and paid the monthly payments to allow her to drive to and from court hearings and other activities safely and on time.

With the help of Angel Tree Ministry, friends made sure there were Christmas trees and at least one present for each child, and other friends and family gave other presents to them. Also, a local charity gave the family fully cooked Thanksgiving meals for several years. Each act of kindness was received with sincere thankfulness as they helped with the heavy emotional and financial burdens we were carrying.

It was clear that planning and income goals was futile until after completion of the criminal court process. Our emotions were raw and continually fluctuating from extreme optimism to dark despair. At times it seemed like God was hiding from us.

Supervision of Children 24/7

About eighteen months after the case began, the investigations discovered no evidence of abuse by Lori and the results were filed with the Washoe County Family Court. Finally, it allowed Lori to have 24/7 supervised contact with her children which meant she could resume her motherly duties and live in the same residence.

At this news, we began interviewing several applicants responding to the advertisement for a live-in babysitter who would be the primary caretaker and supervisor of the children. After several interviews and the court's approval, we hired Marita to be the caretaker and supervisor for all three children five days per week while Lori's husband was at work. She was an excellent choice, a breath of fresh air, and a blessing in many ways. Although Marita spoke very little English, she was especially attentive to the children. She was a good housekeeper and stretched the tight grocery budget by cooking delicious dishes from scratch. Meals usually consisted of economical Mexican cuisine, including home-cooked black or pinto beans, fresh salsa, rice, tortillas, eggs, and fresh cilantro, lettuce, onions, tomatoes, avocados, chicken, and cheese. Strikingly, although the baby had been fragile with breathing problems since she was born, and although she did not like canned baby food, she became noticeably healthier with Marita's wholesome nutrition and nurturing. Once again, contributions from extended family and friends were necessary to pay her wages because neither my son-in-law nor I could afford them.

One weekend when Lori was under house arrest, there was an accident that threw us into a crisis mode needing a potentially life or death decision. Lori's three-year-old son, Timmy, was jumping up and down on Lori's bed when he accidentally fell onto a wooden nightstand causing a significant bump and a laceration that looked severe enough to need stitches to heal properly. When considering treatment options (although I saw the accident) we knew that a trip to the doctor or hospital would result in the prosecutors' office discovering what happened and would try to twist it into another incident of child abuse. For sure, local newspapers and TV news would hyperventilate the story and CPS and police would again investigate Lori for abusing one of her children. After carefully seeing that Timmy had no other symptoms, Lori asked her brother who was a surgeon's assistant to come stitch up the wound. He put several stitches in Timmy's superficial head wound to close it, and it healed with no complications and no visible scarring. Although alarming, this event was an example of the love and grace of God shown to us by the practical help of family and friends.

Complications of Media and Public Hysteria

The unrelenting daily coverage on local and national TV shows and front-page newspaper articles added to the grief and shock of Angie's death and the horrific criminal charges filed against Lori since they only published the prosecution's side of the story. TV anchors and camera crews parked 24/7 for many days in front of Lori's family residence after her release hoping to be the first to get an interview and report breaking news. They did not know that Lori was living on the other side of town at her aunt and uncle's house and her attorneys had instructed her not to talk to the media.

Nevertheless, the coverage was extensive. One local newspaper published forty-six articles about the case within the first twenty-four months. Additionally, other local newspaper published many articles, and endless "breaking news" interrupted regularly scheduled TV programming for many years announcing each step of the legal process, involving all events, statements by prosecutors, and court filings.

They highlighted and broadcasted mistaken information that this was a "Shaken Baby Syndrome" case involving an unsafe child care facility. They repeated the allegations made by prosecutors that Lori had a history of two CPS "complaints" filed against her because of abusing one of her children. Also, the news articles implied that the state and county illegally licensed her to run a daycare center that resulted in the death of the toddler. Because of this propaganda and extensive coverage, public outrage and hysteria were thick in the air around the state. The media and the public tried and convicted Lori in the court of public opinion, long before the criminal trial began. The news broadcasts made it sound as though Lori was a risk to the public at large and they should be informed at once with continual and repetitive updates at every twist and turn of the complex legal process.

The news media repeated all false allegations made by prosecuting attorneys during many court hearings that Lori abused her eldest child and another child attending her daycare center. Neither were true. Instead, the other child had fallen from a highchair while at daycare, hitting her lip and head which could have caused a hairline fracture along the suture line in her skull. However, because this child was at daycare only two days per week (1/15 of the hours in each week), it was uncertain whether falling from the highchair or some other trauma caused the hairline fracture. Besides, Lori notified the parents at once when it happened, and had her own pediatrician examine the infant (while there with her own children) and he saw no reason for alarm.

Lori's attorney told her and the family not to talk to the news media or police officials about anything to avoid feeding into the media frenzy and causing difficulties for the defense team. Those instructions were hard to accept because we wanted everyone to know the real story and set the record straight.

I obeyed the attorney's instructions, but after the trial was over Channel 8 interviewed me for over an hour at their station but they only broadcast a few seconds of the interview. In contrast, the prosecuting attorneys used the media repeatedly and extensively to promote their agenda. Plus, it did not help that the judge approved the news media's motion to allow news cameras in the courtroom during every hearing. In addition, the prosecutor's office helped the grandmother and parents of the deceased child in arranging participation in several local and national TV news and documentary shows. Also, they took part in a daily week-long series on a local channel with an investigative reporter discussing the case and claiming Angie was a victim of *"Shaken Baby Syndrome"* while attending a dangerous and illegally licensed child care facility.

Much of the published information was either mistaken, hyperbole, or misleading and detrimental to Lori's chances of getting a fair jury trial in the county. As publicity increased, the prosecuting attorneys became more aggressive in their efforts to win a conviction. Naturally, winning a guilty verdict in this high-profile case would enhance their chances of promotion to a higher job position, and would aid in the re-election of the existing district attorney by implying he was tough on crime.

Thus, the prosecution of Lori evolved into a joint collaborative political and media firestorm of promoting many false narratives and snowballing public outrage and hysteria. It seemed as the case became more publicized, the more entrenched the prosecuting attorneys became in their determination to win a guilty verdict. Understandably, a not-guilty verdict would cause them public embarrassment and confirm a lack of credibility. Ironically, these specific prosecuting attorneys were well known and well-practiced at distorting statements and evidence to promote their agenda, according to defense attorneys in the area.

Unbelievably, even before the trial began, a website created by the grandmother of Angie said that she was in constant contact with the district attorney's office who was helping with making appearances on national TV such as The Maury Povich Show, The Geraldo Rivera Show, MSNBC Issues Live, U.S. News and World Report, Court TV, and many others. The website also claimed that both her state senator and the Nevada State Attorney

General were helping her tell about the case and promote her goal of getting laws changed to protect children while in daycare.

On her website, the uneducated grandmother also said that her goals were to "educate" people and JURY POOLS about this case, "DAY CARE DANGERS" and the horrors of Shaken Baby Syndrome. She erroneously believed child abuse in daycare centers was rampant and the licensing system needed reform.

Upon reading her statements, I immediately called Lori's attorneys to alert them about these unfair and illegal activities and insisted that they stop her efforts to educate the jury pool and that she removes the statements from her website. The defense attorneys made a call to the prosecuting attorneys informing them to stop her illegal and improper conduct.

Among the most egregious misleading and wildly publicized messages was that my daughter had abused her own child and that earlier "complaints" were filed (implying criminal complaints) against her for doing so. Public records show that Lori had never been charged with child abuse of her own child nor any other child, nor supervised by CPS for remedial behavior to avoid the filing of a complaint. Thus, it is crystal clear that those phoned in allegations to CPS were unsubstantiated and invalid, but the prosecution and news media continued to sensationalize and promote the false narratives.

It is important to remember that between 1980 and 2000 the national TV news media sensationalized several dozen child abuses and child murder cases which created worldwide public hysteria and panic over the subject. Among the USA cases were the following: The McMartin Preschool case (1983-1990 California); Louise Woodward-the British Nanny (1997 Massachusetts); Glendale Montessori Preschool (1986-1989 Florida); Oak Hill (1991 Texas); Susan Smith (1995 South Carolina); Fells Acres Day School (1985-87 Massachusetts); and Country Walk (1985 Florida).

Approximately one month before the beginning of Lori's criminal case, the heavily publicized Louise Woodward (British Nanny) (1997) began. National and local TV shows and print media discussed both cases for many years.

Previously, the McMartin Preschool case (1983-90) alleging thousands of instances of child sexual abuse involving seven childcare workers, created new heights of public hysteria about child abuse and daycare centers. HBO made a TV drama called *"Indictment: The McMartin Preschool Trial"* which aired May 20, 1995 and further promoted the story. After a seven-year-long legal battle, including a trial that lasted over three years, the court dismissed all charges against the defendants in 1990. The case left a path of destruction and emotionally damaged preschool children in its wake, along with the ruined careers of daycare workers. Even though the state spent $15,000,000 trying to prosecute the seven defendants, the charges were proven to be false. Although many factors created the fraudulent charges against McMartin, the major factor was the public hysteria and moral outrage enflamed by the media that generated pressure on law enforcement officials to get convictions. According to the NY Times, Retro Report on March 9, 2014, the McMartin Preschool case unleashed public hysteria over the subject of child abuse. In that same report, several similar highly publicized cases are noted involving wrongful convictions.

Also, in 1995 the Susan Smith case riveted the nation and was in the national news for many years. Susan claimed that her car had been hijacked with her two small children inside of it and they had been missing since then. She appeared on many national TV news programs pleading for the return of her two children. After failing polygraph tests, this psychotic woman finally admitted she had driven her automobile into a lake, drowning her two small children while they were inside it. Upon conviction of murdering her two small children, with evidence of severe mental health disorders, the court sentenced her to life in prison. We were all disgusted by the thought of this happening to two small innocent children. The public's emotions elicited by it were real and understandable and were still in the hearts and minds of the people during Lori's case.

This phenomenon of public hysteria is well established and documented in the psychological literature, such as a research paper published in the IPT (Institute for Psychological Therapies) Journal, Volume 2 – 1990, called "The Phenomenon of Child Abuse Hysteria as a Social Syndrome: The Case for a New Kind of Expert Testimony" from a speech made by Lawrence D. Spiegel, Psychologist, presented at the St. Joseph Children and Youth Conference Center, November 4, 1988. His sixteen-page research results including references is published online at http://www.ipt-forensics.com/journal/volume2/j2_1_4.htm (Accessed 05/21/18).

> There is little doubt among professionals … that we are experiencing a national phenomenon. The issue of child abuse, after having been kept in the shadows for so many years, has finally emerged… with such a fury that some have characterized it to be of almost hysterical proportions.

The article goes on to point out that a contagion of emotional and irrational behavior causes a circular reaction among groups of people, who then similarly act on those irrationalities. It also addresses the roles the justice systems play in determining the veracity of an accusation of child abuse.

We have all seen this phenomenon develop in many high-profile criminal trials, including the O.J. Simpson case, the McMartin Preschool fiasco, the British Nanny (Louise Woodward) case, and those mentioned previously.

The public hysteria and media circus surrounding Lori's case created added stress and anxiety for her and her family, making the reaction of strangers a constant concern. Along with influencing the jury and prosecutors, it hung over Lori's daily routines like a dark thundercloud threatening her peace and security. The adults caring for Lori's small children kept them from watching television or seeing the newspapers, or they would have heard scary stories about their mother, seen her picture and been further upset. This task was not easy, but cartoons, movies, and Disney videos helped keep them distracted when necessary. Our goal was to keep as much of a normal a life as possible for the three young children who were already emotionally damaged by the absence of their mother's daily nurturing.

Privacy at Lori's residence was non-existent as her attorneys told us to be careful of everything we said whether on the phone or in the house about anything remotely connected to the criminal case. He said that although a court order was necessary before "wiretapping" they were only legally mandated to let us know within thirty days after doing so. He said that prosecutors had listening devices that could be pointed toward the house and could hear everything said inside. Although a court order was needed to legally do this, there was no way to prevent them from doing so surreptitiously and illegally.

Attorney Problems
CHAPTER 5

Between the filing of the *"Stipulation to Extend Time for Filing of Petition for Writ of Habeas Corpus"* and a short time before the scheduled oral arguments on it (about three months), Lori's attorney would not return or answer any of our phone calls.

Afterward, we learned that he had taken his family on an extended vacation and left no one running the law practice in his absence. Because of this, feelings of despair and abandonment overwhelmed Lori as she needed answers and reassuring words at a crucial and vulnerable time when her very future and freedom were at risk. Therefore, a profound shift took place in their relationship and it evolved from one of trust to a complete lack of trust and confidence. We felt bewildered and trapped by what we perceived to be his clear lack of professionalism, preparation for trial, ability to conduct discovery, empathy, and ability to communicate appropriately and promptly.

Drawing from my own legal experience, I agreed that his activities were not acceptable by any standard of professional practice and we needed to do something. Out of desperation over those concerns and not receiving a return message or phone call from Attorney Wilson, I suggested that Lori write a letter to the judge informing him about her fears and ask for a change of counsel. This step was very risky as it could backfire against her if she offended the judge by what she wrote. Another concern was that the enormous non-refundable retainer paid to Attorney Wilson for representation through trial would not be refunded. In her letter to the judge, she wrote the following:

Honorable Judge,

I am appearing before you today because I must have Attorney Wilson released from being my legal counsel. Although I retained Mr. Wilson almost seven months ago, it is clear and evident that with only five weeks away from trial, he has done virtually nothing to prepare for it. After many attempts to find out what progress has been made on my defense, I was able to secure a meeting with Mr. Wilson and the investigator on September 22nd to discuss it. My worst fears were realized when I was told that another case was taking precedence that was coming up for trial. Then I was told that my case would now be number one in his office and the other case would be put aside. Mr. Wilson admitted that he had not handled a defense of this nature with such medical complexity, contrary to his first assertions. Interestingly, he claimed that after eighteen years as a lawyer, "most of this stuff is in my head," referring to preparation for such a case. This case is being handled as if it were a petty theft issue. Mr. Wilson was also in agreement that "in hindsight" monies should not have been paid to an expert who specializes in sexual abuse only. This experts' curriculum vitae was not even looked at prior to sending him money.

A few weeks ago, I requested a record of service given and hours that Mr. Wilson had spent working on my case. I was told it would to take about one week to "think about it" and to compose a record. As of this date, I have not received any such record. All together more than $100,000 has been raised and paid to Mr. Wilson's office of which only the unused part that was deposited to offset expenses has been refunded to me in the amount of $18,798.12. But he refuses to be reasonable in my request to return the larger part of monies he received, because of his failure to act in good faith on my case.

The money paid to his office was voluntarily paid by dozens of supporters (some of whom I have never met) across seven states. These people believe in me and my right to have competent legal representation. I am now in a very difficult predicament. As an indigent, I do not have monies needed to defend myself.

Your honor, without those funds being refunded to me, Mr. Wilson is putting me in a position of indigents. I do not have the money needed to defend myself. I seek the court's assistance and advice in this matter.

Sincerely, Lori Watson

Attorney Wilson finally admitted he was in over his head and had never handled this type of case before. He humbly agreed to step down as Lori's defense counsel and to allow the appointment of a new defense attorney.

During Attorney Wilson's absence, and out of desperation, Lori and I had felt it was necessary to do our own research into the dynamics of defending against child abuse and child murder charges. While doing so, we learned from more than one criminal defense specialist that obtaining an acquittal was especially difficult because of the prevailing public hysteria over child abuse and the natural human instinct to protect infants and children. Several credible sources told us that the only solution was to find the real reason for the deceased child's injuries and prove it at trial. In other words, the scales of justice had shifted out of balance, and it was necessary for Lori's attorneys to prove that she did not commit a crime, rather than the state having to prove she did.

Behind the scenes and prior to the judge's approval of the discharge of Attorney Wilson, Lori had already met Deputy Public Defender Justine and was very impressed with her knowledge, abilities, and track record in successfully defending against these types of charges. Based on their conversations, Lori agreed that she should become her defense attorney once approved by the court.

The judge granted Attorney Wilson's motion to be relieved as defense counsel, and because of the lack of enough funds to hire a replacement attorney, he agreed the public defender's office could appoint a new attorney. Attorney Wilson informed the court he was refunding some of the fees paid by friends and family of Lori and the court agreed that any refunded money could be used to pay defendant's expert witness and investigative fees. Based on that understanding, a public defender would be approved and paid for by the state.

One month later at a status conference, the court approved the appointment of Public Defender Justine and her associate, Public Defender Boots to replace Attorney Wilson. It was encouraging that the two new attorneys had significant experience and success in defending against similar crimes and were highly recommended by their peers.

Finally, it seemed as if Lori had a competent defense team. The new team began at once trying to catch up to speed by interviewing Lori and examining all known facts and case documents, including hospital and medical records, and the autopsy report. They arranged for a forensic psychologist to examine Lori to get a better understanding of her emotional and psychological condition. The exam revealed there was no tendency toward abusive behavior in her personality or character. The defense attorneys also arranged for her to undergo a lie detector test which found there was "*NO DECEPTION INDICATED.*" Although the result could not be used as evidence in court, it gave her attorneys confidence that she was truthful and had not intentionally caused the catastrophic injuries to Angie.

Defense Medical Examiner Hired

Once the newly hired attorneys were assured of her truthfulness and her mental and emotional state, they hired a highly accredited forensic pathologist and medical examiner (hereinafter referred to as the Defense ME) who would be instrumental in getting to the truth of the deceased child's injuries. They asked him to compile a report of his findings and conclusions after evaluating all the available medical evidence and investigative records in the case and take part as an expert witness during the trial.

After receiving a copy of the deceased child's medical records and autopsy report, the Defense ME realized that some of them were illegible. Consequently, he traveled to Reno in January 1997 (ten months after autopsy) to visit the hospital to personally obtain a readable copy of all the deceased child's medical records and collect forensic evidence from the coroner's office.

While reviewing the hospital medical records, the Defense ME discovered several pages of Angie's medical records had not been provided by prosecuting attorneys to the defense attorneys in their standard "discovery" package of information. The newly discovered medical records included a Stanford Research Clinic Pathology Report, an AFIP Pathology Reports, and an amended pathology report from the treating hospital diagnosing that Angie had injuries that had been healing for twenty-four to forty-eight hours prior to hospitalization.

After leaving the hospital, he visited Dr. Gray, the Chief Medical Examiner at Washoe County Coroner's office to review the forensic evidence and discuss the newly discovered pathology reports. Dr. Gray told him that he had not seen nor read either of the pathology reports and admitted that if he had, he would have written his autopsy report differently.

The Defense ME continued his forensic investigation at the coroner's office by reviewing the remaining brain tissue and the microscopic tissue specimen slides that had already been prepared by the coroner. While doing so, he noticed that crucial tissue specimens from the left side of the preserved cerebellum (adjoining the fracture site) had not yet been cut and prepared for staining and testing. So, he asked the coroner to cut and prepare tissue specimens from that essential area for him to take with him. At his direction, Dr. Gray prepared six paraffin blocks embedded with formalin-fixed left cerebella tissue specimens for the Defense ME to further examine and diagnose.

Before returning to his home state, the Defense ME interviewed Lori at length at the "crime scene" in her home to see if there were any contradictions in her statements. Among other things, he asked about the short-distance fall that Angie suffered on the day of the tragedy and about the toddler's activities and symptoms the prior week when she became ill after receiving her immunizations. He also examined the crime scene and furniture that was involved in the fall. The doctor felt very confident that Lori was truthful, and he could prove that what happened was not caused by an intentional act of child abuse.

As previously mentioned, pathological findings about the timing of the brain injuries were critical to the defense as the tragedy happened on Monday afternoon and the child was not in her care during that prior weekend but was in the care of her parents, grandparents, or someone else. Additionally, Lori had only known Angie for two weeks and had given daycare for her only ten of the prior fourteen days.

For several months, we expected a modification of the coroner's autopsy report. But to our astonishment and dismay, even after learning about the exculpatory pathology reports, neither the Washoe County District Attorney's office (prosecutors) nor the coroner's office took the courageous step of re-investigating and doing more advanced forensic testing. At the very least, it seemed logical that they could amend the autopsy report to include a reference to the pathology reports and show the cause of death as "undetermined" instead of homicide (at the hand of another.) As fate would have it, Lori's attorneys reported they had discussed that possibility with the coroner and were told that the prosecutor's office would not allow him to do so. Thus, the coroner's hands were tied, and the state continued to prosecute Lori for "Open Murder and Murder by Child Abuse." State prosecutors had no interest in validating or disproving the credibility of the independent pathology reports prepared by three different pathology departments since they believed they had arrested the guilty party.

After returning to his home state, the Defense ME performed his own forensic analysis of the microscopic tissue/cell specimens that he received from the coroner. He also carefully examined all medical records and reports, police reports, witness statements, and court records in the case, as well as what Lori had said and written about what happened. After doing so, he prepared his first written *"Preliminary Confidential Expert Report,"* to defense attorneys, a portion of which is as follows:

> I then visited the Coroner/Medical Examiner Office and examined the microscopic autopsy slides and the retained fixed brain tissue together with Dr. Gray. Dr. Gray admitted to me that he was not aware of the controversy surrounding the surgical pathology specimen and had not examined the surgical pathology slides himself, nor was he aware of the outside consultant pathology reports, and he had not sampled the area in question during the autopsy (he had believed it to have been merely necrotic cerebellum). In my presence and at my direction, he then sampled and processed six cassettes from the area and sent me the unstained slides from those six cassettes (which I subsequently sent out for staining, so that I could review them.)

Upon examination of the more crucial brain tissue specimens, the Defense ME discovered that Angie suffered a significant left posterior fossa subdural hematoma at least six months prior to the incident in question, and that the underlying cause of that subdural hematoma was unknown. He also found that this subdural hematoma had later organized with at least one rebleed which occurred no earlier than twenty-five days and another rebleed occurring approximately two weeks before the tragic events of March 4, 1996. *[Keep in mind that these tissue samples were in addition to those preserved by the operating surgeon and diagnosed by the Stanford Research Clinic, AFIP and the local hospital pathology department.]*

Contrary to common sense and their alleged pursuit of truth and blind justice, it was hard to understand the rigid and immovable posture of prosecuting attorneys and the coroner's office. Their prejudices, moral relativism, and inflexible posturing had developed over many years of pursuing criminals guilty of horrific crimes against children and caused them to paint every defendant with the same guilty brush. Thus, they were unable to recognize good or truth shining as bright as neon signs.

Prosecutors functioned on the belief that *"the ends justify the means"* which allowed them to place their self-directed moral agenda above facts, legal procedures, and statutes. Specifically, as little gods, they were self-empowered to ignore and try to nullify the *"state-of-the-art"* pathology report in Angie's hospital medical records, as well as all forensic evidence.

Since prosecutors had not initially showed the three pathology reports to the grand jury or the defense team (as required by law) for them to suddenly admit they existed and were valid would show that they had not acted in good faith and had withheld potentially exculpatory evidence from the defense. So, the stalemate continued.

One of the ironies of this case is that Washoe Chief Medical Examiner, Dr. Gray had not even read the first hospital pathology report dated March 5, 1996, nor had he read either of the newer two pathology reports before completing his autopsy report a few weeks later. This contradicted his sworn duty and responsibility to review all case files, including medical records and forensic evidence before figuring out a cause of death. At the very least, he had access to the original pathology report (in his file) at that moment in time which should have prompted him to conduct further forensic investigation. It read as follows:

> MICROSCOPIC: Specimen consists of large aggregates of clotted blood. Focally there are large numbers of cells characterized by round ovoid nuclei surrounded by large amounts of clear cytoplasm having the appearance of Oligodendrogliocytes which are focally infiltrated moderate number of acute inflammatory cells. No areas of calcification are identified. DIAGNOSIS: POSTERIOR FOSSA, OLIGODENDROGLIOMA AND HEMATOMA.

In simple terms, this original report diagnosed that Angie was suffering from a rare tumor at the exact spot where the fracture was found, in the lower back part of her skull. To the average person, the diagnoses of a tumor and/or older injuries may seem like a fantasy and highly unlikely, but medical researchers have discovered there are certain types of tumors or cancers that will weaken any adjoining bones and cause a deterioration of them. That condition would have made Angie's skull more susceptible to fracturing from a short distance fall.

When the hospital pathologists were informed that Angie's injuries were from child abuse, they wanted to make sure of their findings of a tumor and decided to consult with the Pathology Department at Stanford Research Clinic. Stanford used very specialized and more modern staining techniques on the surgical tissue specimens (taken from one of the two masses extracted during surgery) to reach their diagnosis. The Stanford pathology report read as follows:

> The specimen consists of fibrous material and blood wherein monomorphous cells often aggregate and stream. The cytology of many of the cells includes some bubbliness of cytoplasm. Both the KP-1 and PGM-1 stains show a fair proportion of the cells to be reactive. There is abundant cytologic degeneration as evidenced by blowing up of nuclei. As a result, lack of uniform staining for macrophages markers doesn't disturb me too much. Some staining for S100 protein can also be attributed to these degenerative changes without indicating differentiation as perhaps along the line of oligodendroglial cells. I do believe that this is all a reactive process and that no neoplasm is noted despite the remarkable mimicry.

This report scientifically diagnosed that the injuries sustained by the deceased child happened between twenty-four to forty-eight hours before her accidental fall on March 4, 1996. The macrophage cells (specialized cells that show the processes of healing) were in quantities and form that could only evolve after that amount of time had passed.

Fortunately, the hospital pathologists realized they would be called to testify in court and decided to verify the Stanford Research Clinic report by sending new tissue specimens to an agency of the US Government [the Air Force Institute of Pathology at the Department of Defense (AFIP)]. They also performed advanced up-to-date testing and examination of the specimens and discovered evidence of older healing tissues. Their report to the local pathologists reads as follows:

> AFIP DIAGNOSIS: M96-1996 Brain, posterior fossa: Fibrin and reactive inflammatory infiltrate consistent with organizing hematoma.

We reviewed the single H&E stained microscopic section submitted in reference to this case. Additional sections prepared from the accompanying paraffin block were stained with H & E and immunohistochemical methods for KP-1, S-100 protein, factor V111 and CD-34. This material was reviewed by the staff of the Department of Neuropathology.

This letter follows our telephone conference of 8 April 1996 to hospital pathologist.

The microscopic sections demonstrate fragments of fibrin and red blood cells infiltrated by rounded cells with abundant clear cytoplasm and bland nuclei, which are positive for KP-1 immunostain and negative for S-100 protein. The infiltrate contains in addition lymphocytes and some neutrophils. The immunostains for factor VIII and CD-34 show no presence of blood vessels. These findings are consistent with organizing hematoma.

Finally, after receiving the report from the Stanford Research Clinic Pathologists, (and conversing with AFIP) the local hospital pathology department corrected their diagnosis by issuing an amended pathology report which read in part:

This case was referred to the Stanford Research Clinic for evaluation. Following special stains, the lesion removed from the posterior fossa represents a fibrinous exudate with an abundance of macrophages, rather than an Oligodendroglioma. The diagnosis is amended as follows:

DIAGNOSIS: POSTERIOR FOSSA, FIBRINOUS EXUDATE WITH ABUNDANCE OF MACROPHAGES, NO NEOPLASM IDENTIFIED.

It is important to remember that the local hospital pathologists acknowledged they were not sufficiently trained or skilled to perform the more highly-advanced staining and testing techniques that were specifically needed to determine the age of an injury and that was one of the reasons they sought consultation with the two cutting-edge research institutions.

After learning about those three unsolicited and highly credible pathology reports, we were extremely optimistic and thought it would only be a matter of time until the state would, at the very least, try to confirm or dispute the three reports with a cytopathologist, a histopathologist, and/ or a hematopathologist. Much to our amazement, we could not have been more wrong. The prosecutors dug in their heels and went ahead as if the two premier research institutions (Stanford Research Clinic and AFIP), and the local pathologists lacked ability and knowledge to give correct diagnoses. Were they (state prosecutors) more competent to decide the truth of the highly scientific forensic matters? Certainly not!!

The question remained: What evidence would it take to prove to prosecutors that Angie had preexisting intracranial injuries and that the injuries resulted from more than one event and that Lori was innocent of child abuse?

Public Defender Problems

Due to alarming and unfortunate circumstances, the professional and personal relationship between Public Defender Justine and Lori did not last very long. She asked Lori to pay for travel, lodging, and tuition fees of $2300.00, to make it possible for her to attend a *"Child Abuse Defense Seminar"* in California. Lori agreed to pay her the money because she was told it was necessary to obtain the latest forensic medical information, litigation techniques and strategies unique to defending her specific type of criminal case. But Lori took steps to check on her new public defender by communicating with a few other attorneys who were attending the same seminar. After the symposium was over, they reported to Lori that her attorney only attended it for a couple of hours. She showed up the first morning, signed the attendance roster and stayed a little while before leaving with her boyfriend for a rendezvous and did not show up at all the remaining two days. When Lori confided in me about what happened, we jointly decided the behavior could not be tolerated and that she should be confronted. When she tried to discuss it with the attorney, she became angry and discounted the seriousness of what she had done. Not accustomed to being challenged by her client, she grew very hostile toward Lori and later made derogatory statements to the judge about her during the hearing to be replaced as counsel.

For the second time, Lori was feeling betrayed and abandoned by her attorney. Although I knew she had a wealth of knowledge and abilities, her personality and character concerned me. Her actions at the seminar proved she did not have the strength of character and dedication that would serve my daughter's best legal needs in an honest, respectful, and diligent manner. Nevertheless, we went into a panic mode with this unfortunate turn of events as it appeared that the wheels had come off the carriage of justice again, and we doubted it would ever roll forward in the right direction or at a suitable speed.

Because of this breakdown in the attorney-client relationship, Lori had no choice but to write a letter to the judge again asking for a different attorney to represent her. Subsequently, Public Defender Justine filed a motion for her and her associate to be relieved as defense counsel. The court eventually granted that motion, clearing the way for an appointment of a new attorney team.

For all practical purposes, our journey was back at the starting line. An entirely new legal defense team (who knew nothing about the details of the case) would be chosen at random at the discretion of the public defender's office and the judge.

Suddenly, Lori was in another vulnerable and precarious position, but there was no alternative. We waited impatiently but did not lose hope as we knew the future was in God's providential hands. We prayed that a competent and ethical attorney would be chosen so that all the newly discovered medical evidence could be introduced at trial or, better yet, the state prosecutors would dismiss the case or amend the charges based on the newly discovered forensics.

Eventually, the court appointed a public defender panel participant, Attorney Crisley, as Lori's lead attorney and a month later they appointed Attorney Snow as second chair attorney. Both were hired under the umbrella of the public defender's office. Although Attorney Crisley understood basic medical terminology and techniques, he admitted he had no experience in defending a client against a murder charge involving child abuse as he had mostly handled civil matters. He was quick to inform us that Attorney Snow was more experienced in defending criminal felony cases and would be a tremendous asset in preparing the case for trial and extremely valuable in making prompt objections to any inappropriate statements and actions of the prosecuting attorneys and/or judge. These talents were crucial in preserving Lori's rights to any appealable legal issues.

Lori and I were cautiously optimistic about these attorneys because they were young, intelligent, honest, and humble men who believed in

Lori's innocence and cared about the outcome. The downside was that trial was scheduled to begin five months later and they would need to burn the midnight oil to be thoroughly ready for trial by then.

Although Lori's new attorneys were in charge, we were still influenced by things we learned from Public Defender Justine and the Defense ME she hired. Therefore, we continued to search for answers about what caused the child's injuries and spent many hours at the public library doing research online and consulting with several criminal defense attorneys. From everything we were learning about the medical and legal issues involved, a not-guilty verdict was highly unlikely unless a jury could be convinced there was an alternative reason for the child's traumatic brain and skull injuries and later death. Our research confirmed that a "guilty" verdict in child abuse and/or child murder cases is more likely than in any other type of case. *"Innocent until proven guilty"* becomes *"guilty until proven innocent,"* and *"beyond a reasonable doubt"* becomes *"if there is a possibility of guilt."* Each time Lori and I tried to explain this to defense attorneys, they simply mentioned the constitutionally mandated requirement that it was the prosecution's job to prove she was guilty beyond a reasonable doubt and the defense did not have to prove she was innocent. In theory, that principle is correct but in the real criminal justice world, we found it had almost never worked that way in child abuse or child murder cases. We thought it was necessary to provide her new attorneys with information we learned about issues relating to child abuse, head injuries, skull fractures and short distance falls in children. This was information that we felt needed to be fully explored by the defense investigators. We hoped they were prying open every lock and turning over every stone to find answers.

Finally, in late summer of 1997 (by now eighteen months after the tragedy) Lori's third set of attorneys, Crisley and Snow, asked me for funds to hire a private detective to investigate the deceased child's home environment and any unsavory characters that were involved in her home life, and search for evidence of negligence or wrongdoing. At a cost of several thousand dollars, a retired FBI agent was hired to go to Reno to investigate.

Upon checking police records of all those who lived in the same four-unit apartment as Angie and her parents, the investigator confirmed with neighbors that the best friend of Angie's parents lived in the apartment directly above them and they spent most of their non-working hours together. Strangely, police records showed this friend was arrested two months after the death of Angie, for manufacturing and selling meth from his apartment but they did not connect this in any way to Angie's brain abnormalities. Although his arrest and activities were documented by a police report and court records (because of the lapse of fifteen months and lack of prompt forensic investigation) this toxic environment could not be proven to be connected to the toddler and her brain injuries. Regardless, it has been scientifically proven that manufacturing meth creates a toxic environment known to cause congenital disabilities and neurological anomalies in a growing child or infant. Although this information said a lot about their living conditions, it was not beneficial to the defense attorneys due to the delay in discovering the information.

Most of the people the defense investigator interviewed who lived near the family would not discuss what they knew as were very sympathetic to the deceased child's parents and hostile. In contrast, one neighbor reported that there were always a lot of people coming from and going into the apartment at strange hours. She also said that at least four adults, whom she believed was an aunt and her boyfriend or husband, living in the two-bedroom apartment along with Angie at the time of the tragedy. The neighbor also reported that several times she saw an aunt (Colleen's sister) hitting and yelling at little Angie, and often saw Angie outdoors without proper clothing in the cold winter weather. However, the neighbor did not want to get further involved and did not want to testify in court. After spending a lot of time and money, we were back to where we started. Exactly why, when and what happened to the child was still anyone's guess!

Because there was no alternative, defense attorneys prepared for trial by trying to prove there were other possible causes for the child's head injuries based on the previously discovered pathological reports from three reputable sources. Certainly, if the writers of those reports testified at trial as unsolicited experts, they would have an undeniable impact on the trial jury and create reasonable doubt. Further, there would be no need to rely upon the diagnosis of the dismissed Defense ME who also found evidence of several older brain injuries.

Lori and I were distressed and disappointed to learn that since being hired, the Defense ME had developed a questionable reputation since he had been charged with tampering with evidence in another case wherein his diagnosis challenged a powerful state medical examiner. Therefore, his further participation in Lori's defense in any manner would reflect poorly on her defense team's credibility. In any case, his diagnosis made a lot of sense considering all other medical facts known about Angie. The tissue specimens he analyzed showed evidence of several older injuries in different stages of healing. Each new day brought new legal and strategic challenges to the defense team.

Multiple Hearings & Pretrial Battles

CHAPTER 6

After the grand jury indictment and Lori's arraignment for murder, unresolved disputes and legal battles between the prosecution and defense precipitated the filing of various motions with the court. Opposition and reply papers were prepared and processed totaling thousands of pages of legal wrangling, even before the trial could begin.

To our surprise and horror, each of those motions and related documents and the court hearings on them generated immediate local and network TV news reports and newspapers articles. When possible, Lori, her family, and many friends attended the oral arguments on the motions, in addition to regularly scheduled status conferences and trial continuances that crowded the landscape.

Of the many defense and prosecution court motions considered and ruled upon by the judge before the beginning of trial, the most important ones were the following:

1. Motion for Bail (granted)
2. State's Motion to Raise Bail (denied)
3. Defendant's Petition for Writ of Habeas Corpus (denied),
4. Motion to Withdraw (1st Defense Attorney Team) as Counsel (granted)
5. Motions to Continue Trial Date, (granted). Motion for Appointment of New Defense Counsel (2nd Defense Attorney Team) (granted),

6. (2nd Defense attorney Team) Motion to Withdraw as Counsel (granted),
7. Motion - Appointment of Defense Attorney Crisley (granted),
8. State's 1st Motion to Admit Evidence of Other Bad Acts (re: CPS 1994 phone calls) during Its Case-in-Chief (denied),
9. State's 2nd Motion to Admit Evidence of Other Bad Acts (re: child who fell from high-chair at daycare), (vacated)
10. Defendant's Motion to Dismiss Indictment for Prosecution Misconduct (denied)
11. Defendant's Motion to Dismiss for Failure to Present Exculpatory Evidence to Grand Jury (denied),
12. Defendant's Motion to Endorse Expert Witnesses, on Order Shortening Time (granted).

As the above list shows, before beginning any criminal trial each party may file *"motions in limine"* that are specifically designed to discuss evidentiary issues that may be unfairly detrimental to one side or the other. After hearing relevant testimony, the judge will decide whether that evidence is prejudicial or irrelevant and thus, whether it should be introduced as evidence during a trial. This process is called a Petrocelli Hearing.

It was earthshaking and stomach-churning to learn the state had filed two motions in limine (items 8 and 9 above) asking the judge to allow the jury to hear evidence of two prior uncharged and unproven allegations of child abuse by Lori. Although both motions were believed legal by the court system, they were highly manipulative and unethical, especially considering several very comprehensive investigations by law enforcement found no evidence of abuse by Lori. It was note-worthy that the state's motion papers made no mention of those investigations.

One of the prosecution motions concerned the child who fell out of her highchair while at daycare and the other one involved two phone calls to CPS more than three years before alleging Lori could potentially have abused her three-year-old daughter. The prosecution also hoped to present what they alleged was evidence discovered when police recently interviewed Lori's six-year-old. Although police collected the evidence by unlawful means (without parental consent) and although it was legally inadmissible, (as it was "fruit from a poisonous tree") prosecutors mentioned it often during several court hearings to influence the judge, without proper objections being made by defense attorneys. The blatant disregard for law and order seemed to go unchecked with no adverse consequences.

It was understood that the purpose of bringing these two motions was to ask the judge to allow the jury to hear about those uncharged and unproven incidents as evidence of habitual abuse and thereby convince them that Lori was a person who routinely abused children and had a depraved heart and callous indifference to human life. With a successful outcome, they would solidify the legal requirements for a First-Degree Murder by Child Abuse charge (under the felony murder rule) and make a murder conviction under those statutes more likely.

Prosecutors Snuffelpaw and Bird refused to acknowledge or mention in their motion papers that after the death of Angie, a comprehensive investigation of Lori's entire life and specifically her behavior with children had been conducted and closed after investigators could find no evidence of any abusive behavior. Otherwise, this same Washoe County District Attorney's office would have filed new child abuse charges against Lori. The filing of these two motions were examples of where legal court procedures were used to undermine the pursuit of truth and justice.

Defense Attorneys Crisley and Snow had to decide what the best strategy and approach would be to fight these two motions. An important consideration was whether Lori's (now seven-years-old) daughter who was the subject of one of the motions should be questioned or asked to testify at a court hearing. The decision was complicated because of the prior interview by prosecution investigators at her school and their distortion of what she said. If the judge granted the motion and the child's testimony was necessary, she would testify "in camera" (in a private informal setting without the public in attendance.) In any case, Lori chose not to risk harming her child mentally and emotionally by placing such an enormous burden on her, although it could have helped her defense. Despite Lori's concerns, it is almost unbelievable that defense attorneys never questioned the child and recorded the conversation to figure out how credible and worthwhile her testimony would be and what Tanasha remembered about her interview by police detectives. This step could have gone a long way to disprove the false allegations of those detectives.

More recently, I talked to my grown-up granddaughter, Tanasha, about the incident and she remembered that two detectives interviewed her at Kindergarten and knew precisely what she said. She asked her teacher to go with her, and the first question by a detective was, "*Does your mom beat you?*" Not understanding his question, she replied, "*Do you mean at running?*" Then he asked, "*Does your mom hit you?*" She replied, "*Sometimes she spanked me, but not anymore.*" She did not understand why they were asking her questions. When I pried further, she had no memory of her mom ever doing anything other than spanking her. Before I explained what the issues and exact wording in question were, it was clear that her memory agreed with the teacher's statements about the conversation that Tanasha never used the word "beat" as the detectives alleged. Also, it was highly suspect that police detectives did not make their usual audio recording of an interview that could prove or disprove the validity of their written report.

After several continuances, oral arguments took place for all motions pending before the judge, including the two "Motions to Admit Evidence of Other Bad Acts." Thankfully, the judge partially ruled against the prosecuting attorneys' motion about Lori's eldest daughter, saying the evidence would have an unfair and substantial prejudicial effect against Lori at trial. Even to the most highly skilled legal professional, there would be confusion as to the applicability and value of any unsubstantiated "bad acts" that were more than three years old.

Much to our chagrin, the judge ruled that the alleged bad act involving Lori's daughter could not be introduced or discussed at trial unless the defense attorneys "opened the door" by mentioning or referring to Lori's good character, in which case the prosecution could introduce those "prior bad acts" as rebuttal evidence.

As it turned out, the judge's ruling was a double-edged sword as it trapped the defense team in an extremely challenging position by making it impossible to introduce evidence of Lori's past or present good character, reputation, or her protective and nurturing attitude around children, and prevented her from testifying at trial without severe complications. Prosecutors would have a field day dragging her name through the mud with those added mistaken allegations of child abuse.

As a result, defense attorneys decided that no testimony relevant to Lori's past or present good character or history whatsoever could be discussed in the presence of the judge or jury for fear of "opening the door." At the time, it seemed like the best defense trial strategy, especially since Prosecutors Bird and Snuffelpaw were unusually adept at distorting and spinning facts to their advantage. Their passionate and highly theatrical arguments in front of the judge and jury were always on the menu, making the smallest crumb of disharmony or contradiction by defense attorneys sound like a recipe for a "Class A Felony."

In retrospect, it may have been a better defense strategy to explore and explain the circumstances surrounding those unsubstantiated CPS phone calls and put them to rest by proving to the court that there was no validity to those accusations. This strategy would have cleared the way for Lori to testify on her own behalf and explain what happened on March 4, 1996. Regardless, defense attorneys made a conscious decision not to go in that direction.

On the remaining "prior bad act" motion concerning an eight-month-old who fell from a highchair at daycare, the judge postponed the hearing and his decision to a later date. Of course, it was very disappointing to prosecutors when the parents of the eight-month-old refused to cooperate with them, causing them to withdraw that motion before the hearing took place. However, prosecutors withdrew the motion on the premise that they could bring up the those "child abuse" allegations during trial if defense attorneys opened the door by discussing Lori's prior conduct or reputation.

As the unlimited power of state prosecutors unleashed dangerously dark storm clouds around us, we wondered what was happening to the continual prayers of dozens of Christian people. Were they going no further than the ceiling? Why was God hiding? Was God not all-powerful? While feeling disappointed that God did not intercede at once and provide a way out of the inexplicable nightmare, I thought of many scriptures that instruct us to be patient and wait for God and his timing.

While all the legal maneuvering was happening within the court system, a storm of public hysteria had been ignited and fueled by non-stop 24/7 TV media and newspaper coverage which inflicted more emotional distress upon Lori and the family. Although repeatedly described as being a child abuser and murderer, the more responsible news anchors would use the word "alleged" but then would go ahead to give very biased and distorted information that it was an open and shut case. Regardless, in most cases, they were merely repeating what prosecuting attorneys were saying in the courtroom or what reporters were reading in the various court documents.

Wisely or unwisely, the defense attorneys decided not to respond to the media to refute the mistaken information, as they believed it would be counter-productive and distorted by the prosecution. Each court status and pretrial hearing brought new anxiety and questions about what other tricks state prosecutors would engage in next, and what would satisfy their appetite for revenge against an accused child killer.

When humanly possible, one or more of my sisters and I would drive from Fresno to attend the soul-piercing and gut-wrenching court hearings to show our solidarity and give emotional support to Lori and her family. A massive sense of darkness and otherworldliness weighed down our spirits each time we approached the courthouse. And we had no choice but to listen helplessly as state prosecutors made allegations against Lori that we knew were based on either outright falsehoods, partial facts, or the prosecutors' imagination or speculation. It took an extreme amount of self-control, not to yell out in court that what they said about my daughter was untrue but that would have done more harm than good as prosecutors could use my words against Lori if a sliver of chance existed. Without a doubt, these prosecuting attorneys intended to win at any price, no matter how long it took, how untruthful they needed to be, or how many children and adults they hurt in the process.

Based on many years of work experience, prosecuting attorneys build their cases on facts and events accurately as reported by witnesses and evidence found by investigators. But in this case, the facts and evidence morphed into new art forms with dimensions and substance that were hardly recognizable. Like a science fiction movie, there seemed to be no limit to prosecutor's flagrant disregard for reality as they distorted relevant facts, forensic science, existing laws, and established court procedures. Albert Einstein once said, "*The difference between stupidity and genius is that genius has its limits.*" But, moral relevancy has no boundaries.

By now, more than twenty months had passed since we entered this criminal justice maze. Lori's attorney informed us that Prosecutor Bird promised the grandmother of the deceased child that Lori would be convicted regardless of what it cost, while boasting that the county and state checkbooks (public funds) were open, implying there was no limit to the amount of money they could spend convicting Lori. This very biased promise was a betrayal of the prosecutor's sworn duty to promote truth and justice and to apply the legal processes equally in an unbiased manner to all people, regardless of her personal preferences and beliefs. We felt betrayed and disheartened and more like second-class citizens.

In my quest for information, I consulted with a retired prosecuting attorney for the US Justice Department with more than forty years of experience. He explained that the outcome of any jury trial depends upon which attorney puts on the most compelling "dog and pony" show and has little to do with the facts and evidence presented. He reminded me that this phenomenon is especially true in highly emotional trials involving the abuse or death of a child since outrage and vengeance rules in the hearts and minds of jurors. Therefore, jurors forget that reasonable doubt should be ruled out before finding a person guilty.

Defense Motions to Dismiss

As part of their pre-trial strategy, defense attorneys filed two motions to dismiss the charges against Lori. The first was a "*Motion to Dismiss for*

Prosecutorial Misconduct," and the second was a *"Motion to Dismiss for the Prosecution's Failure to Present Exculpatory Evidence to the Grand Jury."* Both motions involved the original hospital pathology report which neither investigators nor prosecutor mentioned to the grand jury. Ironically, this original pathology report had a page attached entitled *"Cancer Screening Sheet"* and both pages were attached to the coroner's autopsy report. Police investigators and prosecuting attorneys ignored it or read it but thought it was irrelevant because of the diagnoses made by emergency room doctors.

All the while, police investigators did not follow up with the hospital personnel to discuss the report or to get a copy of either of the three later pathology reports showing Angie had two-day old brain injuries. In summary, while ignoring the three relevant pathology reports, the prosecution selectively presented to the grand jurors the opinions of emergency room doctors and the coroner who claimed that child abuse caused Angie's injuries no earlier than a few hours before arrival at the emergency room.

About two months after the motions were filed, opposition and reply papers were filed, oral arguments were heard. Thereafter, the judge ruled against the *"Defendant's Motion to Dismiss Indictment for Prosecution Misconduct"* and against *"Defendant's Motion to Dismiss for Failure to Present Exculpatory Evidence to Grand Jury."* Although the judge's decisions concerning these two motions may have been based upon the "letter of the law," they did not measure up to the full "intent of the law" which is to promote truth and justice. Regardless of the judge's thinking or legal reasoning, practically speaking these rulings were equivalent to the court sanctioning the well-known habit of prosecuting attorneys only presenting evidence favorable to their allegations and viewpoint to a grand jury, to defense counsels, and to the judge and jury while ignoring all other evidence.

In trying to understand the court's rulings, I recognized that we live in a fallen and broken world with broken people and governing authorities that reflect that brokenness. Knowing that we have no guarantee of a life without trials and difficulties, it was encouraging to know we have a promise of life everlasting in our heavenly home without pain or suffering. Lori and I needed to keep an eternal perspective while traveling through this maze. Otherwise, despair and grief would shatter us into a million fragments and leave us unable to cope.

After the Judge heard oral arguments and ruled upon all pre-trial motions, the trial was set to begin the first week of November, twenty months after the tragedy. Although we knew the trial was on the horizon, nothing could have prepared us for the incredible depth of despair and devastation it brought. Knowing that my daughter and her family's future would hinge on the skills and wisdom of the attorneys, the judge, and the jury was one of the most mind-numbing realities ever experienced. The entire legal process and experience felt like being in the middle of a never-ending EF-5 tornado with no protection and shelter from the pounding rain, thunder, blinding lightning, and winds of 200 mph. Through it all, we relied on promises in the Bible that God was in charge and would give us the wisdom, courage, and strength to continue fighting for what was right.

During this tumultuous time, Lori shared with me that she was having a recurring nightmare of standing alone in the middle of a busy freeway, frozen and unable to move with dozens of automobiles speeding toward her at ninety miles per hour. Each nightmare would end before the approaching cars hit her and she would be jarred awake, traumatized, and shaking with fear of what her fate might have been. Her personal distress, confusion, anxiety, grief, and pain came from many directions such as Angie's unexplainable brain injuries and death, the vast number of court hearings over the prior twenty months, restrictions imposed on her in caring for her young children, financial needs, defense attorney problems, and the uncertainty of the upcoming trial.

Resurging emotions brought waves of indescribable anguish, uncertainty, panic, and despair that were quieted by the Holy Spirit bringing a familiar inner comfort and peace that flooded our hearts and minds. God promised He would not allow suffering beyond our ability to handle it as promised in the scripture at 1 Cor. 10:13(b), [AMP] which says:

> But God is faithful [to His Word and to His compassionate nature], and He [can be trusted] not to let you be tempted and tried and assayed beyond your ability and strength of resistance and power to endure, but with the temptation He will [always] also provide the way out (the means of escape to a landing place), that you may be capable and strong and powerful to bear up under it patiently.

Once we were assured that the trial was beginning shortly, Lori and I wrote letters and mailed or emailed them to everyone on a list I had compiled of friends and family members who were interested in being updated about our struggle. My letter read as follows:

Dear Friends and Family,

Enclosed is a letter from my daughter Lori about the pending trial. Please pray for her peace and calm assurance (in mind, spirit, and emotions) that God is in control and his truth will prevail.

If you can attend at any time during the two-week trial that starts on November 10, in Dept. 7 of the Washoe County Courthouse in Reno, please let me know as I will have buttons with a picture of her and her children for you to wear to show support and ask that you be seated in the defense side of the Courtroom. I will be stationed outside the Courtroom and will provide you the buttons, as I will not be allowed inside as I am on the witness list and may be called to testify. Of course, we understand if you cannot attend. Remember to keep the Judge, jury, attorneys, Lori, and her family in your prayers.

Thanks for your support. Lori's Mom

Lori's letter read as follows:

Dear Friends and Family,

I have contemplated this letter for an eternity, and now it is time to write you. The other day, my son came to me after having a nightmare and said, "Mommy, I had a dream that you went away and never came back to me." He was hysterical. That moment captures the pain and fear that my family and I have been through these past 20 months. We need you now. We are asking for your help in three ways.

1. Would you commit to praying for me, my family and everyone connected with my defense team? On Monday, I go on trial for the charge of murder. If convicted, I could face life in prison without the possibility of parole. The trial will be in Courtroom #7, in the Washoe County Courthouse.

2. Could you attend this trial as part of my support team? We need about 30 people present each day for about three weeks. You would sit on the defense side of the Courtroom. You can come and go as needed. If you can even attend one day, would you please call me and let me know when you can attend. I will reimburse any parking fees to you. There is a parking garage near the courthouse. Any support that

---

you can give to my family during this extremely difficult time would be very welcome.

3. We need encouragement, prayer, and childcare, to name a few. Financially we are devastated. Over $100,000 has been raised and spent on my defense, and it was not enough. We are forced to pay over $1000 per month to either friends or a nanny for the care of our children. Every month we are exceeding our income by at least $1000. As you can see, something needs to change. Could you please pray for this situation?

Something has gone terribly wrong in this United States of America, where all people who are charged with a crime are supposed to be "presumed innocent." My family and I need your physical, spiritual, and emotional strength.

Thank you, Lori Watson,

In response to our requests, many of Lori's close friends and extended family members voluntarily arranged to take time off from their jobs and caring for their families to attend the trial. They prayed for her, her family, and all those involved in the legal process, including prosecuting attorneys.

It has been said that a person's character and reputation is truly revealed by the friends kept during a crisis. If this is true, Lori's character was of the highest caliber as the most gracious and loving Christ-like people stood by her during these very dark days and years.

Christian churches in several states placed Lori and the family's plight on their prayer chains. Many were praying that Lori would be found innocent, that she and her family's needs would be supplied, and the Holy Spirit would bring them peace, strength, and courage. Also, close family and friends who knew about the favorable pathology reports were praying that defense and prosecuting attorneys would jointly do the necessary work to verify that the various pathology reports were valid so the charges against Lori would be changed or dismissed entirely. Why God did not answer the prayers of many hundreds of people was beyond comprehension. Was it not God's will at this point? Did He have a more significant purpose and a refining process in mind for Lori and all of us? Or was it because God was hiding from us as King David asked in Psalms 10:1 (NCV);

> Lord, why are you so far away?
> Why do you hide when there is trouble?

As part of the pre-trial preparation, Lori's attorneys instructed her to have no facial expressions during the trial testimony regardless of how outlandish the accusations were against her. This was especially important when the jury was present since any facial expressions and demeanor might be interpreted by prosecutors and jurors as an unfavorable response and used to undermine her best interest. They also recommended that she wear soft pastel colors that would appear more maternal and likable to the jury. They also forbade us from talking to TV or Newspaper reporters before or during trial, to avoid any further unfavorable media response.

A month before trial began, Lori had attended a seminar presented by *"The National Child Abuse & Resource Center"* by a famous trial and jury consultant firm.. Among many other things, Lori learned that due to the highly emotional nature of the case, jurors would make their decisions on emotions rather than analyzing the evidence and common sense, and that was especially true in circumstantial (no other witness) cases. Defense attorneys needed to passionately emotionalize the defense issues for the jury while proving there was an alternative reason for the child's severe intracranial injuries.

While Defense Attorneys Crisley and Snow were preparing for trial, they learned that the Defense ME previously hired by public defender Justine, was charged by his home state's governing authorities with allegations of evidence and witness tampering in a very complicated and difficult case he had become embroiled in. For obvious reasons, the Defense ME could not be allowed to give testimony at Lori's trial since his legal trouble would negatively affect his credibility. Therefore, he was informed that his services were no longer needed.

While trying to help with trial preparation, with Lori's approval, I sent Attorneys Crisley and Snow several faxes and left voicemail messages emphasizing that all tissue specimen slides and blocks of tissue from the left side of Angie's brain that were prepared by the Washoe County Coroner and given to the Defense ME nearly a year before needed to be analyzed by other credible pathologists. It should not have been a very difficult task to either verify those earlier findings or debunk them. Finding the truth of the histological (tissue) specimens and preparing an aggressive defense was of paramount importance. But since the defense attorneys had stopped communicating directly with me about their intentions or trial strategies, I feared they did not agree.

I knew the attorneys would face problems if they introduced the microscopic histological (tissue) slides prepared by and for the fired Defense

ME, since all expert pathologists are routinely asked which documents and evidence they reviewed in making their diagnosis and opinions. Thus, the prior involvement of the prior Defense ME would be known and defense attorneys wanted to avoid it at all cost. Additionally, the microscopic slides (prepared for and by the Defense ME) were inscribed with identifying numbers and his last name. But this was not an insurmountable obstacle, as a DNA analysis could have proven they were from Angie, and the coroner would have been able to verify that he prepared tissue specimens for the doctor from Angie's left cerebellum.

Regardless, while the Defense ME was still involved he consulted with a well-respected pathologist at the University of Miami and sent him the microscopic tissue slides for diagnosis. In an email to me dated November 1, 1997, (after the criminal court's pre-trial discovery deadline and a few days before the trial began) the UM pathologist wrote as follows:

> I can only surmise that the slides I examined are the ones he indicates. However, they have findings similar to those he describes.
>
> From a trial strategy standpoint, however, I am not able to know whether I would be helpful or not. The child clearly has previous injury. I believe the State's pathologist will readily agree with this. In addition, I suspect he will readily agree that there is an AV malformation (or something like that.... I am not sure what he thinks it is, other than it has been there awhile. I suspect we all agree to that.

This was exciting news but unfortunately the criminal court's pre-trial discovery "cut-off" time had passed before this email was received by me and then sent to defense attorneys. The discovery cutoff made it almost impossible to have the UM pathologist testify at trial unless drastic measures were taken, such as the filing of a motion to get a trial continuance and a last-minute motion to name him as a defense expert witness.

Lori's attorneys told me they believed that since other pathologists had already been hired by both the defense team and prosecutors, it was highly unlikely the court would approve any such last-minute request and her attorneys took no action to explore the veracity of the University of Miami pathologist's findings. Defense attorneys had not realized that those tissue specimens were taken from a specific area of the brain that would have further supported the diagnosis of the other three pathology departments, as well as that of the Defense ME.

As more and more forensic medical evidence surfaced, it became obvious that Angie's injuries most likely originated with the AVMs, or a similar undiagnosed pathological condition, that was further compromised by falling off the kitchen countertop head-first on the hard kitchen floor, the multiple vaccinations she received a week earlier, and the short-distance fall on March 4th. Doctors, including the Defense ME, explained that an undiagnosed pathological or hereditary condition, such AVMs, or some similar anomaly (i.e., tumors) would cause lesions, hemorrhaging, hydrocephalus and increased intracranial pressure that leads to other symptoms such as retinal hemorrhaging, gait disturbances, and loss of consciousness.

Defense attorneys finally realized that winning the case hinged on the medical forensic issues and hired medical experts who began exploring the brain injuries suffered by the deceased child. Lori and I hoped the newly hired defense medical experts would offer answers to many critical forensic issues, such as the following: Was the child's rather minor fall on that Monday secondary to a primary head injury or some undiagnosed pathological condition? What was the correct description of the skull fracture when the child was first admitted to the hospital? Were the severe hydrocephalus, swelling, and bleeding conditions initially caused by the multiple immunization shots? Or were the injuries triggered by some other preexisting pathological disease or nutritional deficiency? Was there indisputable evidence of several farther advanced healing in the child's brain of at least 24 to 48 hours old?

It was agreed that funds returned by Lori's first attorney would be used for trial expert witnesses and investigative costs, but by the time trial arrived those resources were almost depleted. Although defense attorneys had discussed hiring a biomedical or biomechanical engineer to explain the dynamics and consequences of the toddler's short-distance fall, we received no requests from Lori's attorneys for money to hire one. Perhaps if there had been enough time to prepare thoroughly, the defense attorneys would have done so.

Finally, prosecuting attorneys had nine medical experts who would give their opinions at trial while the defense only had three. The twelve experts included two pediatricians, the Washoe County Chief Medical Examiner (Coroner), an ICU pediatric specialist, two pathologists, a neuropathologist, a pathologist, two neurosurgeons, an ophthalmologist, a pediatric radiologist.

It was revealing that the state subpoenaed only the doctors from the hospital who were favorable to their theories and ignored the other treating doctors who did not support their position. Bizarrely missing from the state's witness list were the two hospital pathologists who diagnosed prior head injuries and the two hospital radiologists who initially reviewed Angie's CT scans.

Not having the hospital radiologists who read the first pre-surgery CT scans testify was of concern mainly because he diagnosed there was a linear fracture that was not depressed, in contrast to a post-surgery diagnosis of a complex fracture system by the second radiologist. The second hospital radiologist compared them to the pre-surgery CT scans and reported the changes as;

> AP and lateral skull films show widened coronal and sagittal sutures. There is a craniotomy defect posteriorly and a shunt tube in place on the left."

Under "Conclusion" he diagnosed;

> Apparent widening of the sutures and postoperative changes in the occiput and an intracranial line on the left.

Obviously, the reason why the state prosecuting attorneys did not intend to call any of the hospital radiologists or pathologists to testify at trial was that they would undermine the state's claims about the severity of the child's initial skull fracture and head injuries and imply that prior injuries or other issues could have caused them. The unanswered questions were: Which skull fractures happened before surgery? Which part of the fracture happened when the surgeon drilled into the fragile splintering skull and removed a part of it to alleviate brain pressure?

It was regrettable that defense attorneys did not choose any of the treating hospital radiologists to testify as experts at trial to highlight and explain the differences in the before and after surgery CT scans.

Regardless, after the deadline to do so, the defense team asked the court for permission to appoint hospital pathologist, Dr. Moss to testify concerning the evidence of old healing tissue as diagnosed by the Stanford Research Clinic, AFIP, and his department. The court approved the request and allowed Dr. Moss to testify as a non-paid medical expert for the defense without being paid.

Altogether, defense attorneys subpoenaed thirty percipient witnesses and paid Dr. Coyote, Forensic Pathologist, and Dr. Sparks, a Pediatric Neurosurgeon to testify as expert witnesses, in addition to Dr. Moss, the local pathologist.

In addition to appointing nine paid medical expert witnesses, the State of Nevada's prosecuting attorneys subpoenaed forty percipient witnesses to testify, including first responders such as police, detectives, paramedics, and everyone who visited Lori's house on the day of the tragedy.

The fact that the state called nine medical expert witnesses to testify compared to three by the defense attorneys could send an unspoken signal to jurors that the state had better and stronger evidence on their side; and therefore, were able to hire more medical experts. More likely, the defense attorneys' failure to find and appoint more medical experts was due to insufficient time (less than five months) to prepare adequately for trial by attorneys who were admittedly inexperienced in defending child abuse or child murder cases. Aside from all that, these defense attorneys were handling several related essential motions along with servicing several other clients and trials in the interim.

In contrast to the minimal experience of Lori's defense attorneys, the prosecuting attorneys bragged about having more than fifty years of experience prosecuting child abuse and child murder cases and had been prosecuting this same case continually since it began twenty months before. Also, prosecutors already had the names and contact information of many previously hired medical expert witnesses and on short notice would frame their testimony in a manner that would support the state's theories if they had wiggle room to do so. That was an easy challenge since they never testified to a reasonable degree of medical certainly after examining all available evidence.

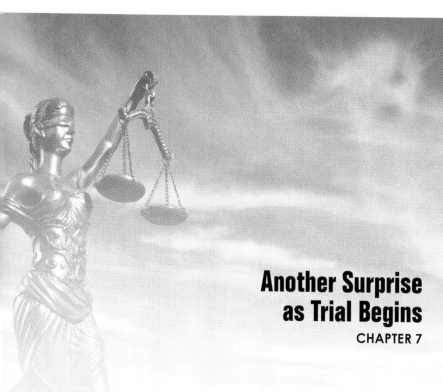

Another Surprise as Trial Begins

CHAPTER 7

On the first day of trial the proceedings became more confusing and ominous when prosecuting attorneys filed an Amended Indictment. This was a total shock to everyone and Defense Attorneys Crisley and Snow objected strenuously since it upgraded and limited the charges to only include *"First Degree Murder by Child Abuse."* It read as follows:

> Defendant did, on or about March 4, 1996, then and there willfully, feloniously, without authority of law, and with malice aforethought, kill Angie Rison, a human being, to wit: by the Defendant subjecting Angie Rison, a minor child being approximately 14 months of age, to acts of child abuse, including, violent shaking of the body of Angie Rison and/or throwing the body of Angie Rison against a hard surface and/or the striking of the body of Angie Rison with an object and/or other manner or means unknown, which resulted in the death of Angie Rison on or about March 6, 1996.

The Amended Indictment was incomprehensible since the same prosecuting attorneys had previously instructed the *grand* jurors that the *trial* jurors would decide whether conviction of First Degree Murder or a less serious charge, such as Involuntary Manslaughter, Negligent Homicide, or Second-Degree Murder, was proper. Ironically, those instructions contradicted existing state laws that demanded the grand jury decide what specific crime has been committed.

Even if this Amended Indictment was legal, it was highly unethical considering the prosecutor's prior instructions to the grand jury. It sent a strong message to the defense attorneys that the prosecutors would only be satisfied with a First-Degree Murder by Child Abuse conviction. Unfortunately, the Amended Indictment worked against some of the defense's prior trial preparation and strategy in very profound ways.

Emboldened by the judge's prior rulings in their favor (i.e., the defense's Petition for Writ of Mandate, Motions to Dismiss, and other motions) wherein he ignored laws requiring that the elements of malice aforethought (premeditation and deliberation) must be found before prosecuting for First Degree Murder, prosecutors filed the Amended Indictment. More specifically, the system and the judge ignored existing Nevada statutes that did not (at that time) classify child abuse as a felony, nor was it counted as a felony in the "felony murder" statute.

We were perplexed and alarmed by the Amended Indictment and had many questions, such as: Why was it done? Were lawful procedures followed? Where was the new evidence that could have prompted this change? Since court rules and discovery laws instructed the state to give all known evidence to the defense on a prompt basis, where way was the new evidence? Regardless, the "powers that be" in the Washoe County District Attorney's Office decided they had the authority to do this, even without discovering any new evidence or impaneling a new grand jury.

In keeping with their usual *"Modus Operandi,"* prosecuting attorneys thought this pretrial strategy would pressure Lori into making a confession and pleading guilty to a lesser charge, since this technique had worked with many other defendants. But it did not work as Lori was determined to be acquitted.

Counterbalancing our concern about the *"Amended Indictment"* was our belief that all elements of First Degree Murder must be proven beyond a reasonable doubt, and from our perspective an acquittal was possible.

The jury selection of ordinary non-professional citizens began at once after filing of the Amended Indictment and took several days to complete. Prior to the judge calling the jury into the courtroom, state Prosecutor Snuffelpaw unexpectedly raised a question to the judge about the admissibility of the various pathology reports from the local hospital, Stanford Research Clinic, and the AFIP Pathology Department. He asked the judge to rule that they could not be discussed or introduced at trial or mentioned during opening arguments because they had not been authenticated by affidavits from the various custodians of record.

After several arguments from both sides, the Judge ruled the issue would be dealt with during the trial but even then, they could only be introduced as documents being relied upon by defense expert witnesses to form their opinion and *could not otherwise be introduced as evidence or trial exhibits.* It was crystal clear that Prosecuting Attorneys Bird and Snuffelpaw did not want the jurors to know about them or consider them to be significant or reliable evidence.

[Note: Although not mentioned in court, this problem arose because defense attorneys had failed to authenticate the evidence by subpoenaing the four pathology reports from the three pathology laboratories or medical facilities, with instructions that they send a copy of each under seal and certified under penalty of perjury by the custodians of records, directly to the court. This misstep by defense attorneys gave prosecutors a legal way to keep their true significance hidden from the jurors - and reduced the defense expert's testimony to mere opinions.]

After that discussion and while the jury was not present, prosecuting attorneys announced to the court that the grandmother and mother of the deceased child had made several appearances on news and TV shows discussing the case and wanted to know if the defense intended to raise that issue during trial. Defense attorneys responded they were not concerned and did not think it was an issue. They had been too busy practicing law and preparing for trial to be aware of the extent to which prosecutors had worked with the family to arrange TV and media promotions and tell their version of what happened. Lori and I, along with friends and family, had watched many of the TV news and various current event shows helplessly from the sidelines while the publicity promoted by the District Attorney's office convicted Lori of murder in the court of public opinion.

After resolving the two issues outside the presence of the jurors, the judge called them into the room and announced that trial was now is session.

Trial Opening Statements

Prosecuting and defense attorneys presented their opening statements as a preview of the evidence each side expected to introduce during trial. Prosecutors portrayed it as an open and shut case with no room for reasonable doubt. Commenting on every tortuous opening statement made by prosecutors would serve no useful purpose except to say they were rife with hyperbole and distortions of foundational facts and evidence. As expected, female Prosecuting Attorney Bird repeated the same thoughtless clichés in her opening statement in a very emotional and dramatic way as she had done in many prior court hearings, by saying:

> .... the amount of force that would have been needed to cause the injuries to this 14-month old baby would be like dropping a child from a two-story building onto her head, onto cement.

The allegations against my daughter were shocking and devastating, causing me to become nauseous and light headed. With every ounce of my being, I wanted to stand up and scream out that they were wrong, but I knew that would be counterproductive. Unable to respond, I realized we were prisoners of the powerful Nevada criminal justice system and circumstances that only God had the power to defeat.

In their opening statements, defense attorneys disagreed with everything said by prosecutors and said they would show evidence that the child had prior injuries and was reinjured on the day of the tragedy and were not caused by anything Lori intentionally did. Although their words were right on point, they were not presented with the authority, conviction, or emotion to match the dramatic opening statements by prosecuting attorneys. This was not a good sign.

Although I was allowed to listen to both opening statements, defense attorneys could not allow me to hear any trial testimony as they had listed me as a witness just in case I was needed. I was banished to the court hallway, where I saw the strange behavior of Angie's father. He was acting like a scared rabbit with excessive and erratic body movements while constantly looking over his shoulder as if he was paranoid or trying to avoid impending doom.

Also, I overheard Angie's mother angrily saying to her sister that she could not stand her mother and she was moving out of state to get away from her. I wondered what life was like at home for little Angie and if an unhealthy home had caused her to feel needy and neglected, and that was why she was so clingy to Lori and bonded so quickly with her.

Percipient Witnesses Testify

Because I was not allowed to attend most of the trial, it was necessary for me to read two dozen trial transcripts to know exactly what was said and by whom. It is impossible and unnecessary to discuss all the testimony and evidence contained in the tens-of-thousands of pages (some of which held contradictory testimony), but the most important facts, issues and testimonies inspired this writing, including an account of the most egregious and unpredictable actions of prosecuting attorneys who were sailing in the stormy seas of moral relativism.

Testimony of thirty percipient witnesses was heard first. They included the parents and friends of the deceased child, and first responders, police officers, and others who saw Lori or visited her house on the day of the tragedy. Their testimonies produced no evidence that was significantly meaningful because none of them was present with Lori the entire day or present to verify the accidental fall of Angie. However, although asked in various ways, visitors that afternoon did not see any unusual or out-of-control behavior by Lori as alleged by prosecutors.

It was clear that while preparing for trial, prosecutors had collaborated with first responders to claim that Lori's written statement was missing an hour during which she committed the murder and for which she did not give an account. Their statements were supported by a "Trial Exhibit" they claimed was a true and correct copy of her statement, but they omitted page two which clearly showed an hour was not missing.

No witness testified that Lori was upset or showed any signs of anger or hostility on the day of the tragedy. Police investigators, paramedics and other visitors at her home said it was neat and clean, nothing seemed to be out of place and there was no sign or evidence of any struggle or violence.

Therefore, detectives testified they were not able to find and confiscate any evidence showing that a violent crime had been committed, and thus did not seal off the so-called crime scene nor preserve it for further forensic study which would have been standard protocol.

It was obvious from the very beginning that the defense needed a witness who could testify that Angie had suffered an earlier primary traumatic brain injury or could present proof of some biological defect or medical condition that caused the injuries. Since that did not happen, the defense was compelled to rely solely on the ability of medical and forensic specialists to examine all the available medical evidence before testifying

Expert Testimony Scrutinized
CHAPTER 8

A s previously mentioned, prosecuting and defense attorneys jointly had a total of twelve medical specialists to testify as "Expert Witnesses" during the trial. Because this was purely a circumstantial case (meaning there were no collaborating witnesses to prove or disprove the charges), the trial became a classic battle of medical experts who gave their opinions about what caused the deceased toddler's skull fracture and the underlying severe brain injuries.

The following is a summary of the opinions of the twelve medical "expert witnesses" who testified about the relevant forensic issues. All the named experts mentioned below are fiction and the product of the writers' imagination. If there are currently doctors with similar names, that is purely coincidental and the same are excluded from this narrative.

Dr. Kowiak, ER Pediatrician for Prosecution

Dr. Kowiak was the doctor who initially treated Angie upon her arrival at the hospital emergency room. Although he did not see any external injuries, bruising, or swelling of her head, he thought she was suffering from a neurological devastation and ordered CT scans of her head. Three hours after the child became comatose, radiologist read the CT scans that revealed a linear skull fracture, tissue swelling and an extensive collection of blood within the brain.

The pediatrician opined that within three to six hours before arrival (between 10 a.m. to 1 p.m.), Angie had suffered a non-accidental trauma after which she would have been lethargic and that he believed an intentional violent trauma equivalent to falling from a two-story building was necessary to cause the injuries. He made this determination although he had no training or experience as a forensic pathologist, pediatric neurologist, medical examiner, biomechanical or biomedical engineer who usually would qualify to make such diagnosis.

Dr. Gray, Coroner/Chief Medical Examiner for Prosecution

An autopsy is designed to be an *unbiased forensic* medical and scientific process consisting of a post-mortem examination of a corpse to determine the cause and manner of death and to evaluate any disease, pathological condition, or prior bodily injuries that may have contributed to it. In violation of that process, Dr. Gray testified that he was comfortable with being influenced by the police investigators who routinely attended autopsies to give him insight into what caused the injuries. Amazingly, the doctor admitted he wanted their input to point him in the right direction and testified that was his usual procedure when doing an autopsy. It was clear that the coroner was acting as if his office was an extension of the police department and prosecutors instead of an independent investigative agency as needed by state law.

His testimony underscored the belief that the defense team should have had a pediatric forensic pathologist attend the autopsy to balance the influence and sway of police investigators. Without a doubt, if Lori and I had known how the medical examiner/coroner performed autopsies, we would have put more pressure on her attorney to hire an independent pediatric forensic pathologist to attend the autopsy, ask probing questions, and make sure all relevant forensic evidence was secured.

Dr. Gray rationalized not preserving a sample of the fractured skull bone by saying that he could not see evidence of healing and thus, there was no reason to keep a bone specimen. This statement conflicts with other forensic medical examiners and pathologists who reported that its impossible to see with the naked eye evidence of bone healing for several days or a few weeks. Instead, such bones need to be microscopically examined by appropriate bone pathologists to diagnose the age of the fracture.

Dr. Gray claimed he was unaware of the hospital pathology report of March 4, 1996, when he prepared his autopsy report. However, a copy of that original report was attached to his autopsy report provided to the grand jury. When asked if he had seen the subsequent Stanford Research Clinic transmittal letter, the AFIP, or the amended hospital pathology report all diagnosing an older injury, he incorrectly testified that he heard about them but had not seen them. Since no attorney asked the right follow-up questions, he was not forced to admit that he had seen them when the Defense ME visited him during his trip to Reno in January 1997 (more than ten months after preparing his autopsy report.) This was memorialized in the *"Attorney Privileged Work Product Report"* given to Public Defender Justine, by the Defense ME while he was still working for the defense team. The coroner had also discussed them with Public Defender Justine while she was still defense counsel.

Regardless, the chief medical examiner admitted that if there were an abundance of macrophages (evidence of older healing), the injuries would have been at least a day or two old. Amazingly, he also testified that he could not read CT scans but would sometimes look at them *"to try and figure things out."* This was why he was uncertain about whether the fractured skull bone was depressed or not and why his report did not specify what type of skull fracture it was, e.g., whether depressed, diastatic, linear, basilar or a growing fracture. Since he had not read the hospital radiology reports and could not accurately diagnose CT scans himself, he was relying on hearsay (from an undisclosed radiologist) to describe the autopsy and hospital CT scans instead of having a skilled pediatric radiologist read them for him.

Very candidly, the chief medical examiner testified that since there was no pattern to any of the injuries, it was impossible for him to figure out how the injuries were inflicted on the child. That statement directly contradicted his prior testimony during the grand jury hearing, and his *"Opinion"* in the autopsy report (prepared nineteen months before) when he said as follows:

> It is my opinion that the decedent came to her death because of closed head injury with a fractured skull, blunt trauma to head, homicide (at the hands of another.)

His trial testimony shows to me that he was now remorseful about his hasty autopsy report and wanted to minimize the impact of it on the jurors, especially since he had known about the prior three pathology reports for ten months. Regardless of his opinions, the higher authorities would not allow him to reexamine the evidence and consider amending the autopsy report.

Dr. Vo, Pediatric ICU Specialist for Prosecution

Dr. Vo was director of the ICU section of the local hospital and a board-certified pediatrician and critical care specialist who first examined Angie and viewed the CT scans taken one and one-half hours after the unconscious child with a reported head injury arrived in the emergency room. Obviously, this hospital was not a *"Level 1 Trauma Center"* and was not prepared to handle life or death situations quickly and efficiently.

It is notable that Dr. Vo had recently attended Dr. Bork's (another expert witness in this same case) seminar about how to recognize child abuse. In keeping with what she learned at the seminar, she decided that the injuries were non-accidental and most likely occurred on the afternoon prior to arrival at the emergency room. Although the CT scans revealed swelling at the back of Angie's head, she did not see any external signs of physical injury or abuse.

When questioned about the amount of force needed to inflict Angie's wounds, she replied as follows: *"Probably falling from a two-story building or a three-story building onto a concrete floor on the back of your head."* However, that was an irresponsible and uneducated statement because she had no training or experience as a medical examiner, forensic pathologist, pediatric neurologist, nor as a biomedical or biomechanical engineering. Her testimony would be equal to a disaster clean-up response team member testifying as an expert meteorologist or accident reconstructionist concerning the wind force and weather patterns needed to create the disaster and destroy a building without the right ability and knowledge of how and what the building was made of and its prior condition. Likewise, Dr. Vo was not trained or experienced in answering questions about the amount of force needed to cause specific skull fractures and brain injuries.

Dr. Moss, Clinical Pathologist for Defense

For obvious reasons, state prosecutors did not subpoena Dr. Moss, a pathologist at the treating hospital to testify for the prosecution. More importantly, after the deadline had passed to appoint expert witnesses, *defense* attorneys asked for and obtained permission from the court to name Dr. Moss, as an expert to testify concerning his department's review and diagnosis of the histological (tissue) slides prepared from one of the two masses removed during surgery.

Upon first examination of the microscopic tissue specimen extracted from the spot near where the fracture was found, Dr. Moss and his staff diagnosed a rare brain tumor, called an Oligodendroglioma. When Dr. Moss and his department were told that the case involved a child abuse/murder victim, they decided to consult with the prestigious Stanford Research Clinic to make sure of their diagnosis, because he realized that he and other pathologists at the hospital would be compelled to testify during trial about their findings.

Therefore, he instructed his staff to cut a preserved tissue specimen and a paraffin block from one of the two masses of brain cells/tissue or blood clots removed during surgery and send them to Stanford Research Clinic for consultation. Per their usual protocol and practice, they made the referral to Stanford Research Clinic without providing them with any personal history of the specimens to prevent any bias in forming a proper scientific diagnosis. He testified this adhered to Koch's rules (standard industry practice) about how to do a scientific study and arrive at a correct diagnosis.

Dr. Moss testified that he knew his pathology department was not equipped or experienced enough to process the more sophisticated types of stains needed for a more precise diagnosis of cancer and aging of tissue samples. That knowledge prompted the consultation with the Stanford Research Clinic, which was at that time one of the cutting-edge cancer research and pathology institutions in this country.

After receiving the responsive pathology report from Stanford Research Clinic diagnosing an abundance of macrophages, Dr. Moss prepared another paraffin block and microscopic slides of the tissue and sent them to an agency of the US government, the AFIP (Air Force Institute of Pathology) to get a third diagnosis. The referral transmittal included no history of the specimens per their usual practice. Without being influenced by the history of the specimens or the prior diagnosis of the local pathology department, both the Stanford Research Clinic and AFIP diagnosed an organizing hematoma with an abundance of microphages that were at least twenty-four hours old. Therefore, the local hospital pathologists amended their original report to comport with the two more advanced testing and diagnoses.

As mentioned, prosecuting attorneys tried to prevent those four reports from being introduced as evidence or discussed in any manner during trial. After much discussion and heated arguments, the judge ruled that defense expert witnesses would be allowed to show and discuss them as documents they reviewed and relied upon in preparing their testimony.

But they could not be introduced as exhibits of evidence to the jury since the respective pathologists' custodians of records had not authenticated them by sworn affidavits.

Dr. Moss testified that although both Stanford Research Clinic and AFIP Pathology Departments agreed about the evidence of older injuries, but they disagreed as to the results of the S-100 staining diagnosis. *(Note: S-100 is a specific stain used to diagnose malignant melanoma, carcinoma of the artery, certain tumors, and epidermal differentiation.)* The Stanford Research Clinic tests showed positive for S-100 protein, but the AFIP test did not.

> [Note: Since each of the two institutions were given separate paraffin blocks holding preserved tissue, they could have been obtained from different tissue masses. Further studies were needed to determine whether a tumor or other anomaly was also present.]

Dr. Moss testified that it was unfortunate that he was not given the bone fragment taken from Angie's skull to test and analyze it for an in-growth of blood vessels and excessive hemosiderin, a degenerating pith from blood that begins to form very quickly and becomes microscopically visible in a day or two, and he could have also looked for early fibrosis and scarring within the skull fracture. In part, he testified as follows:

> We could find evidence in the skull fracture which would rule in or rule out, with 100% certainty, the presence of this injury as having occurred or not – the skull fracture having occurred or not having occurred more than three to five days before. ......but we didn't have the bone, so we don't have the evidence.

Dr. Moss pointed out that the AFIP (Air Force Institute of Pathology) Report was agreed upon by their entire Neuropathology Department (not just one pathologist) and they jointly diagnosed that the abundance of macrophages showed the injury was at least forty-eight hours old. They also diagnosed that there was fresh blood in the specimens they reviewed.

Since the AFIP pathologist in charge of the department who signed the report was a member of the US Military, he could not be forced to testify during a civilian trial and the subject tissue specimens could not be returned to the hospital, since military law prevented such from happening. [Note: Since then, the AFIP will no longer will do pathological testing for civilian entities or persons.]

Dr. Moss testified he believed it was days earlier that Angie suffered a primary fracture that was catastrophically re-aggravated by a simple fall or something that would not normally aggravate or cause bleeding. He said the first bleeding could have either progressed slowly or speedily, depending on circumstances and that it could have spontaneously begin bleeding again without any later triggering event, as he had seen happen in other cases.

Dr. Blank, Forensic and Neuropathologist for Prosecution

The testimony of Pathologist Dr. Moss was followed by the testimony of Dr. Blank, a Forensic/Neuropathologist, whose specialty was child abuse by SBS and head injuries. She was a rebuttal witness to discredit the testimony of defense experts and to confirm the state's allegations.

Dr. Blank opined that a rotational force caused the injuries by slamming the child's head against a wall or flat object. She did not believe the tissue samples removed during surgery, nor any of the other microscopic specimen slides she examined held macrophages but instead were internal granular cells from the cerebellum. She said that she made that diagnosis by reviewing the autopsy report, medical records and the histological (tissue) microscopic slides made available for examination.

Although Dr. Blank was a forensic pathologist, she admitted incompetence in a very critical area. When cross-examined by defense attorneys, she responded that she was not familiar with the specific specimen staining done by Stanford Research Clinic and AFIP (KP-1, PGM-1, and S-100) and did not know the purpose for using them. She also contradicted other experts by saying, *"we do not have a large amount of experience with what a degenerating macrophage would look like."*

She lost a lot of credibility by speaking about issues that revealed her ignorance. This was another instance where requiring expert medical testimony be sworn to a reasonable degree of medical certainty could have prevented mistaken and misleading opinions and declarations being made to the court by medical experts.

[Note: There are many sub-specialties within the field of pathology due to the complex nature of human anatomy. This case needed the most up to date knowledge and training in the areas of cytopathology (the study of cells), histopathology (the study of tissue), hemopathology (the study of blood issues), and osteology (the study of bones), and Dr. Blank was untrained and uncertified in those subspecialties.]

Contrary to the testimony of Dr. Blank, other medical pathologists testified that many cells look very similar under a microscope and the only way to know for sure what they are is by specialized staining and testing, and by the company they keep. Over several decades, the staining and interpretation of cell and tissue specimens have progressed into using hundreds of different stains for various purposes. Moreover, if a correct diagnosis is possible by simply looking at different unstained tissue specimens under a microscope there would be no need for specialized specimen staining.

Was the lack of credibility and ability of this witness noticed by the jury? Only time would tell.

Dr. Bork, Neuropathologist for Prosecution

A few days before trial testimony began, the court allowed the prosecution to designate Dr. Bork as a last-minute expert witness. Secretly, prosecutors arranged for the expert to receive and examine two H&E stained microscopic tissue slides and one unstained slide (from the hospital) to prepare for testifying about her findings. Since these highly unusual actions were in direct conflict with the state's laws concerning predetermined discovery deadlines and rules, Lori's defense attorneys objected to them. In response, the judge allowed the doctor to only testify and give her opinions on the other two histology slides she examined but cautioned that if the prosecution decided to introduce the results of the late testing (done after trial began), the defense could raise the proper objections at that time.

Ironically, the judge allowed the prosecution's last-minute medical expert witness to testify because they claimed they had not previously been able to obtain the local hospital histological slides for testing and this expert's testimony was needed to "level the playing field." This statement was utter nonsense because the state was the custodian of all evidence and had over twenty months in which to prepare for trial (while the defense attorneys only had five months). Plus, the state had already hired eight other professional medical experts to give their opinions.

Dr. Bork was very eloquent and self-assured in her delivery, and her opinions sounded very credible and convincing. It was clear that she had tons of experience being an "expert witness." She used an overhead projection of photos of the hospital microscopic slides as well as other examples to explain what she knew about them and why she believed the tissue specimens did not have evidence of healing for more than just a few hours.

Her testimony was based primarily on the autopsy report and her review of the coroner's microscopic tissue slides (not including ones made for and by the Defense ME) and two of the H&E stained slides prepared from one of the two masses removed during surgery. She testified that she had examined the microscopic tissue slides prior to her appearance and disagreed with both Stanford Research Clinic and AFIP and said there was no evidence of macrophages, although she was not certified or experienced as a cytopathologist or hemopathologist. The most important question "at issue" was whether the slide (or any of the slides) showed a two-day-old injury or were there just internal granular cells with no evidence of healing or macrophages.

It was unfortunate that no expert recognized that it was possible that the single slide from the hospital examined by this neuropathologist (and others) may have been taken from a different tissue mass (as two masses were removed during surgery) and may have consisted of differing properties; and proper testing of each mass separately could have produced conflicting diagnoses. Unfortunately, because the masses were not kept separate, no expert witness could have known which tissue mass was used for each of the microscopic tissue or cell specimens being discussed. As previously mentioned, the hospital surgeon described the two tissue specimens removed during surgery as:

> One container labeled 'posterior fossa subdural hematoma' has within two portions of friable grayish-brown tissue measuring 1.2 cm and 1.4 cm in greatest dimension, respectively. Each is entirely submitted.

A critical detail not emphasized enough by defense attorneys was that the H&E stains used by the local hospital and examined by Dr. Bork were not sufficient to properly detect macrophages and the age of necrotic tissue, because they were not stained with the more highly sophisticated stains that AFIP used (KP-1 and S-100 protein, factor YEI, and CD-34) nor the ones used by Stanford Research Clinic (KP-1, S-100, P.M.G-1).

It was unfortunate that the identifying number of the tissue specimens being discussed and projected onto the overhead projector by the expert witnesses was never read into the court record. Therefore, it is uncertain as to which of the thirteen slides of the brain/cerebellum was being discussed at any given time. However, the slide shown by the enlarged photos of a microscopic specimen was one that was stained and diagnosed by local pathologists, since the microscopic tissue specimens examined by the Stanford Research Clinic had not yet been sent to defense attorneys. Their transmittal letter showed the slides were delivered to defense attorneys a few days before trial ended.

In keeping with the prosecution's goals, Dr. Bork testified that the microscopic tissue specimens she examined, including the H&E stained histology slide projected on the overhead screen, did not show "macrophages" evidencing older injury, but were made up of internal granular cells instead. It was obvious that she was not aware that more advanced staining techniques were needed, and defense attorneys did not strongly emphasis that defect in her testimony to the jurors and the judge during their cross-examination of her.

Dr. Coyote, Forensic and Hemopathologist For Defense

This defense medical expert, Dr. Coyote, was the only expert witness who was an experienced and trained anatomical pathologist also board certified in the subspecialties of hemopathology and forensic pathology. He was the only expert testifying who lectured nationwide in both the fields of hemopathology and child abuse. Although he had testified in 400 other trials as an expert, only two of them were in favor of the defense.

Dr. Coyote gave his opinions to *"a reasonable degree of medical certainty"* after reviewing the entire police report with attachments, statements of witnesses, hospital medical records, x-rays, CT scans, diagnostic and pathology reports, autopsy report, photographs, and microscopic tissue/cell specimens at both the coroner's office and the hospital pathology department. He believed the severe symptoms Angie experienced (the week after her immunizations) were indicators of an existing brain injury. And he refuted the opinions of the state experts by testifying that more specialized staining and examinations used by the

Stanford Research Clinic and AFIP Pathology Departments revealed the specimens were not positive for internal granular cells, but they were positive for enough macrophages to show necrotic tissue that was at least 24 to 48 hours old at the time of surgery.

Dr. Coyote said the Stanford Research Clinic Pathology Department transmittal letter dated November 25, 1997, (provided during the last week of trial to defense attorneys) underscored those facts wherein it said:

> Enclosed please find 2 slides, an immunostain for myeloperoxidase and a trichrome preparation. The former is a hematologic stain that I'm sure your consultant will be interested in. Her interpretation would be of great interest to me since I had not expected the cells to be reactive. Certainly, the staining does underscore the fact that brain was not present in the specimen. The trichrome preparation also supports that notion in showing absolutely no evidence of an underlying stroma (connective tissues, vessels, etc.)

The doctor gave other reasons he disagreed with state experts who said the slides from Dr. Moss held only brain tissue by explaining:

> Q. ATTORNEY CRISLEY: Okay. Go ahead to the next photo.
> A. WITNESS: This is another slide prepared from Dr. Moss' slide again showing the cells that we're discussing.
> Q. ATTORNEY CRISLEY: Let me ask you here. You testified that you know the cell by the company it keeps. Can you explain to the jury, in this circumstance, if they were looking at these granular cells that have become an issue, what differences would you see, or would you see any differences?
> A. WITNESS: First of all, I would expect to see brain tissue. When you look at this under the microscope at a higher magnification, some of these cells don't have round nuclei. They have nuclei that look like clover leaves. Those are polys. Those are a normal part of the blood, not a normal part of the brain. So, the fact that

there are other blood cells in here and no other elements of the brain is what I'm referring to.

Q. ATTORNEY CRISLEY: Okay.

A. WITNESS: Okay, actually this shows, if I may, this shows what I have described a bit better. These are the cells we are talking about. These you can see it under higher power here, all these cells in the background are blood cells, these round pale structures that don't have a nucleus. Clearly see here there are sheets of them. So, perhaps, now, when you asked before if I could go back and show the brain?

He also agreed with other experts who testified that after any traumatic brain injury the blood vessels are fragile and can bleed again, either spontaneously or with minor trauma.

Although Dr. Coyote explained the technical and medical issues involved, the jury's verdict would hinge on which expert and attorney sounded more passionate, more persuasive, and likeable as they did not understand medical vocabulary nor forensics enough to make informed decisions. Without a doubt, neither the jury, judge, nor anyone else in the courtroom were educated or experienced enough in the related medical specialties to understand the testimony of medical experts. And if one of them had testified that one or more of the microscopic tissue/cell specimens was taken from the brain of a gorilla, they would not have known any better.

Dr. John Benson, Neurosurgeon for Prosecution

Dr. Benson had no other or hidden agenda but to tell the truth since he was the neurosurgeon who performed emergency brain surgery on Angie to try to save her life which began three and one-half hours after arrival in the emergency room. He gave some interesting details that conflicted with statements made by prosecution medical experts and their coroner who claimed the pre-surgery CT showed a compound skull fracture with depression. Dr. Benson carefully described it this way;

There was a quite *extensive linear fracture* from the foramen magnum all the way up. It was separated widest inferiorly and tapering back together superiorly.

The surgeon also testified that instead of finding a depressed fracture, (caused by bashing in the skull) that it was elevated on the left side compared to the right side. When the prosecuting attorney asked him, *"In your operative report, one side of the fracture was elevated, not depressed, correct?"* He replied, *"Right. One side was not pushed way in.... There was a little bit of separation in an in-out direction as well as lateral."*

Furthermore, Dr. Benson's testimony conflicted with statements made by other state experts and the coroner who alleged the defendant's actions (not the surgeon's) created a complex fracture that pushed the skull bone into the brain. Conversely, the operating surgeon made a revealing statement when he described it as a serious linear skull fracture and made this observation:

> ... little jaggedness to the edge, cracks, and splinters in the bone, edges are sharp. They will tear your glove.

Did the surgeon's drilling into the unusually brittle skull bone cause the linear fracture to become complex with three prongs? Did that explain why the CT scans taken after surgery showed a complex fracture?

Scientific research has proven that skulls of fifteen-month-old children are ordinarily pliable and not brittle. So, is it possible that Angie was suffering from a brittle bone/collagen defect or another pathological disease that had not yet been diagnosed but could have been with proper forensic investigation at autopsy?

In his haste to save Angie's life, the operating surgeon discarded the skull bone fragments (of calvarium in the occipital area) adjoining the fracture. (Neither did the coroner's office think to preserve a sample during autopsy.) The accidental loss of these valuable pieces of evidence was unfortunate because bone pathologist could have resolved the issues concerning the timing of the skull fracture and added credibility to the four pathology reports showing older injuries.

The surgeon's description supported another defense medical expert who testified that internal edema (swelling), hydrocephalus (fluid retention), and bleeding over a longer period created extreme intracranial pressure pushing the bone outward causing it to fracture, much like an over-inflated balloon will pop when lightly impacted or touched. This internal pressure would explain why there were no current external contusions, damages, or lacerations that one would expect to see if the fracture was caused by one or more intentional violent acts as alleged by the prosecutors.

Since Dr. Benson was the operating surgeon, his unpaid testimony along with conclusions of Dr. Moss (and the four pathology reports by other pathologist) created reasonable doubt of any intentional abuse. But, would jurors understand them that way?

Dr. Sparks, Neurosurgeon - For Defense

Dr. Sparks is a famous neurosurgeon who had performed over 500 surgeries during his career. He was the Chief Neurosurgeon at Northwestern Hospital who once taught neurosurgery at Harvard Medical School and another university. He previously authored and published no less than 200 scientific journals (including fifty chapters in textbook and sixteen textbooks) on neurosurgery or neurological issues concerning the head and spine.

After examining all the medical records, CT scans and hospital records, along with a history of the events leading to the child's demise, he recognized that Angie suffered a prior head injury that was injured again on the day in question.

Dr. Sparks gave the following testimony during questioning by defense attorneys:

Q. In your experience, as an expert in neurosurgery, can any types of tests be performed on like say that piece of skull that was removed to date or figure out the time and injury occurred

A. Yes.

Q. Tell the jury what could have been performed on that piece of skull.

A. Yes. One of the inconsistencies in this case to me is that when the child came to the hospital in extremis and the CAT scan was done, it showed the skull fracture and showed the bleeding. The head was very carefully examined and there was no external evidence of trauma noted on any of the records, at least that I reviewed. Now if a child had just fallen with enough force to fracture the skull, in my experience, I would have expected external evidence of head trauma.

I would have expected either a large, what we call cephalhematoma, which is bleeding under the scalp, so the scalp is all boggy in that area or at least some swelling in that area and most probably some bluish discoloration due to the bleeding and bruising in that area. So, one of the inconsistencies that I have trouble reconciling is how a child could have had an injury of that force that day to sustain a skull fracture and then have no external evidence of trauma. Well, to answer, in terms of how that could be, one of the possibilities, I'm not saying it absolutely happened, but one of the possibilities is that this skull fracture was sustained some days before and that is the major fracture that caused the linear fracture and that the scalp had healed up and then some more minor trauma maybe on that day had occurred that in turn moved this now more unstable skull because it was already fractured and caused some additional bleeding,

Well, the way to absolutely answer that question is to examine the fracture site. If that fracture site had occurred a week before or days before and certainly more than a week earlier, it would already be undergoing healing, and, in the early stages, it would be a fibrous healing and if it had occurred several weeks before, it would already start to have calcium forming. So, the pathologic examination of that skull fracture would be absolutely crucial, in my opinion, to understanding when the fracture happened.

Q. Okay, now I just need to make sure everybody is understanding what you are saying. Would somebody by the naked eye be able to look and see these you called them fibrinous?

A. Fibrous union. No, they would not.

Q. So say, for example, you were the treating physician and you went in and took this piece of skull out of her head off the back of her skull and did what Dr. Benson did in this particular case, would you have been able, with your bare eyes, to look at that and tell when in fact that fracture had happened?

A. No, most probably not.

In summary, he believed that if there had been an impact to her head that afternoon forceful enough to cause the injuries, he would have expected to see external evidence such as a contusion on her scalp or bleeding underneath the surface of the skin, but none was seen by doctors or reported in the medical records. And based on the totality of the medical records, he believed there was significant evidence to show that Angie was re-injured on the day in question, by the reported short-distance fall which caused more bleeding and re-fracturing. His diagnosis was supported by the symptoms the child suffered with for most of the week after receiving her immunizations, and the three pathology reports from three separate laboratories showing older healing tissues.

The doctor also testified that if her injuries were *only a few hours old,* her hydrocephalus (collection of cerebral fluids) would not have been as great as the operating surgeon described. He said it would have taken from twelve to twenty-four hours (not two to four hours) after the flow is cut-off to create that kind of pressure in a child of that size and enlarge the ventricles (where fluid is held) to that extent because cerebral fluid is naturally generated at a very slow, prolonged rate in a child of that age.

Then, Defense Attorney Crisley went way out on a limb by buying into the two-story fall theory held by the state. He showed the witness a picture of the two-story apartment building stairs and walkway where the deceased child lived and asked the doctor a hypothetical question; *"If a child fell from that second story balcony, could it result in the same kind of head injuries the child had?"* The doctor replied in the affirmative but said it would have happened several days prior to admission to the emergency room to give time for the outward contusions and swelling to diminish.

This hypothetical question later came back to haunt the two defense attorneys after the prosecutors sent their investigators to the apartment building, (for the first time, twenty-one months after the tragedy) to ask questions and try to find evidence of it happening. When they found none, Prosecutor Bird ridiculed the defense in the presence of the jury by saying they were trying to invent evidence and were grasping at straws. This over-the-top tactic by prosecutors diminished the defense attorney's arguments and the testimony of this very capable neurosurgeon in the eyes of the jury and overshadowed all other more critical aspects of his testimony.

Several pieces of evidence (including pathology and medical reports), along with Dr. Spark's personal knowledge and work experience reinforced his analysis and conclusion that Angie's physical symptoms did not correlate to either of the state's suggestions as to what caused the child's injuries and death. His opinions were formulated to a reasonable degree of medical certainty after completing a comprehensive investigation.

Dr. Jay, Pediatric Radiologist for Prosecution

Dr. Jay was chosen as an expert to testify in support of the prosecution approximately *four months before* he received the toddler's X-rays and CT scans for review and diagnosis. Since he had testified for the prosecutor's office in several other cases he was expected to testify in a manner favorable to their theories.

He was not the hospital radiologist who reviewed the CT scans that started two hours after 911 was called. After examining the hospital CT scans, he diagnosed what he called a depressed skull fracture meaning that the edges were not even with each other. He did not use the words "complex fracture" and only described the fracture line as one line extending laterally from base of the skull to the inion (protrusion at the back of the head.)

The attorneys did not ask several germane questions such as whether the fracture involved the naturally occurring suture lines (a diastatic fracture), and whether any of the many scans showed evidence of coup-contrecoup (both sides of the brain) bruising or swelling or other damage. But, he did not describe finding any such findings.

Strangely, the radiologist said that Angie's lateral ventricles in her brain were larger than what would typically be expected in a child of her age. The question was not asked whether that condition appeared to be the result of obstructed drainage of cerebral fluid over a longer period than a few hours or was due to some pathological defect or condition.

Ironically, the doctor surprised the prosecutor by refusing to say unequivocally that Angie could not have walked around after suffering her skull fracture, although she asked the question several ways. Because of his inability to say what prosecutors wanted, Prosecutor Bird cut the questioning short and did not press him for more definitive answers. His testimony was revealing and striking because he did not equivocate about radiological findings that did not comport with what prosecutors were claiming.

Dr. Wick, Pediatrician for Prosecution

Dr. Wick was a pediatrician licensed as a medical doctor in California forty-seven years before the subject tragedy. Since that time, he had not been trained or certified in any other specific medical specialty but spent the latter part of his medical career studying work of others who researched child abuse issues, conducting seminars, and obtaining various grants to further his endeavors. He became a well-paid and self-acclaimed expert on child abuse by speaking at conferences, writing textbooks, and teaching other doctors and law enforcement about the subject.

Although the doctor had testified over fifty times for prosecutors, he said he had *never* testified for anyone's defense. Based on his prior testimonies for state prosecutors, they knew they could count on him to frame his testimony favorable to their position. The prosecution, defense, and the judge accepted his testimony as an expert in pediatrics and child abuse although he was not trained or certified as a forensic medical examiner, pathologist, radiologist, histopathologist, cytopathologist, biomechanical or biomedical engineer. Regardless, he gave trial testimony that should have been restricted to those specialists, and there was no such thing as a board-certified child abuse expert in the medical industry.

When Defense Attorney Snow objected to his testimony into other medical specialties, the judge ruled that his would be allowed. [This doctor's highly acclaimed reputation and experience presenting seminars about child abuse had without merit spilled over into other medical specialties without him completed more advanced training and certification.] The judge's ruling allowed him (as a non-pathologist or forensic specialist) to say to the jurors that each of the three pathology reports were all wrong in their diagnosis of the older injury, despite the cutting-edge advanced staining techniques and knowledge used to determine the age of necrotic tissue.

It was peculiar that Dr. Wick's opinions concerning the skull fractures were based primarily on the autopsy report (which was based on someone else's radiological diagnosis.)

> (Note: The Washoe County Chief Medical Examiner, Dr. Gray, had testified under penalty of perjury that he did not know how to read x-rays or CT scans, but said he *would sometimes sort of look at them to try and figure them out.*" Strangely, this expert did not consult directly with any treating radiologist nor did he ask any other radiologist to review the CT scans and admitted he had not read all of Angie's medical records before forming his opinions.)

Regardless, Dr. Wick seemed quite uncertain as to the nature of fractures revealed on the CT scans (whether it was a compound or linear fracture) when he said the following,

The best description of the fracture comes from the autopsy. The fracture is also visible although not completely visible in the CT scans (before surgery) and it is visible to some extent in the X-rays -- of the plane X-rays of the skull that were taken, but they were taken after the operation (after surgery) and the piece of skull was removed at operation...

His testimony reminded me of the ancient "Telephone Game" played at parties; an example of how repeating small misconceptions can make an enormous difference in the final message making it misleading beyond recognition

Dr. Hope, Ophthalmologist for Prosecution

A new theory about how Angie was injured was introduced during the last week of trial by the state's rebuttal expert witness, Ophthalmologist, Dr. Hope. This highly credentialed and experienced ophthalmologist who had already testified several times for the state was called as a last-minute rebuttal witness to persuade jurors that SBS (Shaken Baby Syndrome) was responsible because of the retinal hemorrhaging noticed during autopsy.

Dr. Hope said that the retinal hemorrhaging was caused by violently shaking (SBS) the child and then slamming her head against a hard surface that caused the skull fracture and other brain injuries. Nevertheless, there was physical evidence and testimony that contradicted the doctor's statement. Such as, it is accepted among forensic examiners that if a toddler's skull has been fractured by violently slamming the head against a hard surface there would be coup-contrecoup brain injuries, torn ligaments, bruising and or handprints caused by grasping and swinging the child at an excessive speed. Additionally, there would have been a contusion or laceration at the point of impact. The only contusion on the child found by medical personnel, first responders, and the coroner was a small one near one of her knees.

Later, upon cross-examination by defense attorneys, Dr. Hope testified that she did not have time to read the medical records before taking the stand and was unware of contradictory evidence. Instead, her opinions were based solely on the autopsy report. Defense Attorney Crisley pounced on that fact and pointed out her dubious conclusion to the jury saying that she was another prosecution expert who had given an opinion without knowing all the facts.

Also, since Dr. Hope had not read the medical records, she was unaware of the extremely high blood glucose level discovered by doctors upon admission to the emergency room, and unaware of the extreme pressure in the brain, both of which lead to extensive bleeding in the eyes.

Summary of Expert Testimony

During the whole criminal process and particularly during the trial, prosecuting attorneys were like champion chess players who kept steps ahead of the defense by manipulating and conflating critical issues and evidence. This included switching from alleging different methods (shaking, striking, throwing or unknown means) of inflicting injuries on Angie depending on which expert was testifying and the point they were trying to make.

The prosecution's medical experts gave several conflicting opinions about what specific act caused the deceased child's traumatic head injuries based on their feeling, thoughts, and impressions. But each of them did so after analyzing only a small fraction (per their testimony) of available evidence, instead of studying all medical records and forensic evidence as most courts require. Defense Attorney Snow lodged an objection with the court about that type of expert witness testimony and asked that their opinions be stricken from the record. After several discussions of applicable statutes and case law with the attorneys, the judge ruled against his objection and allowed all the questionable medical opinions to be heard and considered by the jury. The intricacies and complexities of various medical specialties, including forensic pathology and all its subspecialties were unknown to the court. That knowledge would have affected the rulings.

It is a common practice during trial preparation for state prosecutors to coach their experts to testify in favor of the prosecution. In this case, the common theme was that Angie was the victim of non-accidental trauma(s) within a few hours before her arrival at the emergency room which resulted in her demise. However, each of the them gave a different opinion about several key issues, including the distance a fall would have need to be to cause the head injuries the deceased toddler sustained. For example, the coroner thought that a fall from a minimum of eight feet was necessary, another expert claimed ten feet, and others said that falling off a two-story building (fifteen to twenty-five feet) was the distance needed to inflict a similar skull fracture and/or clinically important traumatic brain injury.

Although prosecution experts could not agree about which type of abuse Lori committed to inflict the mortal injuries, they all opined that Angie's injuries were *irrefutable* evidence of child abuse deliberately inflicted upon her within a couple of hours before arriving at the emergency room. Strangely, upon cross-examination by Defense Attorney Crisley, several of them contradicted themselves by saying that the skull fracture and brain injuries were also consistent with an accidental fall, but not a short-distance one.

The state medical experts were sending an unspoken message that greater physical injuries are always inflicted by intentionally shaking, hitting, or throwing a child than is possible from accidentally falling a short distance, even with a pre-existing brain injury and a weakened condition. Ironically, they were also sending a subliminal message that a short-distance fall could not, under any conditions, crack a skull or produce life-threatening intracranial injuries.

In almost every regard, defense medical experts disagreed with prosecution medical experts. The most significant dispute was whether there were "macrophages" (cells that aid in the healing process) in the tissue/cell specimens showing that a brain injury occurred no earlier than twenty-four hours prior to brain surgery. Defense experts also argued that a pre-existing skull fracture could have weakened her skull and made it more susceptible to re-fracturing by the short-distance (roughly four feet) fall and caused re-bleeding, increased swelling, and hydrocephalus. Of course, the state's medical experts claimed that was not possible.

During trial, the prosecution attorneys and expert witnesses went ahead as if the tissue specimens under discussion and examined by the experts were equal in all respects to those analyzed by the Stanford Research Clinic and AFIP. Conversely, they ignored that Dr. Moss (the local hospital pathologist) had explained that the Stanford Research Clinic and AFIP forensic tissue specimens were both prepared and examined by using more advanced cutting-edge staining methods (not available locally) that were exclusively able to figure out the age of the necrotic tissue. More importantly, no medical expert witness was able to examine the *same* microscopic tissue specimen slides as the Stanford Research Clinic Pathology Department since they had not been returned to the defense attorneys until a few days before trial ended.

A major problem with the state's medical experts was that neither of them was a histopathologist, hemopathologist or cytopathologist. Therefore, they did not have enough knowledge and training to know exactly what tissue testing procedures should have been used to discover and diagnose the age of dying tissue. Upon cross-examination, Dr. Blank, the prosecution medical expert pathologist, confirmed this fact when she admitted to not being familiar with the tissue stains used by the Stanford Research Clinic and AFIP and that what they were used for would have to be looked up.

As previously mentioned, since the exact slide identifying numbers were never read aloud into the court record, it is sometimes difficult to know specifically which one was being referred to or was projected onto the overhead screen. But it appeared that only a few of the tissue specimens were reviewed by experts and discussed during trial and did not include some very crucial ones prepared for and by the Defense ME almost a year earlier.

It was highly irregular and against court rules, that neither the prosecution nor defense listed any of the microscopic tissue or cell specimen slides (nor photos of them) on their exhibit lists, although they were discussed at great length. Therefore, exactly how many of them existed, the identifying label on each, and the significance of each was never listed on the exhibit list by prosecution or defense attorneys. Regardless, much later during a court hearing, Prosecutor Bird admitted she had seen approximately thirty of them. The truth is that records and photographs taken by the defense at the close of the criminal trial documented a total of forty-eight forensic microscopic tissue/cell slides existed (including the ones prepared almost a year earlier through the efforts of the Defense ME). [Note: Those forty-eight slides were sent by defense attorneys to those helping Lori in the wrongful death civil case seeking monetary damages.]

Conflicting trial testimony and evidence existed about the severity and cause of the skull fracture. This was obvious when comparing the operating surgeon's report, the hospital, pre-surgery radiology reports, and the testimony of experts during trial. Some state experts said that the pre-surgery fracture was not depressed or complex but described it as a linear fracture. Conversely, the coroner, prosecuting attorneys, and the rest of their experts kept saying that the pre-surgery fracture was a complex fracture and depressed based on their review of the post-surgery scans and autopsy report. However, defense attorneys did not point out to the jury these inconsistencies and the conflating of that evidence by prosecuting medical experts.

Another crucial area of disagreement was that defense medical experts claimed extreme intracranial swelling and pressure elevated the fractured bone, instead of it being (depressed) as the prosecution claimed. They also believed the amount of intracranial pressure and other conditions could not have developed within a few hours but would have taken from twelve to twenty-four hours to develop based on the known speed that cerebral fluid is generated in a child of that age. Of course, state experts disputed this by saying that a sharp blow (blunt force trauma) first pushed the bone into the child's brain and the resulting swelling and pressure elevated it.

Medical records, CT scans and X-rays of Angie showed there were no multiple fractures (meaning broken bones on other parts of the child's body), no contusions, no torn ligaments in the neck or upper back, no "bi-lateral" skull fracture (both sides of the skull), and no coup-contrecoup brain injury (bruising on the opposite side of the brain), which would have existed if there had been a sudden and violent impact to her head. Neither was there bruising where hands would have grasped the child, no fresh welts, or bumps where the flesh would have contacted a hard surface, as well as no blood or other residue found on any object had there been a violent traumatic event.

The normal protocol for expert testimony dictates that each medical specialty should testify next to each other, so their questioning can effectively point out areas of disagreement or agreement and make cross-examination more meaningful. Because that did not always happen in this case, it created a disadvantage for the defense.

There were other important issues overlooked by all medical experts and attorneys during their forensic analysis and discussions. They ignored that there were two separate distinct tissue masses removed during emergency surgery (and put in one container) and sent to the hospital pathology department for diagnosis. Since the microscopic slides sent to Stanford Research Clinic and AFIP were prepared and sent to them at two different times, it is entirely possible that each of the two specimens may have unknowingly been prepared from separate and distinct tissue masses. Thus, they may have each had different properties and structures.

It is ironic that most of the state's medical experts testified when they had not reviewed all the medical records of the deceased child and that the experts mostly relied upon the Autopsy Report to form their "expert" opinions. Therefore, they formed their opinions "in a vacuum" without examining all available medical evidence and historical data.

After the trial was over it was discovered that neither the defense or prosecution experts had personally examined all the forty-eight (48) histological slides available which included the microscopic tissue specimen slides prepared by the coroner for the fired Defense ME nor the ones prepared from the paraffin block sent to him later by the coroner. Later, it was also learned that most of the slides prepared by the coroner were actually "smears" of the tissue specimens, (and not taken from the injury site) instead of actual "tissue slices" that would have revealed the actual structure of the specimens and made a more correct diagnosis possible.

Following the testimony of dozens of percipient witnesses and one dozen medical experts, the prosecution and defense rested their cases and prepared for closing statements which were to be summaries of crucial evidence already presented along with reasons why they were vital for the jury to consider.

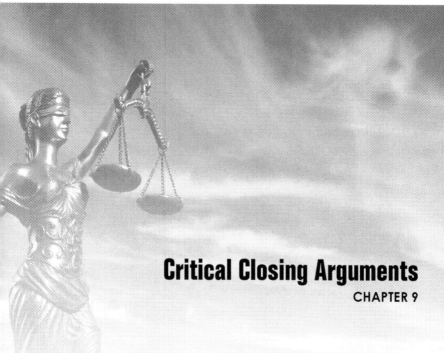

Critical Closing Arguments
CHAPTER 9

Closing arguments lasted an entire day and mostly focused on the various medical expert opinions concerning the timing and cause of the child's traumatic brain injuries. A major topic was whether there was evidence of prior injury as shown by three pathology reports and testimony of defense experts.

Throughout the trial and closing arguments, the complicated medical forensic issues were confusing to prosecuting, defense attorneys and expert witnesses, as they repeatedly conflated the differing roles of various medical specialists, especially pathologists (i.e. clinical, anatomical, cytological, histological, hemopathologist, forensics) and their respective duties and limitations.

Also, prosecutors and their experts conflated the various types of tissues and cells, as well as the specific histological stains required to diagnose certain conditions and aging of necrotic tissue. I believe, that because of their moral relevancy mindset, they intentionally did so to mislead and confuse the jury and achieve the "greater good" of winning a conviction.

Below are summaries of the most important aspects of the prosecution and defense closing arguments.

Prosecution Closing Arguments

As customary, the two prosecuting attorneys were first to present their closing arguments with each of them presenting half of the total. Prosecutor Snuffelpaw began first by trying to debunk the findings of macrophages (older injuries) by the local hospital, Stanford Research Clinic and AFIP. While ignoring direct expert testimony given about proper pathological testing protocol, he claimed their diagnoses were untrustworthy and meaningless because the pathologist had not been informed about the emergency room doctors' theories of non-accidental injury. The prosecutors and experts inferred that world renown ultramodern pathology institutions did not know how to conduct scientific analyzes of tissue and cell specimens.

When describing what happened on the afternoon of the tragedy, Prosecutor Snuffelpaw spoke about boiling points and events that trigger child abuse. Surprisingly, his arguments were not based on actual evidence or testimony presented, but were merely the product of his own imagination in declaring:

> Lori Watson is a person that reached that boiling level on March 4th, 1996, and all those things I just told you, the child throwing the bottle, getting food in her hair, getting food on her clothes, needing to be cleaned, the infant crying, the two-year-old trying to play, needing to get the children down for a nap, having somebody else coming over. There is an awful lot going on. You are trying to cleanup. Those are all things in Lori's statement that was played to you and that's going to go back with you. Listen to it again, if you want to, and you will see all of that and, more importantly, you'll see all of it having occurred right around lunch and immediately thereafter. A lot of triggering events coming to bear at one time.
>
> What you need to understand is that the State is not telling you in this case that Lori Watson is a cold-blooded premeditated murderer, that she premeditated and planned to kill Angie. We're not saying that at all. I'm not submitting to you that that's what the evidence shows. We are not saying that she premeditated and planned to abuse Angie. We're simply saying that it happened,

that she did abuse her, and that's what the competent evidence tells you in this case. For whatever reason, she reached that point and for whatever reason, Angie was there and for whatever reason, her aggression went towards Angie and the acting out went towards Angie and the abuse went towards Angie and Angie died. That's the harsh reality of this case and when that happens in Nevada, it's First Degree Murder. It's that simple."

Those statements contradicted actual testimony and evidence because nothing in Lori's handwritten or recorded statements to police showed there was a boiling point that could have led to killing Angie in a fit of rage. Neither was there any such "boiling point" ever mentioned or alluded to by anyone else who visited Lori that afternoon. There was only typical children's behavior she dealt with routinely. Classifying them as "triggering" events was nonsense to all who knew Lori, since she was an experienced and loving mother, not prone to fits of rage at children or anyone else.

Prosecutor Snuffelpaw repeatedly told the jurors that Angie's manifestations were uncontroverted findings of child abuse (SBS) based on statements of their medical experts, Dr. Blank, who became famous and made huge profits by obtaining government and industry grants and presenting seminars for the benefit of other medical experts and prosecutors. The primary message of his seminars was that a certain triad of symptoms, i.e. (1) severe brain swelling and/or diffuse traumatic axonal injury; (2) bleeding under the membranes which cover the brain, and (3) bleeding in the layers of the retina, were incontrovertible evidence of SBS in the absence of other physical injuries. This false teaching resulted in the discounting or ignoring of all reported claims of short-distance falls or pathological conditions that should have been forensically considered before filing criminal charges.

Prosecutor Snuffelpaw argued as follows:

> Those are the hallmarks of non-accidental trauma. Those findings alone show you that a child has suffered non-accidental trauma and what did Angie have? She had every one of those. I'm not talking about medical opinions now. I'm talking about uncontroverted findings. She had subdural bleeding, she had subarachnoid bleeding, she had retinal hemorrhaging. The type of

retinal – that should have been over there. I got kind of spaced off. I apologize for that. The specific type of retinal hemorrhage, there was testimony about specific types of retinal hemorrhages that are pathognomonic for child abuse.

Contrary to the prosecution and their medical expert's statements, even at that point in medical history there were many documented controversies and disagreements among pediatric specialists and research scientists about the triad of injuries (especially retinal hemorrhaging) as always being "pathognomonic." (Meaning a particular disease is present beyond any doubt.) Numerous peer reviewed medical journals at the time cited a variety of pathological and/or anatomical defects or conditions that are sometimes mistaken for (non-accidental trauma) child abuse and/or SBS and should be considered and ruled out before making a diagnosis.

During closing arguments Prosecutor Snuffelpaw also chose to ignore that there was no evidence of other fractures nor physical injuries on Angie to support the state's theories. Specifically, there were no damaged, torn, or strained neck muscles (whiplash), no coup-contrecoup head injuries, no contusions, and or bruising found on the child's body that would have resulted from grasping and violently shaking a twenty-pound toddler.

The second half of the prosecution's closing statements was delivered by Prosecutor Bird who distorted Lori's written and verbal statements to police. She claimed that Lori gave conflicting information about timing of events and said an hour was missing from Lori's account. This theory was promoted by reading (only pages one and three) of Lori's handwritten statement, but the missing page two explained the time line very clearly and showed there was not an hour missing between the time she put the toddler down for a nap and the time paramedics were called. Additionally, prosecutors ignored Lori's audio taped interview by police that also clarified the issue.

Prosecutor Bird summarized the forensic testimony of medical experts, including the timing and exact nature of the head injuries Angie sustained. She said that all the state experts determined there was indisputable evidence of non-accidental (child abuse) trauma when she said the following:

The skull fracture in Angie, there was testimony by
Dr. Blank and Dr. Coyote acknowledged the literature

about the skull fracture that, I believe, was authored by Dr. Blank.

What are you looking for in a skull fracture to tell you whether it is inflicted or accidental? Eight characteristics that you look for and you only need one or more to make it indicative of inflicted non-accidental trauma. Those eight characteristics are depressed fracture, a diastatic fracture, a fracture width greater than three millimeters, complex configuration to the fracture, nonparietal fracture, associated intracranial injuries, bilateral fractures, and multiple fractures.

She further claimed:

Six of those eight characteristics were present when you only need one telling you that this was an inflicted skull fracture, not an accidental injury.

Her argument that only *one of those symptoms* was necessary to diagnose child abuse was not supported by testimony of any trial expert nor by any published medical research on the subject. Furthermore, she claimed that six criteria were present. But her own medical experts and Lori's medical records showed only three (not six) of the criteria were present, (non-parietal injury, associated cranial injuries, and more than three millimeters widening of suture line.) The presence of the three other criteria was disputed by experts' testimonies, (depressed, complex fracture, diastatic-fracture.) And finally, two of the criteria definitely were not present, (*bilateral and multiple other fractures*). Such distortions of details could greatly influence jurors who are not educated in medical forensics and terminology.

Prosecutor Bird made every effort to ridicule and discredit the testimony of defense medical experts, saying they were in over their heads, and made other disparaging remarks about Dr. Moss who issued the "Amended Pathology Report" showing Angie was suffering from a two-day-old intracranial injury. She made an argument that he reached his diagnosis in a vacuum (without knowing the description and history of the tissue he was examining) and concluded that it was misleading to him and the other pathologists and made their diagnoses unreliable. Strangely, she ignored the testimony that it is proper protocol to <u>not</u> inform pathologists of the history of a tissue specimen (per established scientific protocol) to keep from being influenced one way or the other while doing their testing, observations, and diagnoses.

Prosecutor Bird misinformed the jurors that Dr. Moss changed his opinion when she said:

> Now what happened in pathology? Well, Dr. Moss did an examination at first and Dr. Moss was called as the defense witness, ladies, and gentlemen, but I would submit that his opinion is more in line with the State's case. He said the only examination he did and, remember, after he got these reports, which we will talk about later from the Stanford Research Clinic and the AFIP, he changed his opinion just on those reports. He didn't do anything. He just said, well, I've got these reports. I'm going to change my opinion. I mean, Dr. Moss, if the Stanford Research Clinic and AFIP tell you to jump off a cliff, are you going to do that? No, of course not, but he changed his opinion in a snap just because he did, but, in his opinion, he said he was experienced; he can tell the difference between blood and tissue.

Contrary to those statements, consider the actual testimony of Dr. Moss that shows his careful professional attention to his duties. The trial conversation between the doctor and Defense Attorney Crisley is as follows:

> Q. Just so the jury is straight, after March the 14th, when the Stanford Research Clinic letter was sent, you received and looked at it; is that correct?
> A. That's correct.
> Q. What did you do as a result of looking at this diagnosis from the Stanford Research Clinic, which was different from your original diagnosis?
> A. Obviously, this is a serious discrepancy, and I was still reasonably uncomfortable. I wasn't totally comfortable with -- even experts make mistakes. I make mistakes. It's normal to make mistakes. It's not normal to cover them. It's not normal to hope that ill consequences never get revealed. It's not normal to not admit it, because you

don't want to go to court some day and admit a mistake even if it didn't hurt anybody. We sent this to the Stanford Research Clinic. The Stanford Research Clinic refuted our diagnosis. I was still uncomfortable with it. I took it upon myself to send it to another expert organization, totally separate from and not a part of the Stanford Research Clinic, separate people, separate state; specifically, the Armed Forces Institute of Pathology, which is about as close to the bottom line of expertise in anatomic pathology that you can get in the United States.

Prosecutor Bird spent extensive time painting word pictures of the various pathologists at local hospital, Stanford Research Clinic & AFIP and the defense pathologists as being unreliable and irresponsible, and wrong in their diagnosis of pre-existing healing tissue. Conversely, the trial transcript shows the doctor's statements were clear and unequivocal with extreme professionalism that left no room for misunderstanding.

Prosecutor Bird distorted the testimony of Dr. Moss concerning the various histological stains the Stanford Research Clinic and AFIP utilized to diagnose the aging of tissue when she argued as follows:

> How does one of them do this S-100 stain on this sample and it's positive and then the other one does that same stain on this sample and it's negative? What did Dr. Moss say when I asked him if the two blind consults are in conflict? He said, well, you are in trouble and that's what you are here, ladies and gentlemen. If you are relying on those at all, you are in trouble because the reports themselves conflict with each other. Nobody can tell you essentially what they mean. Nobody can tell you what kind of controls were used. They have to do with some type of control to know that what they are doing has any meaning and nobody can tell you anything about that. They didn't even send what they looked at back. So, nobody can even review it. Nobody can do anything with those. They are inherently untrustworthy, and I submit to you not at the fault of those clinics, but because of the way they were setup and because of that, they are not informed opinions and you should not give them any

weight in this case and that leads to one of the biggest problems with Dr. Coyote...

In direct contradiction to those arguments, Dr. Moss had testified competently during trial about the various stains and what they were used for when responding to questions from the prosecution attorney. The testimony went as follows:

Q. For instance, what is an S-100?

A. S-100 is a specific stain that used to be used to diagnose malignant melanoma, and then somebody figured this out, an S-100 stain stains 100 percent of papillary carcinoma of the artery. Then we figured out it stains a lot of other things, polys it's like neurospecific inlays. It used to be called NSC, and it was thought very specific for us for a certain type of lung tumor. NSC now -- for pathologists now stains for everything. So, we don't use the S-100. This is an evolving science. It's only been around for 20 years. But KP-1 and PGM-1 are two stains that are thought, by current standards, to be specific and are reliable for macrophages or histiocytes.

It is hard to believe that attorneys who spent decades prosecuting child-abuse and child-murder cases did not hear and understand that the differences between the two pathology reports only related to the S-100 stain, and that stain was not even used for discovering macrophages and aging of tissue. Even currently, the S-100 stain is used to diagnose various cancers, as well as tumors, including "gliomas." This term refers to all glial tumors in general (primarily glioblastoma, astrocytoma, oligodendroglioma, and ependymoma) but the term is also used sometimes instead of astrocytoma.

The prosecutors' lengthy closing arguments consisted of carefully selected pinpricks of trial testimony while not mentioning the tons of contradictory evidence and testimonies. Their arguments were followed by the defense closing arguments, and then the state presented a rebuttal closing argument.

Defense Closing Arguments

Defense Attorney Snow began his closing argument by saying;

> As we sat through the evidence in the case and as I listened to the closing arguments, I was reminded of what we all spoke to you about during the voir dire process, as we were asking you questions, and I kind of talked about it a little bit during opening –statement where I told you, as a father that has a little girl and as a citizen in the community, I too am concerned about child abuse and we talked during voir dire about the natural knee jerk reaction that some of us may have to feel a duty to hold somebody accountable.

Then he reminded everyone that none of them can know whether there were macrophages (older injuries) shown on the microscopic slides under discussion and they would need to rely upon expert medical witnesses whose testimony created reasonable doubt. He explained the defense expert witnesses were very capable and qualified to testify concerning the available forensic pathological evidence, despite the claims of prosecuting attorneys.

Defense Attorney Crisley presented the second half of closing arguments for the defense. At one point, Prosecutor Bird interrupted him and cleverly slipped in information previously ruled as not admissible. It involved the judge's prior ruling concerning prosecutors' violation of standard trial rules (discovery cut-off) when they obtained a newly H&E stained tissue specimen from the local hospital and tried to have it tested and interpreted by one of their expert witnesses for testimony at trial. *[Strangely, this attempt at testing was made although these very experienced prosecutors who knew the rules of the court and the judge's ruling that the results of the testing could not be discussed unless defense attorneys opened the door.]* Despite the judge's prior ruling, Prosecutor Bird took the opportunity to claim that the defense attorneys were trying to hide relevant evidence. The conversation between the attorneys and the judge went like this:

DEFENSE ATTORNEY CRISLEY: Now, if Dr. Bork or Dr. Blank (prosecution experts) had other tests that they were ready to come in and say refute these, they didn't. They didn't do any tests, remember.

PROSECUTING ATTORNEY: Your Honor, I'm going to object for that also. As this court knew, there were other test performed and the defense said we do not want that to come in front of this jury and those tests did not.... (interrupted by the Judge)

THE COURT: Ms. Bird, Ms. Bird. (trying to stop prosecutor)

DEFENSE ATTORNEY: Judge, just for the record, it's clear those tests were done the week before the trial.

THE COURT: Let's talk about the evidence that was presented at the trial

DEFENSE ATTORNEY: There was no evidence presented through Dr. Bork or Dr. Blank that they performed tests conflicting with these reports of the AFIP and the Stanford Research Clinic. And, curiously, Dr. Blank, Dr. Blank came in here and said I'm an expert in this area. I know what everything is. I'm never wrong, but I have no idea what KP-1 and CD-34 are. I don't know what the stains are. I would have to look it up

This interruption of Attorney Crisley by the prosecuting attorney was immediately objected to by Defense Attorney Snow, who asked that a mistrial be declared, but the judge ruled against him saying he did not think it was prejudicial enough to make a difference in the trial outcome. However, this was another incident where Prosecutor Bird showed a lack of respect for the law, the judge's ruling, and legally established discovery cut-off rules and procedures that both sides were compelled to respect.

Attorney Crisley reminded the jurors that prosecution medical experts had formed their opinions without knowing the full history of Angie's prior illness and injuries, and therefore their opinions were unreliable. He explained that there were significant disagreements between the various medical experts in response to important questions. To highlight the conflicting medical opinions and show that plenty of reasonable doubt clearly existed about how and when Angie was injured, Attorney Crisley presented a hard to read hand drawn chart of the conflicting testimony while explaining to the jurors that their job was to make a verdict on that basis.

Although the following chart is not an exact replica of the chart he prepared by hand, it has the same information and clearly proves there were controvertible facts and evidence showing plenty of reasonable doubt.

Can a child ambulate (walk) after a skull fracture?	Can a subdural hematoma spontaneously rebleed?	Were they aware of full extent of prior week's illness?	Could a fall have created same injuries?	Was there evidence of old injury on the specimen slides?
Yes – 6 No – 2 Did not know-1 Not asked – 3	Yes – 7 No – 1 Maybe – 2 Not asked – 2	Yes – 2 No – 8 Not Asked – 2	Yes – 9 No. 1 Maybe – 1 Not Asked 1	Yes – 3 No. 3 Not Asked -6

When Attorney Crisley finished speaking, Lori and I were convinced that a not-guilty verdict would be the outcome and were encouraged and felt uplifted by that possibility. Next, the prosecution presented their final rebuttal arguments. This is normal routine, but it can be very unfair to the defendant when there is no chance for them to refute a prosecutor's final statements.

Summary of Rebuttal Arguments

As Prosecutor Bird began the state's rebuttal arguments, my pounding heart dipped into my stomach in fear of what spin she would put on the facts of the case and what new allegations she would make. Lori, her friends, and family members in the courtroom were having the same thoughts and feelings.

In summary, Prosecutor Bird's rebuttal statements were passionate, comprehensive, and immensely convoluted. To start with, she erroneously claimed that all experts agreed (she excluded defense experts' testimony) there were no old brain injuries and they all happened on March 4th, and Lori was the guilty party. As expected, she argued that defense medical experts were in over their heads and unqualified, but the state's medical experts were far superior and more trustworthy.

She made more false allegations and convoluted arguments not supported by trial testimony or evidence. One example of this was when she passionately argued that Lori had a "bad baby room" where the playpen and Solo Flex machine were and where she put "bad babies" when she got frustrated with them. She claimed that room was where the child abuse/murder took place, alleging Lori became angry, out of control and bashed Angie's head against the solo-flex machine because of unusual stress she said Lori was experiencing. A portion of her passionate and very theatrical statements to the jury reads as follows:

I would submit to you that she wasn't worried about this baby when she snapped and wanted to quiet a screaming child. Maybe Angie had gotten into something. Remember Dr. Wick saying that, in his belief, the object was horizontal rather than vertical. Ladies and gentlemen look at this Soloflex machine right next to the crib with the bottle and the one toy. Look at that horizontal bar. Would taking a baby and bashing her head on to this horizontal bar result in the kind of fracture system and the injuries that we saw? You bet it would. How about bashing her head against this seat here on the Soloflex because she won't shut up and you take that baby and just whack her down as hard as you can. Would it hit below the inion and crack this baby's skull and cause it to go into the brain and ooze out? **I submit to you that's what killed Angie and child abuse is an ugly thing, ladies and gentlemen,** and people don't like to believe that it exists, but it does and people do take babies and do smash them into furniture. Because when you bash a baby's head up against an object, it quiets them down, they are quiet, they don't cry any more. That's when she found her not breathing right, when she found her color wasn't that good, and that's when she knew that something was very, very wrong and mixed that fact with fiction when she called 911 and said Angie fell and hit her head. She didn't fall, but she knew it was a head injury and she knew something was wrong.

Despite her statements, there was no evidence presented to the jury that (1) Lori snapped or was upset with Angie for crying or screaming or that Lori exhibited any unusual or stressful behavior, (2) the Soloflex machine was involved in any manner, (3) Lori had a bad baby room, (4) there was evidence of coup-contrecoup brain injuries that would have resulted by sudden deceleration upon impact, or (5) the child had bruises or handprints that would have resulted from hanging onto the twenty pound child while swinging her to bash her head against the Soloflex machine.

Several dozens of Lori's supporters in the courtroom were outraged and shocked by the female prosecutor's closing rebuttal arguments. Our heads were spinning as we left the courtroom muttering among ourselves and asking, *"Where was the evidence that caused her to make those unfounded statements?"* Neither Lori, her attorneys, nor anyone else had heard any testimony close to what she was alleging.

Prosecutors had a self-imposed license to morph medical expert testimony, laws, and evidentiary facts into new definitions and art forms when doing so assured the conviction of someone believed to be a murderous child abuser and a scourge on society.

When Defense Attorneys Snow objected to each of the state's various unfounded allegations, the judge merely overruled his objection and then reminded the jury that:

> What the attorneys say is not evidence, and prosecutors have a right to express their opinion, and the jury should rely on their own memory of the actual testimony.

In a few instances, the judge sustained an objection raised by defense attorneys and instructed the jury to disregard the prosecutor's statements. Regardless of the judge's admonition, spoken words are like air we breathe that cannot be un-breathed. Passionate words by prosecutors (whether true or not) which enflame the emotions, imagination, and outrage of jurors against an accused child abuser cannot be erased from their consciousness.

Prosecutors Snuffelpaw and Bird gave passionate closing and rebuttal arguments that can best be described as "Merlin's Magic Show" because evidence magically appeared or disappeared, and sometimes reappeared in another form when needed to support whatever point they were trying to make at that moment. Their very zealous and theatrical magic show could convince and inspire any juror, without a stellar memory and analytical mind, that Lori was a guilty monster whom they should erase from the face of the earth. Without a doubt, these state prosecutors knew they are habitually considered the voice "of the people" and that the public and jurors are inclined to accept their statements as the unadulterated and absolute Gospel truth. Thus, a prosecutor's statements always have greater weight of credibility with jurors than those of defense attorneys.

As customary, the state's rebuttal closing arguments allowed no opportunity for Lori's attorneys to refute or challenge the new unfounded allegations and left her in a very unfavorable light in the eyes of jurors. It was a combination of false statements, new unfounded allegations (not based on evidence presented) and a distortion of evidence and opinions presented by medical experts.

After three and one-half weeks of trial and five hours of closing arguments, on the afternoon of December 2, 1997, the judge gave jurors instructions and sent them to the jury room to decide Lori fate.

Attorney Crisley told us to always stay near the phone and he would call the minute the jury reached a verdict because Lori would be expected to appear in court at once to hear the verdict read.

After we left the courtroom and considered the totality of the closing arguments and testimony that showed plenty of reasonable doubt, we concluded that an acquittal would be the verdict. It is safe to say that we were feeling very optimistic about that possibility. But when we remembered that approximately 90% of the time juries render a guilty verdict in child abuse/child murder cases, we became unsettled and anxious. We wondered whether the jury would make the decision based on the passion and excitement displayed by prosecutors or on the actual medical evidence and expert opinions presented? We knew the jurors did not understand complex medical and forensic investigative techniques and scientific terminology that would enable them to analyze whether the expert medical witnesses knew what they were talking about. This reality was also very unsettling.

It was very quiet at home that evening and there was little discussion as we waited nervously. Knowing that life is not always fair and bad things do happen to good people, I was not confident of what the verdict would be. I did not know what God's purpose was in allowing this entire tragedy to happen but knew he must have a good reason or purpose for it all. I kept thinking of the various scriptures that say, "*the truth shall make you free*" while praying for a just jury verdict. Also, several Christian churches and prayer groups, local friends and family members were also praying for a "not guilty" verdict and an end to the nightmare.

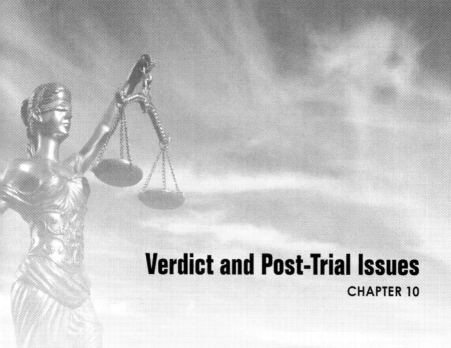

Verdict and Post-Trial Issues

CHAPTER 10

Lori received a phone call around eleven the next morning to appear in court as quickly as possible since the jury had reached their verdict. Since the jury had not taken very long to deliberate we were concerned because her attorneys had informed us that if a verdict came quickly, it would be a guilty verdict.

As promised, I phoned several of our friends and family members to let them know to come quickly to the courtroom and to call anyone else who might be interested in attending.

A foreboding heaviness filled the atmosphere as we approached the courtroom. making it difficult to think or breath. Our family and friends took seats on the defendant's side of the gallery and shortly afterward the judge took the bench.

An unthinkable scene unfolded as the judge asked Lori to stand up and the clerk to read the verdict. The clerk's words sounded like they were from the bottomless pit as she read, *"We, the jury in the above entitled case, find the defendant guilty of First Degree Murder by Child Abuse."* A loud gasp of horror and disbelief echoed across the room and tears flowed down the faces of shocked friends and family.

Lori looked like she had been stabbed in the heart and almost passed out as her knees buckled as she slumped to her seat. Her face was painted with shock, disillusionment, sadness, and terror and a river of tears flowed down her face. Despite everything, there was no anger or bitterness in her face and I thought that if she was prone to explosions of anger (as the prosecutors alleged) this would have been the time it would have erupted.

After the clerk read the verdict, the jurors were polled one by one at the request of Defense Attorney Crisley. Then the Judge thanked and excused the jury and announced that the case was being referred to the Washoe County Department of Parole and Probation for the customary personal background investigation and pre-sentencing recommendations.

A dramatic scene unfolded as the judge allowed Lori a few minutes to say farewell to friends and family before being ushered from the courtroom by deputies. An emotionally shattered Lori, barely able to walk, was escorted from the room in handcuffs and taken directly to the county detention center where she would be held until sentencing. She looked back tearfully and said, *"I love you."* I threw her a kiss and tearfully replied aloud, *"I love you too."* Words cannot describe the agony and helplessness I felt. She was a child who had consistently maintained a high moral character and always loved children. How could she have been found guilty of committing First Degree Murder by Child Abuse?

It is impossible to describe how confounded and disappointed I was with the verdict. As we left the courtroom, my heart and my head were racing in overdrive trying to understand what had happened. A horde of TV and news reporters followed close behind with cameras and microphones trying to get a response from someone. The guilty verdict was like a Hindenburg Blimp explosion, destroying my staunch belief in the jury system, and the last ounce of trust I had in the criminal justice system. Gone were the preconceived notions that had shielded me from the brutality and inequity of it all.

Immediately after the hearing was over, Lori's husband, her brother, sister, aunt, uncle, and I met with Attorney Crisley privately to discuss what the next step should be. He was clearly devastated by the guilty verdict as seen by the tears that gushed down his youthful face when the verdict was read. He and Attorney Snow really believed in Lori's innocence and expected an acquittal based on reasonable doubt they had shown to jurors. He informed us they would be filing proper motions to ask the judge to set aside the guilty verdict, as he felt the jury did not consider all the facts. He had assumed the jury would be able to correctly evaluate the evidence he presented, but he was wrong.

Several days after incarceration, Lori was finally allowed to make a phone call from jail. She mentioned that when she left home to hear the verdict that morning she had not hugged and kissed or said goodbye to her baby daughter, thinking she would be back home that same day.

For sure, our prayers were not answered the way we expected, and my faith was shaken to the core. Lori's family and friends also expressed this same sentiment. My natural reaction was to ask God, *"Why this verdict?" "Was it my sins that brought this about?" "What did Lori do to deserve this?" "What are your plans for us?" "Where will it all end, will Lori spend the rest of her life behind bars?"* I got no answers.

Waiting for Sentencing - Incarceration

Shortly after Lori's arrival at the county detention center, she sent me a letter with a request that I send it to friends and family who believed in her innocence and had shown support for her. Her letter gave a small glimpse into what life was like behind bars in the local jail and showed her undying faith and belief in prayer, even while experiencing extreme disappointment. It reads as follows:

Dear Friends and Family,

I don't know where to begin. First of all, thank you for all of your support for myself and my family. There are a few things I need to remind everybody about. I cannot receive anything by mail except pencil or pen handwritten letters, cards without any glitter or ribbons, etc.

And I can receive drawings by colored pencils only – no watercolor or Crayola drawings. I cannot receive any paper, stamps, envelopes, etc., to write back. If you would like to send paperback books or journals, please have them sent from a book store and have them sent to the Chaplin.......... Also, unfortunately all photographs are stapled right through the middle and tends to destroy them, although please send them anyway. So, if you want to send me a copy of anything it probably needs to go to the attorney, so he can have a contact visit and bring them to me. If you would like to put a few dollars on my books, then I can order envelops and writing paper to write you back. My husband has that information. If you wish to write me, my address is: Lori Watson #00014523, Washoe County Detention Center, Reno, NV 89512. I can only have 2 visits a week from friends/family, etc. But two people can come each visit. Visiting hours for me at this time is at 9 a.m. and 8:30 p.m., on Tuesday, Thursday and Saturday, and I believe at 1 p.m. on Sunday. I really crave and covet all visits and letters from you all. Please write me and visit me as often as you can.

Everyone – I thought and believed that this nightmare would be over by now for sure. Please pray for God to display a miracle through the judge or however God wants to work it. When there is a court hearing date set for upcoming motions, it could be very helpful if anyone could attend. The more people the better. My husband will be getting the dates and times soon.

Everyone – I thought and believed that this nightmare would be over by now for sure. Please pray for God to display a miracle through the judge or however God wants to work it. When there is a court hearing date set for upcoming motions, it could be very helpful if anyone could attend. The more people the better. My husband will be getting the dates and times soon.

I would like all of you to know that your prayers must be helping guard my mind, heart, and soul. Because this place is so terrible that without you, I don't know how I could stand it. There is great human suffering in this place. Inmates scream and howl all night and day long. I am in a concrete and steel cell with 3 other women. There is a toilet and sink combo which sits in the middle of the room. There are 4 steel beds, which have a mat the consistency of a newspaper, which you lay on. The pillow is the same way. We have 2 cotton blankets because we were so cold, and the guard brought us another blanket. There is a window that runs along the top of the wall and is about 5" high in 2 parts. If I stand up, all I can see is the sky because the window is so high up. My window looks out over 1st Street between Badger and Lewis. If I stand on top of the bed, I can see the ground, and the prostitutes, and nasty men who purposefully stand and expose themselves. It makes my stomach sick.

Meals are served at 5 a.m., 11 a.m., and 4 p.m. The food can be palatable at times, but for the most part is awful. It is served on these brown soaking wet plastic trays, and the food is slopped on and running down the sides. We don't eat at a table. I have to wipe the bottom of the tray off with toilet paper and put the trays in our lap while sitting on a bed. We never know if we're going to get out of the cell during a day or not. I wear the same clothes for 1 week before we are stripped and have to change clothes. There is no music. If we are let out of the cell, we can take a shower, or get some hot water or make a phone call. There are no wash clothes to wash with, and a button in a very nasty shower has to be continually pushed to get the water out. The same towel has to be used all week. It's cold in the cells so most of the women try to sleep and stay wrapped in their blankets all day. At night they wake up and for the most part, stay up all night and tell horrible stories about prostitution and drugs, etc. It's like Chinese torture all night long. Some of them like to play cards, some read books -- mostly romance and science fiction. I can't get into that book selection at all. They read 12-14 hours a day to escape reality and to pass time I know that everyone out there is doing all they can for the legal case, but in here where time seems to stand still, I wonder and worry a lot.

My greatest pain is knowing that my innocent precious children have had their mother ripped from their lives and they want their mommy to come home to them. I can't believe I'm in the United States of America. Last night at 3:30 am, four officers barged in the cell and ordered us out. They went through everything in the room including all personal stuff. When they were done, the sheets, underwear, snacks, letters from family, etc., was tossed in a pile on my bed. It was so violating, so humiliating and makes you feel like total scum of the earth.

Now on the good side, I was put in a room with a Christian who was prosecuted by the same prosecutors. I believe she is an innocent victim. Maybe all this is part of His divine plan, but I do wish He would work quickly. I love you all. I'll write again soon.

Lori Watson

Post-Trial Motions and Sentencing Hearing

Meanwhile, the Defense Attorneys Snow and Crisley were diligently working to change the course of things by preparing and filing two motions asking the court to reverse the jury verdict. The two post-trial motions filed by Lori's attorneys were extremely important to a proper defense and her rights to appeal to a higher court based on certain irregularities and improper court rulings that had occurred during trial. Lori's attorneys worked very quickly to prepare the motions and filed them with the court two weeks after the verdict.

One was a *"Motion for Judgment of Acquittal, or, in the Alternative, New Trial,"* It asked that the judge declare an acquittal or grant a new trial because the jury was presented with plenty of reasonable doubt, but they did not recognize or consider it.

The other was a *"Motion for New Trial Based Upon Prosecutorial Misconduct."* Even if these motions were not immediately successful, they were necessary before an appeal could be filed at the Nevada Supreme Court.

The prosecutions' opposition and response papers filed with the court concerning these two defense motions consisted of hundreds of pages of complex and convoluted legal arguments. Their gobbledygook reminded me of W. C. Fields when he said, *"If you can't dazzle them with brilliance, baffle them with B.S."* Certainly, state prosecutors had learned that technique very well and were experts at it.

Unfortunately, several weeks after it was filed the judge denied the first defense motion so there would be no acquittal of the charges.

The court hearing on the motion that asked for a dismissal of the charges because of prosecutorial misconduct along with sentencing was continued for another week. That motion concerned the improper and prejudicial statements made by prosecutors during closing arguments of defense Attorney Crisley (concerning late forensic testing of tissue specimens by prosecution experts.) It was disappointing that none of the other egregious statements made by prosecutors during closing arguments (and otherwise) were included in the motions, such as presenting new undocumented and unsubstantiated evidence that was never introduced during trial that would have influenced the jurors to reach a guilty verdict.

Emotions were running high as many friends and relatives of Lori packed the courtroom to hear the oral arguments and offer emotional support. We were all listening intently, and prayerfully as oral arguments were presented by both sides. After discussions, the judge denied that motion also because he thought the prosecutor's statements were not sufficiently prejudicial to have made a difference in the trial outcome, and then went ahead to the sentencing phase of the hearing.

As expected during the sentencing phase, the deceased child's father, and aunt told the judge that Lori should receive the longest sentence allowed by law. Strangely, the mother asked that Lori spend one year in prison for every year of Angie's life. Although I understood their agony of losing a child to circumstances beyond their ability to understand or control, it was doubly perplexing and gut-wrenching to know their anger and desire for revenge was directed toward the wrong person. Would they ever know how much Lori loved little Angie and that she would never have done anything intentionally to hurt her?

When the grandmother took the stand, she read a poem to express her grief, and then recounted the numbers of minutes, hours, and days that the deceased child had lived and said Lori should receive the harshest sentence possible.

Although I asked for permission to speak in support of Lori at the sentencing hearing, her attorneys did not respond to my request. Therefore, no one spoke up on behalf of Lori during sentencing. The attorneys' actions perplexed me, but perhaps they felt that my words could sound like an excuse for her alleged crime and inflame the judge to impose the maximum sentence. At that time, there were three possible sentences for First Degree Murder, either a life sentence in Nevada state prison without the possibility of parole, life in prison with the possibility of parole after twenty years, or a fifty-year sentence with the possibility of parole after 20 years.

Although the Washoe County Probation and Parole Department's written report to the judge showed Lori had no prior criminal record of any kind and recommended a light sentence, the judge gave her the greatest sentence which was life in prison in prison with the possibility of parole after serving a minimum of twenty years because of the violent nature of the perceived crime.

Lori's attorney asked, and the judge agreed she could remain at county detention center in Reno until he was able to hear and decide on the defense "*Motion for Bail Pending Appeal.*" During the hearing on the motion to grant bail, defense attorneys were blind-sided when the judge said that he had received confidential information from an undisclosed source that Lori had violated the condition of his prior release order that restricted her from visiting or contacting her children without supervision, but he gave no opportunity for Lori and her attorneys to dispute that report.

The judge's decision to not grant bail was extremely disappointing because he had previously indicated that he was inclined to release her on bail pending an appeal and we were optimistic. It was a complete shock to Lori as she had not violated the judge's order, nor received any notice from her case worker or anyone else in authority that she violated the court's order. *Irrespective of the so-called report, we knew that if she had violated any of the conditions of her release or those imposed by CPS she would have been re-arrested and hauled into court, which is the normal legal process.* This confidential report was an effort by those opposing her release, watching her every move, and trying to catch her in a violation.

Lori could only think of one occasion that might have prompted this report to the judge. It concerned one afternoon when she drove to the family home to shower and get ready for her second part time job, instead of driving across town to her usual residence at her aunt and uncle's house and backtracking to that job. While doing so, her CPS caseworker came to the door for an impromptu visit. Lori went to the door with a towel on her head, they talked for a while but there was no reason to give her a written or verbal warning. Someone was watching her every move and decided it was a violation but did not know that her case worker had allowed her to be there during that time providing she was being supervised. It appeared that the reporting party or entity did not want to be revealed but was someone from the prosecutor's office. Here again, manipulation and moral relativism decided the course of events. Obviously, the family of the deceased child and the prosecution opposed releasing her on bail and there was no limit to what they would do to keep her behind bars, including manipulating the judge, and widely publicizing against her release in TV and print media.

While incarcerated, Lori had a lot of down time to consider what went wrong with her trial and discussed it with me several times on the phone. As we all know, hind-sight can be daunting and overwhelming as it sometimes creates 20/20 vision on some issues but distorts others where there is a lack of adequate information or understanding.

For very good reasons, she took the time to write her attorneys a lengthy letter naming ten problems she saw with their trial strategy, including the inadequate manner the forensic evidence was handled and presented. Whether right or wrong in her assessments, she needed to vent and let a lot steam off her chest.

Her most important disagreement concerned the fact that her attorneys did not consult her before filing two pre-trial motions, one was to "*Dismiss Indictment for Prosecution Misconduct*" and the other a "*Motion to Dismiss for Failure to Present Exculpatory Evidence to Grand Jury.*" She felt those two motions should not have been made because doing so prematurely revealed the defense trial strategy to the prosecution and unnecessarily elevated the importance of the pathology reports; and caused prosecutors to be better prepared by hiring several medical expert witnesses that they otherwise would not have hired.

Her disagreements with her attorneys were primarily based on things she learned at a seminar one month before trial began, called *"Allegations of Child Abuse, The Law, The Science, The Myths, The Reality."* This seminar was conducted by a well-known criminal trial consultant and featured various other legal and medical specialists. At the seminar, Lori learned valuable information about the intricacies and nuances of successfully defending against child abuse/murder charges, but it was too late for the information to be useful to her attorneys as the discovery deadline and exchange of information by the two sides had already passed.

Since, in my profession, I had previously helped with several huge trial preparations, I knew that her attorneys did not have enough time to properly conduct discovery, strategize and thoroughly prepare her defense. Especially since during that same time frame, they were also conducting other trials and servicing other clients and could not devote much of their time preparing for the murder trial. Regardless, after careful thought and emotional anguish, Lori decided that she did not want Attorney Crisley and Snow to represent her any longer. With anticipation of filing an appeal to the Nevada Supreme Court, she wanted a more seasoned appellate attorney to handle it and wrote a letter to her attorneys and the judge informing them of her decision. Naturally, the change of attorney would need court approval and he would be chosen from a public defender panel of attorneys experienced in processing criminal appeals. The hiring of the appellate attorney would involve a written motion to get the judge's approval and could not happen immediately.

In the interim, no one had informed us that Lori would need money for personal needs, such as medical treatment, prescriptions, phone calls, over-the-counter meds, extra clothing, snacks, tennis shoes, reading and writing material, stamps, drinkable water, and toiletries, etc., while incarcerated. Those expenses created added stress to the family budget deficit as the prisoner's price for those items was double what they cost at Walmart or Target. Regardless, my family and I supplied her needs by foregoing other obligations and using credit cards to deposit money into her account monthly.

Once Lori was out of solitary confinement, the types of inmates selected to share her cell at the county jail caused her more misery. She wondered if they were chosen to make her as miserable as possible (as further punishment because of the nature of her conviction.) Over a period of several months, her cell was like a revolving door, bringing either hardened criminals, drug addicts, mentally ill, or prostitutes that shared the four-person cell with her. Several of the women should have been hospitalized because they were suffering from life-threatening acute medical conditions and withdrawal symptoms, such as DT's, seizures, tremors, infected needle marks, open sores, healing scabs, rashes and itching skin caused by either alcohol or drug abuse. Many of them with infections, pains, chills, and fevers, screamed out for help hours on end, day, and night, but there was no help or medical aid provided to them by the jailers. The only comfort and help that Lori could offer her cell mates was to give them the jail flavored water to drink, speak encouraging words, and try to relieve their distress by washing their sores with water, and placing a wet towel on their foreheads to relieve the pounding headaches.

She told me about one roommate who was pregnant and went into labor and although Lori repeatedly asked for help, the jailers deliberately ignored the woman. By the time jailers called an ambulance, it was too late, and the baby arrived on the way to the hospital. Lori wondered what would happen if she had a medical emergency in this very hostile cold-hearted environment.

Letter from Prison

After six months of enduring dreadful conditions at the county jail, Lori was transferred to a state correctional center for women that was built and run by a private company under contract with the state. As a newcomer in a group of forty women, she was surprised to learn they would be treated as humans and not like animals in cages. In a letter to friends and family she expressed her delight and surprise at the humane treatment she received at this private care facility. In part, she wrote as follows:

Dear everyone

I decided that I had better write you, so you wouldn't worry about me too much. They transferred me to a Nevada Women's Correctional Facility. What is unique is that this is not a state-run prison. It is a correctional care facility. The difference between this and a governmental run place is light years. This is more like the military. Everyone is extremely nice, courteous, and no foul language. The officers say things like; Good Morning, how did you sleep last night? How was breakfast? Is there anything I can do for you? We are in shock. When I first got here we had the warmest, luxurious shower, clean white towels, and washcloths, brand new 7undies and 2 bras, 8 socks, shoes, 4 pants, 1 top, 1 sleep shirt, 1 pair thermal underwear, 1 jacket, lotion, toothpaste, toothbrush, deodorant, and envelopes and writing supplies. The whole place is immaculate. The Chaplin came up and took our hands and prayed with us right when we got here. The warden came up and smiled and said "hi" to each one and shook our hands. This week we've seen the dentist, doctor and been checked from top to bottom. They prescribed something for the terrible rashes that exists on my hands and feet. When they tried to get blood, it was a disaster because of dehydration and, I don't have surface veins, and my blood was so thick it would not come up in the needle. The nurses were shocked. It took eight attempts. I had bandages all over my arms and I was bawling. They put me on daily aspirin, since my blood was way too thick.

I have a lot to tell you. The showers are heaven, as hot and as long and as soapy as you want. They have soft water here that is white and clean. We could not believe the food that is delicious. We ate like savages for days, real juice, milk, coffee, fried chicken, salads, vegetables, fresh rolls, so-delicious. The nurses, doctors, teachers, etc. eat in the same cafeteria with us, just like in college…

Its real strict, in the rooms we must be spotless and ready for inspection at any moment and if you break a rule there are very severe consequences, which I won't elaborate on. The dentist is going to fix my crown that broke and whatever else needed. It was a real clean office with a waiting room with music playing. We have been in total shock. The doctors say such things as, pardon me, excuse me, sorry to keep you waiting, just like the real world…

…They keep telling us that they are not here to punish people, that is not their job. Their responsibility is to house people while they "do time." ….. just the opposite from county jail.

She concluded the letter by saying;

There are lots of Jesus loving people here too, and lots of bogus child abuse cases!!!

Love Lori

Once Lori passed the risk-assessment process (several months after arrival) at the prison, she could order a fan, radio, CD player, and small TV to be shipped directly from the designated retailer at our expense. She was instructed to keep all receipts for her belongings because if she could not show one for any item upon inspection, the item would be considered contraband and confiscated by the guards and never returned. If they thought it may have been stolen, she could possibly be sent to the "hole" until the mess could be sorted out.

Several times she mentioned that there was very little reading material and books in the prison library. But the chaplain offered books and magazines that were educational and inspirational to prisoners. When I learned of the shortage of books, I contacted a charity that gives books to prisons and arranged for shipment of four boxes of books to the prison chaplain. However, I was unaware that the warden had to approve the books, so they sat in her office for several weeks until the warden finally gave approval to allow prisoners to read them.

For individual prisoners, the normal process of receiving books starts with a prisoner making a request to the warden and, if approved, the prisoner communicates with a friend or relative on the outside to order the books and send them directly to the prisoner from an approved book retailer. The rules changed from time to time, about which retailer could be used, how many books were allowed, and whether pre-approval from the warden was needed. As would be expected, certain types of inappropriate books and magazines were prohibited and confiscated by the mailroom.

When mailing letters and photographs to Lori, there was a limit on the number of pages and pictures that could be included in each envelope. At first, she could have twenty printed or hand-written pages at a time, but later the rules changed and only ten pages of material could be sent. Also, ten photographs (no larger than 8 x 10) was allowed. No stickers or glue (except for stamps), colored ink, glitter or ribbons were allowed on letters or cards. It was disturbing to learn that instead of returning inappropriate items to the sender, they were just trashed by the mailroom personnel without notifying anyone.

It took time and effort to make sure we were following all the rules and regulations imposed by the Nevada Department of Corrections when trying to communicate with Lori and/or supply her with money to order items that would bring her a little comfort. Fortunately, several friends and extended family members also occasionally deposited money into her account so she could have basic needs met and know that she was not forgotten.

Collect phone calls from the jail were very costly and soon my phone bill was over $400 per month which put an added strain on my already tight budget. Regardless of the cost, I could not refuse Lori's collect calls knowing she was emotionally distraught and needed to talk on a frequent basis. My constant concern and goal were to communicate openly with Lori about what was happening without re-traumatizing her. I always tried to be aware of her ever-changing moods and spiritual needs and give her the encouragement she needed. Most of the time, I would only listen to her expressions of grief, anxiety, and confusion and not give her any feedback or advice, unless she asked. The important thing was for her to be able to talk about her deepest fears and disappointments, as well as her dreams for the future.

Eventually, a Google Voice phone service provided me with a number having the same prefix as the prison making the calls less expensive as her calls were re-routed from the prison to cell phone at no extra cost.

In the world outside the prison, other issues were developing that needed careful attention and a lot of effort to protect Lori and her family from permanent financial ruin and loss of freedom. They involved two civil lawsuits filed against her and her husband, and the appeal of her criminal conviction.

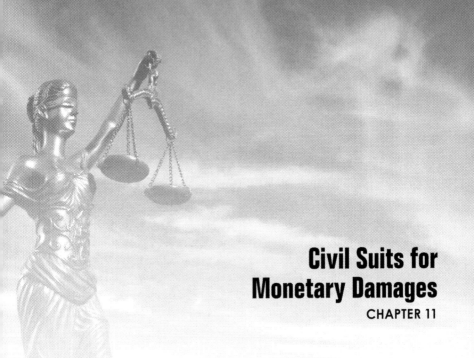

Civil Suits for
Monetary Damages
CHAPTER 11

Shortly after her arrest, **Lori gave me Power of Attorney to file a** claim on her behalf with her daycare's general business liability insurance carrier, Jefferson Insurance, to ask for payment of criminal attorney fees and costs. Since she was unable to do so, I sent the insurance claim form to them and several phone calls and letters were exchanged trying to convince them. But after conducting a cursory investigation of her claim, the insurance company refused to give coverage for Lori's defense attorney because of the alleged criminal act which the policy excluded from coverage.

As we feared might happen, word got around about Lori's Business General Liability Insurance policy. Our tormented journey became more treacherous and complicated with two civil lawsuits seeking monetary damages against Lori and her family. One lawsuit was filed by the parents of the deceased child, Angie Rison, alleging wrongful death and negligence, seeking monetary damages against Lori, her husband, and a close friend who wrote a letter recommending the licensing of the daycare center. The suit also named the Washoe County Department of CPS and Youth and Family Services, the County of Washoe, and the State of Nevada, as defendants alleging negligence in licensing Lori's daycare operation.

The insurance company decided not to give coverage to Lori in the Rison civil case and Lori's ability to defend herself and conduct proper medical and forensic investigations was severely compromised. Thankfully, the policy named Lori's husband as an additional insured and he was also named in the lawsuit. Thus, the insurance company agreed to pay his attorney fees as well as all damages that might be awarded jointly and severally (between himself and Lori.)

The parents of the eight-month old who fell from a highchair at daycare filed the second civil action. It requested monetary compensation because of alleged negligence by Lori while caring for their child. The insurance company agreed to provide Lori and her husband with a civil defense attorney and coverage against any potential award of damages in this case, because a criminal act did not trigger it.

Although both civil cases were hugely unsettling and stressful, we were hoping that the discovery phase in the Rison litigation would give an opportunity to discover new and indisputable evidence that would finally prove my daughter's innocence beyond a shadow of a doubt. There was a glimmer of hope that it would be an opportunity to discover evidence that would fully explain what caused Angie's catastrophic brain injuries, whether from a prior accident, neglect, abuse, or because of an undiagnosed genetic defect, nutritional or pathological condition.

Since Lori was representing herself (in Pro Per) as a defendant in the Rison case, I agreed to prepare and file with the court (and serve on all parties) an *"Answer to the Complaint."* Otherwise, the court would enter a *"Default Judgment"* against her and we resolved not to allow that to happen. We decided to also file a *"Cross-Complaint/Counter-claim"* against the Risons for misrepresentation, breach of good faith and fair dealing.

After researching the Nevada civil process and working late nights, I prepared the legal documents and sent them to Lori for reviewing and signing. Although she did not have the training or resources to do the paperwork, she reviewed each document for accuracy of content and telephoned me with questions or needed revisions. Once a document was acceptable she would sign and return it to me to complete the legal processing of it.

This litigation consumed hundreds of my non-working hours for more than one year. I reviewed all case documents and pleadings, prepared discovery, explored medical issues, and drafted court and discovery documents in the proper format, communicated with attorneys, hired an investigator, sought advice from medical specialists, and tried to find proper expert witnesses.

Also, we were hoping to have an opportunity to conduct depositions (testimony under oath) of Angie's parents to ask them several specific questions under oath about several known events, specifically the following: (1) the baby's fall from the kitchen counter top while in her baby carrier, (2) a more precise account of their activities the prior weekend and (3) their possible visit to the mall that weekend, (4) what happened at home before and after Angie was taken to get her immunizations, and (5) how many "minor falls" there were and when and where they happened?

At the beginning of this tragedy, I began researching the various medical and forensic issues related to Angie's injuries that were central to Lori's defense. The Rison civil case further sparked my curiosity and drove my search for answers. Each of the medical experts who testified in the criminal trial held conflicting opinions. There was still much information about very complex medical and forensic issues connected with short-distance falls and Shaken Baby Syndrome that needed to be explored and evaluated. I hoped that enough irrefutable evidence would result in a civil judgment that criminal prosecutors could not ignore.

It had been our goal that each of the thirteen microscopic tissue specimens of the victim's cerebellum (brain) would be examined by proper medical experts (i.e., cytopathologists, histopathologists and/or a hemopathologists) who would be questioned under oath and add credibility to the prior diagnoses of older injuries and hopefully make a future criminal trial unnecessary. Although I discussed this with the attorney for Jefferson Insurance and their investigator many times, they never bought into the idea of conducting a thorough forensic investigation and Lori had no leverage to demand it.

Regardless, the lack of financial resources did not hinder me from reviewing all the medical records, reading the criminal trial transcripts, and discussing the various issues with other medical experts and attorneys. There was plenty of evidence and clues (in addition to several pathology reports) that Angie also suffered prior brain injuries that were caused either by an accidental or intentional head trauma, pathological condition, genetic or metabolic disorder or a combination of any of them. The defense medical experts in the criminal case, and other pathologists, believed this was what happened.

During the civil case, there were several important issues and circumstances to be explored, including the following:

> Angie's severe and rare reaction to her first MMR (Measles, Mumps and Rubella) shot along with the DTAP-Diphtheria, Tetanus, Pertussis (whopping cough), and HIB (Haemophilus

Influenzas-Type B) vaccinations shortly before the day of the tragedy?

➤ Angie's falling while in her baby carrier from the top of the kitchen cabinet where the mother placed her, Angie landing on her head.

➤ The macrocephaly (a large head – at 95%) at birth in relation to her small body size, where intracranial complications can eventually mimic Shaken Baby Syndrome.

➤ The reported environmental hazard of methamphetamines in the apartment building where she lived (even while her mom was pregnant) as shown on public and police records.

➤ The bruise on the hollow part of Angie's cheek seen on the first day of childcare.

➤ The pathology reports from three unbiased pathology departments (the local hospital, Stanford Research Clinic and AFIP) plus two expert criminal defense pathologists, along with two other pathologists who diagnosed older injuries and/or an anatomical or pathological condition at the site of the skull fracture in Angie's brain.

➤ The lack of external bodily and/or fresh scalp injuries that would go with any violent intentional act as alleged by prosecuting attorneys, who speculated that Lori acted in a fit of rage with a force equivalent to a fall from a two-story building (approx. 25 mph.) onto concrete.

➤ The prior injury as shown by the "fading out" bluish bruising at the back of Angie's head under her hairline that could only be seen by her mom in the emergency room on the evening of March 4, 1996, and reiterated in the Washoe County Autopsy Report? (i.e. Was it from her fall off the kitchen counter while in her baby carrier?)

➤ Based on the description of the child's physical attributes (being under weight, short stature, large head size, rubbery skin tone and condition, wide eyes), whether a possible genetic disorder, pathological condition and/or nutritional deficiency (i.e. Vitamin K, C, D, Iron and/or Calcium, etc.) could have caused cranial defects, vascular problems, or the brittle bone condition that predated the short-distance fall at Lori's daycare.

After many discussions with the attorney and investigator for Jefferson Insurance, and various pathologists who had reviewed all the facts of the case, I believed that one or more events may have caused the traumatic brain injuries and symptoms described by the treating physicians. The following are possible scenarios:

> There was no preexisting skull fracture: The hydrocephalus, edema and subdural bleeding were caused by a preexisting pathological condition that resulted in extremely high intracranial pressure and injuries to her brain tissue, making it more likely that a minor accident such as jumping up and then falling and hitting the edge of the coffee table or the floor caused a skull fracture and a re-bleed.

> There was a pre-existing skull fracture and refracture: The subdural bleeding, hydrocephalus (accumulation of cerebral fluids) and edema (swelling of the tissue) originated from an undiagnosed pathological condition, such as Arterial Venus Malformations (AVM), a tumor, or other vascular or bone malady caused by either prenatal chemical contamination, malnutrition or by a genetic disorder. The resulting high intracranial (brain) pressure caused the skull to fracture without any other mechanism and was re-fractured by the reported simple short-distance fall, much like an overinflated balloon pops when squeezed lightly.

> There was a pre-existing trauma (accidental or non-accidental) that caused a primary skull fracture and intracranial bleeding, hydrocephalus (accumulation of cerebral fluids) and edema (swelling of the tissue), that was further compromised by an underlying undiagnosed medical condition such as AVMs, a tumor or other vascular and/or cerebral anomaly caused by either prenatal toxic chemical exposure, malnutrition, pathological condition or a genetic disorder, or the numerous simultaneous immunizations administered the previous week, all of which were further compromised by her fall on the day of the tragedy.

> Result of Immunizations: Several simultaneous immunizations given to Angie the week before could have caused the subdural bleeding, hydrocephalus and tissue swelling in her brain (with or without an underlying pathological condition) increasing the brain pressure enough to cause a skull fracture by a short-distance fall, as reported.

Lori and I were hoping to enlist the services of a prestigious pathologist at the University of Miami who diagnosed that the tissue samples he reviewed contained evidence of several older healing lesions caused by

AVM's that are most often congenital. In an email to me a few days before the criminal trial began, he gave that diagnosis and later telephoned me to discuss the significance of his findings. He informed me that when AVM's are in the brain, they often cause spontaneous bleeding, swelling in the brain, gait disturbances, and increased intracranial pressure that can also cause retinal hemorrhaging such as Angie experienced. You may recall that many of those symptoms are the identical ones customarily and historically cited by many emergency room doctors, expert witnesses, and prosecutors as "irrefutable evidence" of "Shaken Baby Syndrome" and/or other forms of intentional child abuse.

Medical specialist said that if AVMs were present, they would have triggered or increased Angie's (extremely rare and severe) adverse reaction to simultaneous injection of seven immunizations; DTAP (Diphtheria, Tetanus, Pertussin -whopping cough), HIB (Haemophilus Influenzae-Type B), and her very first MMR (Measles, Mumps and Rubella) that she received six days before her fall. More importantly, the US Center for Disease Control and disclosures of the manufacturers recommended not to administer the shots if the child has a head injury or neurological problem because that could trigger dangerous complications. Their literature also warned about the dangers of administering multiple immunizations simultaneously.

Eventually, because Lori had no civil attorney in the case, the pathologist from the University of Miami refused to take part in the case as an expert witness. This caused the discovery process on Lori's behalf to stall and I redirected my efforts to searching for an attorney who would work on a pro-bono basis.

Premature Settlement Conference

Before the true source of Angie's traumatic skull and brain injuries could be fully explored by proper medical experts, the court and the two insurance companies for the individual defendants decided that a mutual settlement conference was in order. Therefore, about one year after the two civil cases began, the court scheduled a settlement conference for both cases and all parties were ordered to personally attend. Since the insurance carriers had the unilateral legal right to settle (per the terms of the insurance policies) without approval by the insured defendants, the decision was totally in their hands.

We knew that if Lori did not consent to the agreement and continued to fight without the help of an attorney and expert witnesses, she faced the possibility of having a huge monetary judgment imposed against her. Therefore, to make sure Lori was legally protected during the settlement conference it was necessary to hire an attorney to make a *"Special Appearance"* for settlement negotiation purposes only. The civil attorney I worked for agreed to appear on her behalf as he had extensive experience in negotiating civil settlements with insurance companies.

For Lori to leave the prison and attend the mandatory settlement conference, it was necessary for the attorney for Jefferson Insurance to obtain a special order from the Washoe Criminal Court instructing the prison to transport Lori to and from the settlement conference. Lori was very happy to be outside the prison, breathing fresh air, seeing the trees, flowers, clouds, sun, and the city skyline instead of depressing gray prison walls. On the way to the conference, the prison guards going with her were kind enough to drive around the city for a while, so she could have more of the experience. Once she arrived at the settlement conference, one of the Jefferson Insurance attorneys told her to choose what she wanted for lunch and they would treat her. She had been craving Kentucky Fried Chicken, so that was what they ordered. I realized that her choice of lunch was significant. I remembered that her first job was at the neighborhood KFC, which brought her a sense of personal independence and freedom that she craved so intensely as a teenager. She later gushed to me about how good the fried chicken tasted.

The attorney I sent to represent Lori at the settlement conference was instructed to object to settling until the depositions of both the mother and father of Angie could take place, so they could be questioned about the child's fall in her baby carrier from the kitchen counter top, and to get answers to other important questions. However, attorneys for the insurance companies chose not to agree to this request and went ahead with settlement discussions. They made it clear their desire to settle was based on economic considerations, the exculpatory pathology reports, and the reported short fall of Angie on March 4, 1996.

Due to circumstances beyond Lori's control, including her financial vulnerability, she and the attorney agreed it was best to sign the settlement agreement after a draft of it was faxed to me for review. After a few corrections, all the individual parties in both cases and the two insurance companies signed a global settlement agreement and release of liability. The settlement resulted in the Rison family and/or their attorney being paid $500,000 as damages without any requirement that Lori admit to any wrongdoing. We were extremely disappointed at the quick settlement of the Rison civil case which made it necessary to find another avenue to confirm the forensic pathology reports in our possession and discover what really happened to Angie.

However, the settlement by the individual defendants and insurance companies did not include the Rison's (plaintiffs') claims against the daycare licensing agency (the Washoe County Department of Child Services and Washoe County) and that part of the litigation continued.

After the settlement agreement was signed and entered on the court record, the county agencies being sued by the Risons filed a *Motion for Summary Judgment* based on malicious prosecution (meaning the plaintiffs filed a frivolous lawsuit with no legal basis.) The court granted their motion, dismissed the case in its entirety, and ordered the plaintiffs to reimburse the state for attorney fees and costs for nearly $8,000. Considering the large amount of settlement funds, this should not have been an impossibility, but they refused to reimburse the county. As a result, the court issued valid bench warrants for both parents that were valid for ten years. The warrants were mysteriously recalled even though no reasons (arrests, payments, or court appearances) were logged on the court record allowing a legal recall of the warrants. It is likely that prosecutors made a deal with a judge to get the warrants recalled without a payment or compensation of any kind.

Interestingly, a few years after the settlement, defense investigators discovered that the settlement money paid to the Rison family was spent on several very expensive motor vehicles and since then the family appeared to be living in poverty. The Risons were divorced and living separately in different states, and Colleen, the mother, was working in a topless bar in the Midwest to support herself and three children.

While the civil cases were continuing through the civil court, Lori's appellate attorney was preparing the criminal appeal seeking a reversal of her felony conviction of First Degree Murder which carried a life sentence. Since the civil cases were now over, our primary focus turned to the criminal appeal process.

Nevada Supreme Court Intervenes

CHAPTER 12

The local criminal court had previously approved the appointment of Attorney David Smith to represent Lori in preparing and filing the Notice of Appeal and Opening Brief requesting the overturn of her conviction of "*First Degree Murder by Child Abuse.*" According to other local attorneys, Attorney Smith was the best in the area with a great legal mind and a tremendous track record of success. He impressed me as a very modest congenial professional who was cautiously optimistic about the possibility of having her conviction overturned.

It was our continual prayer that the Nevada Supreme Court would review the case, reverse her conviction, order a new trial, and compel the prosecutors to drop the false charges based on the more recently discovered forensic evidence that substantiated and was in line with the prior three pathology departments' diagnoses and written reports.

While incarcerated at the local jail, Lori wrote a letter to Attorney Smith expressing frustrations and agony over her dilemma. Here is a portion of her long letter telling of her misery and concerns:

> Dear David Smith,
>
> I know that you are a very busy attorney, so I hope that you don't mind if I write to you regularly. I feel compelled to write because I am

extremely depressed as it is my daughter Tanasha's birthday today and this is the first time that I have not been there for her and coordinated her birthday party. She loves her birthday parties. My daughter is so smart, beautiful, and artistic. I have been extremely blessed with my children. My greatest pain now is that they are in pain because they miss me terribly. I try to divorce myself from thinking about them, but I can't help reviewing in my mind over and over that I've always put the care and welfare of my children and husband first. I've practically worshipped my family. I love to take care of them & cook & clean and be a mommy. It just seems so terribly tragic and unfair for us all now. And I am angry at the system and the DA's office. They say that they are searching for the truth. If they were, they would have done more research when they found out about the Stanford Research Clinic report before the grand jury met. And I've always wondered why they had a grand jury in the first place. Were they worried that there might not be an indictment (charges forwarded for trial) if there was a preliminary hearing?

By the way, I want to let you know that I believe that a few of the jurors could not reach an unbiased opinion because one of them worked at coroner's office and one of them worked with the neurosurgeon. I am very seriously interested in composing some sort of questionnaire for the jurors designed to indicate that they decided to guess on things that they had questions on in their minds. There surely must be some sort of precedent on this issue. I'm asking you to pull out all the stops in this case and try everything even if you don't think that it is probably going to be successful. I hope that you've realized that it is therapeutic for me to write or talk. The last few days, it seems as though I've been crying constantly. Even though I've started taking Zoloft for depression, now I am very depressed.

On that fateful day, when we ran out of the house to get into the car and head for the courthouse because the verdict was in, I really didn't hug my baby, because I believed that this nightmare was finally over and that I would be back in an hour to celebrate with my children. I have analyzed everything over and over, and still can't believe that upon them enough about the significance of reasonable doubt. I think I would be a better attorney than most criminal defense attorneys in this town. What's really disgusting is that it's all about money and politics. I feel really alone now, it's like my life is not important enough for anyone the jury came back with a guilty verdict. I don't think it was impressed

to stick their neck out and help another human being who might have
been wronged...

Lori Watson

Plagued by extreme emotional agony and desperation, three days later
Lori wrote another heart-felt letter to her appellate attorney. Portions of that
letter are as follows:

Dear David Smith,

I am in so much agony. Please don't be upset at me for writing to you
again. I feel a lot, that no one believes that I am not a murderer. I keep
thinking that for some reason I deserve all this torture. Maybe I yelled at
the kids one too many times, or maybe I wasn't obedient to my husband
like I needed to be. I can't believe that I've been convicted of 1st Degree
Murder.
I need you to believe in my innocence. I've heard that you are a good
attorney. Other attorneys say you are the best, but I don't know if that is
enough. I need you to believe in your gut that I am innocent of murder.
I don't really believe that you can fight for me and my precious children
until you believe that. I'm asking you to respond to me on this issue.......

Then she goes on to say:

I want you to realize that the evidence of older injury that I mentioned
above, which was unsolicited from the defense was not brought before
the grand jury. Although prosecutors knew about it and decided upon
himself that it wasn't relevant, then he never gave the reports to the
defense at all. Oh, I forgot something very important; there was initially
a pathology report written by two pathologists at the local hospital
in which they say Angie had a brain tumor and sent the specimens
to Stanford Research Clinic for consultation. That report (Amended
Pathology Report) by the doctors was completed and in their file way
before the grand jury met, because it was in the bound volume that
was sent to my attorney's office in the very beginning before thegrand
jury hearing took place. But that report was purposefully withheld from

the papers sent to the grand jury for review. That is very important to me. It's not that it was not given to the prosecutors, it's that the report was taken out of what went to the grand jury. I find it very hard to swallow that prosecutors who specialize in these issues of blunt trauma, would not know the significance of a report that said Angie had a brain tumor at the very location of her fracture! Additionally, I cannot believe that they were aware of the existence of "sheets of macrophages" and didn't know there was something wrong. Why didn't they ever give it to the defense then? And the female prosecutor was formerly a nurse for goodness sake. She knows what macrophages are for sure.

Also, Attorney Crisley has in his possession a bag of clothing, shoes, and bottle or cup that was left at my house. The paramedics cut the clothing off Angie, but the detectives never took it with them. That stuff stayed at my house for one year before Pete's detectives finally got it from me. Could you please get an order to preserve the following items and please don't let them get discarded? 1) bag of Angie's belongings at Pete's office; 2) remainder of brain, blood, serum from coroner's office; 3) slides in Dr. Moss's safe at the hospital pathology department; 4) please subpoena photographs and negatives from coroner's office. (this was never done); 5) please subpoena photographs and negatives from the homicide or criminalist (this was never done); 6) the (forensic) slides at Tony's or Pete's offices!

The negatives are extremely important here. First of all, in the autopsy report, it is noted that Angie had a faded-out bruise with no distinct edges on the back of her head. God keeps bringing this to my mind. I feel this is an extremely overlooked point. Why have we never seen this photo that was taken during autopsy? How can a 48-hr. bruise be faded out (barely visible)? An expert on bruises needs to look at that photo.

Also, when you review Dr. Spark's testimony (the neurosurgeon) you will see that he notes that the intracranial pressure was too high for Angie to have just sustained an injury. He talked about several points why Angie had an older injury.

Do you think that because the judge has been doing civil cases, that his perception of reasonable doubt is off? His usual standard is "the preponderance of the evidence" –not reasonable doubt.

Please make sure visually that the slides that Defense ME cut and analyzed and wrote on with a black marker, are in fact still in the box with the others. Lori Watson

Once she was transferred to the state prison with access to a law library, Lori began researching the various statutes and case laws concerning the application of the "felony murder" rule, as well as the history of the various Nevada Revised Statues and the legislature's intent. She wrote the legislature to obtain records of their intent and discussion when revising the murder statute to understand how the revisions related to the charges against her. She also researched each of the other issues that she felt was irregular which the "Opening Brief" should address. When she did not have access to a relevant precedent setting case law publication, she would ask me to send her a copy of it.

Lori was in constant contact with her appellate attorney and they exchanged the results of their individual research by phone and letters. They became a team working toward the best possible supreme court decision. Her attorney respected her intelligence and logic and it uplifted her spirits and gave her a sense of purpose.

After the "Appellate Opening Brief" was filed with the court, I reviewed a copy of it and noticed several minor inaccuracies in his *"Statement of Facts"* concerning certain events and important timing issues. Those minor factual errors were concerning, and I wondered why Lori was not sent a final draft for approval before serving a copy on the interested parties and filing it with the Nevada Supreme Court. Based on my own work experience I knew that the preparation and filing of an appeal brief by the deadline is a huge undertaking and time constraints may have prevented the communication. Regardless, the attorney's legal arguments addressing constitutional issues were more important and we hoped and prayed the higher court would agree with them.

Trial Court Decisions and Verdict Challenged

The Appellant's Opening Brief challenged the trial judge's decisions and the jury verdict by requesting relief from the guilty verdict, based on seven different issues. Some of which violated Lori's constitutional right to a fair and impartial trial and her right to receive equal protection under the law. Some of those constitutional issues are mentioned here, but others are not. The Appellant's Opening Brief addressed the following issues:

1. Aforethought Instruction Was Unconstitutional and Mandates Reversal of Watson's Conviction
2. It Was Error to Deny the Lesser Included Instruction of Involuntary Manslaughter
3. It Was Improper Comment on Watson's Right to Remain Silent for The Prosecutor to Question Jurors About Her Not Testifying
4. There Was Not Sufficient Evidence Produced to Convict Watson of First Degree Murder
5. Improper Closing Argument During the Trial Mandates a Reversal of the Conviction
6. The court Should Have Granted the Motion to Dismiss for Failure to Present Exculpatory Evidence to The Grand Jury
7. The Cumulative Error During the Proceedings Denied Watson a Fundamentally Fair Trial

It would be necessary for the Nevada Supreme Court Justices and their law clerks to review thousands of pages of the trial court records, plus the appellate opening brief, the responding briefs and reply briefs before making a decision. After doing so, in a unanimous decision published in 1999, the justices decided as follows:

> OPINION
>
> Lori Watson was convicted of first-degree murder by child abuse for the death of toddler Angie Rison. The district court jury found Watson guilty and the judge sentenced her to twenty-five years to life in prison with the possibility of parole after twenty years. Therefore, this court reverses the guilty conviction of Watson and remands the case for a new trial because of defective and omitted jury instructions.

The Nevada Supreme Court reversed the guilty verdict based on several fundamentally wrong decisions at the trial court level, saying they were not lawful and violated her constitutional rights. Namely, (1) not allowing the jury instruction that allowed the jury to consider a lesser offence such as 2nd degree murder, negligent homicide, or involuntary manslaughter, and (2) a flawed jury instruction gave a mistaken legal definition of what fundamental elements were needed to charge and convict someone of "*First Degree Murder by Child Abuse.*"

Jury Instruction No. 8, used by the trial court which the higher court ruled as unlawful, incorrectly stated:

> Certain classes of murder carry with them conclusive evidence of malice aforethought. One of them is murder committed by means of child abuse. Therefore, a killing which is committed by child abuse is murder of the first degree regardless of whether the killing was intentional or unintentional.

Under the "DISCUSSION" section of their publication, the justices continued:

> In this case, evidence presented at trial showed that Angie's death may have occurred from circumstances that would have supported an involuntary manslaughter conviction. Defense medical experts testified that a tissue specimen taken from the area near Angie's skull fracture showed that the injury may have occurred days before and that the injury may have been aggravated on March 4th. According to the evidence, the deadly injury could have occurred during a fall, or by some other mechanism besides child abuse. In such a circumstance, the child's death would not have been a product of malice aforethought but possibly a result of neglect or endangerment. Because there is enough evidence to support a jury instruction relating to involuntary manslaughter, the district court's removal of the instruction from the jury's consideration was in error.

The justices also unanimously ruled there was a lack of evidence to support a conviction of *"First Degree Murder by Child Abuse"* by saying:

> There is lacking an overwhelming evidence of Watson's guilt in this case. The case against Watson relies almost exclusively on the medical evidence. The various medical experts provided conflicting testimony. Some of the medical testimony suggested that the victim may have already been injured before being placed in

Watson's care. The jury may have concluded that Watson committed child abuse, aggravating an earlier injury, in which event there would be no malice aforethought.

Although it was assumed the justices would review all issues raised in *"Appellant's Opening Brief"* and give answers to each of them, their analysis and opinion only addressed three (1, 2 and 4) of the seven issues complained about. There was no reason to further analyze and decide on issues 3, 5, 6 and 7 as they already had enough legal reasons to overturn her conviction and order a new trial. The justices declared:

> CONCLUSION:
> Reversal of Watson's conviction is mandated because of the improper jury instruction on malice aforethought and the omission of the involuntary manslaughter jury instruction. Where the issue of guilt must be determined by an evaluation of directly contradictory expert testimony, errors such as those discussed above deprived Watson of her right to due process. Thus, this case is remanded for a new trial.

The justices also mentioned that prosecutors made unsupported prejudicial remarks without any factual basis during closing argument (see no. 5 above) that violated Lori's rights to "due process," by saying:

> Watson cited numerous instances of prosecutorial misconduct, they include arguing facts not supported by the evidence and improperly vouching for the strength of the State's case. In view of the disposition in this case, we do not discuss them, but we assume such arguments will not be made in any retrial.

It was regrettable that the justices did not or could not make an order or ruling that would prevent prosecutors from repeating the same dastardly deeds. Neither did they impose any punitive assessments or damages of any kind, perhaps because no laws existed that would allow them to do so. However, time would tell whether the Nevada Supreme Court's statements would put a stop to the prosecutors' egregious behavior during the next trial, and thereby abide by the court's ruling.

When explaining to news reporters and the deceased's family the reason why Lori's conviction was overturned, prosecutors erroneously claimed that Lori's conviction was overturned because of "technicalities," implying the decision had very little legal or factual basis. This was no surprise and a face-saving attempt, but their "spin" did not comport with reality as these so-called "technicalities" speak to the foundation of all citizens' constitutionally guaranteed right to a fair trial and equal protection and treatment under the law.

In addition, the Nevada Supreme Court recognized the fundamental legal principle that a person is presumed innocent until proven guilty of the crime charged with, "beyond a reasonable doubt" and that principal was not adhered to by the trial jury. As mentioned, too often jurors respond emotionally rather than logically when examining the facts surrounding a child's injury or death, and this case was a very good example of that dynamic.

For all practical purposes, the Nevada Supreme court decision meant that the original grand jury indictment, as well as the Amended Indictment prosecutors issued right before trial began, were also invalid since no evidence of malice or premeditation was presented to the grand jurors for consideration. Perhaps because of lack of oversight or applicable laws, those were not the precepts that prosecutors and the local criminal court adhered to.

Additionally, the higher court's ruling specifically meant that the judge at the trial court level misunderstood and misapplied several state statutes and constitutional laws. Therefore, they had no choice but to reverse the jury's verdict because, without those errors, Lori would not have been found guilty.

The prosecuting attorneys (District Attorneys) filed a petition asking the justices to reconsider their ruling that required a jury instruction to consider a conviction of a lesser offense than First Degree Murder by Child Abuse although they knew the Nevada Supreme Court ruling was unanimous. The petition cited the fact that a copy of Lori's audiotaped statement taken by police was not included in the court appellate record sent to the justices and argued since her statement did not include any sign of committing any lesser offense, the Nevada Supreme Court had erred in making their determination. The irony of their logic was that Lori's audiotaped statement did not allude to or show that she had committed *any* criminal act at all, whether major or minor! Once again, the Washoe County District Attorney's office and their prosecuting attorneys functioned as if they had Glaucoma of the heart, mind and soul and were incapable of properly recognizing or analyzing relevant facts.

Procedurally, the state prosecutors had every legal right to file the petition for reconsideration, but after reading its faulty logic, it seemed more like a legal strategy to keep Lori behind bars as long as they could. Their petition was denied, but the filing and processing of it caused a delay in sending the case file back to the local court and thus delayed her release from prison by about eight months.

Defense Motion for Release on Bail

After the case jurisdiction arrived back at the local level, the court held a status check hearing and Attorney Robert Long (a panel attorney from the public defender's office) was approved to represent Lori in preparation for a new trial.

A short time later, Attorney Long filed a motion with the court asking for an order allowing bail to be posted until completion of a new trial. As expected, the state filed opposing papers, and a defense response was prepared.

Finally, after all motion papers were filed and oral arguments were presented to the court, the judge granted the motion and allowed Lori to post bail for the second time in the amount of $100,000, so she could return home to her family pending the outcome of a second trial. The terms of release included house arrest which meant she could not leave her residence and must wear an ankle monitoring bracelet under the supervision of the probation department. In addition, she was instructed to always be available by phone at her home and pay supervision fees on a weekly basis. Although the restrictions placed on her by the court were cumbersome, there was great relief that she would be able to go home and be a mother to her children.

We were surprised to learn that the $100,000 bail bond previously posted would not cover Lori's second trial and a new bond would need to be purchased and posted. This brought added stress to the family's financial woes because of the 10% bond premium and the associated processing fees. Thankfully, one of my sisters and her husband pledged their Reno home for the second time as security for the bond, and she and others helped to pay the fees and premiums.

After Lori had been living under house arrest for eight months, her attorney asked that the judge change her release to *"Intensive Supervision,"* instead of wearing an ankle bracelet and forbidden to leave her home. He agreed to the request with these four conditions; (1) she could home school her own children, (2) no other children were allowed in the home unless accompanied by another adult who had not been convicted of child abuse, (3) she could not do any babysitting and, (4) she could not earn any money by any means that involved children. This intensive supervision included checking in at the jail once each week, paying supervision fees, and being subjected to impromptu visits from probation officers.

Lori accepted the terms of release ordered by the judge with no objections, as she had previously written him a letter pleading that she be released on bail with restrictions until a new trial.

Prior to the overturning of her conviction, the family division of the same court system had closed their case and ended all restrictions and supervision of her children since they found no evidence of abuse in her history.

Lori and her defense team were constantly wondering what would happen next. Would state prosecutors proceed based on the existing Amended Indictment for First Degree Murder? Would they drop the First-Degree Murder charge and offer a plea bargain to a lesser charge? Would they ignore the opinions of the Nevada Supreme Court and continue with the same faulty criminal charges against Lori? Would they honor and abide by the Nevada Supreme Court's rulings and re-amend the indictment to "Open Murder" which would allow the jury to consider less serious offenses?

Also, it was hoped that prosecutors would stop inventing evidence, and distorting facts and circumstances, especially during closing arguments, since the higher court chastised them for making statements and arguments not supported by evidence.

At the very least, the moral and honorable action would be for the state to prosecute the case on an "Open Murder" theory. But since the prosecutors' moral compasses were directed by relativism, they continued in their illicit behavior of prosecuting for a greater crime than the evidence called for, instead of adhering to the precepts decided by the Nevada Supreme Court. This dilemma reminded me that prosecutors were not obeying the "Golden Rule" which is a principle found in many sacred writings and specifically in Matthew 7:12 (AMP), which says:

So then, in everything treat others the same way you want them to treat you, for this is [the essence of] the Law and the [writings of the] Prophets.

We waited impatiently, hoping that at some point the state would act responsibly and do the right thing. Continuing for more than a decade, the uncertainty and unpredictability of the state's next move placed constant mental and emotional strain on our entire extended families, and more directly on Lori, her husband, and children. How could any of us make any significant career or other personal life choices when the criminal justice system had the final word about our future? In addition, the criminal case demanded our constant attention, either attending and/or waiting for the outcome of each motion and court hearing.

It was our continual prayer that the state would complete a thorough forensic medical investigation and figure out the true cause(s) of the deceased child's primary and secondary head injuries, the result of which would once and for all exonerate Lori.

On a very personal level, my very strong daughter, Lori, did not let the unresolved criminal charges hanging over her every move prevent her from being productive and working to help support herself and her family. Although emotionally distraught by circumstances beyond her control, she obtained several part-time jobs that paid minimum wages. A few times, she was forced to quit a job when a fellow company employee learned of her criminal case and she would then find a replacement job. Her attorney had recommended that since her conviction had been reversed she could honestly say she had not been convicted of a felony on employment applications.

With God's help and a clean conscious, Lori met each set-back and challenge with courage and determination. Since she was very intelligent and hard-working, she took advantage of what she learned by obtaining a Landscaping Certificate in prison and re-landscaped her front yard with a desert scape theme. When neighbors saw the transformation, several of them asked her to do the same for them. Eventually, this allowed her to obtain more landscaping jobs and save enough money to buy a small landscaping and lawn care service business. Her husband who was unemployed at the time did most of the labor although she recruited new clients. But several months later she decided she could make more than minimum wage by running the business full time and could increase the number of customers. After asking for my advice, she quit the two part-time jobs and her business acumen became clear as she daily increased the company's revenue with hard work and determination.

Regardless of her business success, life connected to the criminal justice arena was out of control, and it was foolish to believe otherwise. Although the reversal of her conviction was a blessing, God seemed to have no control over the prosecutor's office.

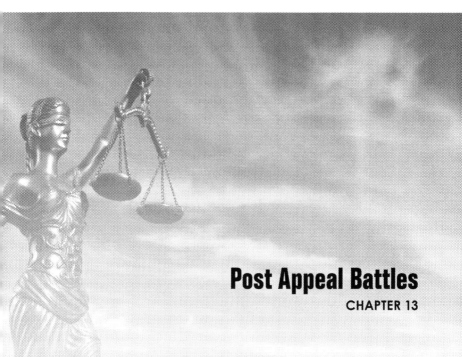

Post Appeal Battles
CHAPTER 13

L egally and practically speaking, nuclear war was raging between state prosecutors and Lori's defense attorney and it seemed all the warheads were in the state prosecutor's arsenal and was aimed at the destruction of Lori and her family. They were determined to prosecute Lori for a second time and were not interested in discovering the truth about what really caused Angie's death. It was as if the Nevada Supreme Court Decision did not exist and they could prosecute Lori for a second time on the same faulty Amended Indictment for First Degree Murder by Child Abuse.

Consequently, Attorney Long filed a pretrial *"Motion to Dismiss the (Original) Indictment"* based on several legal principals and issues that the Nevada Supreme Court previously ruled as applicable to the facts of the case.

For some unknown reason, the motion did not mention or address the Amended Indictment for First Degree Murder issued and filed with the court on the first day of trial in 1997. Instead, relief was requested based on the following legal issues concerning the original Grand Jury Indictment:

1. The Grand Jury did not Convene and Deliberate in Accordance with the existing Nevada Statutory Scheme Regarding Murder and Child Abuse.
2. The Indictment Must Be Dismissed as the Grand Jury was Also Improperly Instructed on the Varying Degrees of Murder and their Responsibilities in Returning an Indictment.

3. The Indictment Must Be Dismissed as the Grand Jury was also Improperly Instructed on the Definition of Child Abuse Given with Respect to Murder.
4. The Indictment Must Be Dismissed for Failure to Present Exculpatory Evidence to the Grand Jury and for Prosecutorial Misconduct.
5. The Indictment Must Be Dismissed for Conformance Between the Eighth Judicial District Courts.
6. Balance of Equities Favors.

Defense Attorney Long attacked the validity of the original grand jury indictment by arguing, among other things, that prosecuting attorneys gave the grand jurors the same jury instruction they had given to the trial jury, and therefore the case should be dismissed.

In the state prosecutors' opposing papers, they argued that their instructions to the grand jury were proper because the indictment had alternative theories of either open murder or murder by child abuse. Also, they argued that the same written jury instruction (that the Nevada Supreme Court ruled as illegal) *had not* been given to the grand jurors (although historically that instruction had always been used) but they offered no proof of any alternative boiler-plate instruction they could have provided to the grand jury.

Although the actual jury instructions were lost, state prosecutors had verbally explained to grand jurors (prior to deliberation) that when a child dies from child abuse, the elements (malice aforethought-premeditation or deliberation) of murder are not necessary as it is automatic first-degree murder since the "felony murder rule" applies (killing someone while committing a felony). When a juror asked the prosecuting attorney for clarification of the felony murder rule, he erroneously explained as follows:

> A JUROR: "I have a question before you get started with two parts that you need to explain to me in language that I can understand."
> PROSECUTING ATTORNEY: Okay.
> A JUROR: About malice aforethought and premeditation and deliberation.
> PROSECUTING ATTORNEY: .... After other explanations, stated:

"You'll see in the Indictment that it's pled under one of or both of two theories. It's an alternative. Number one, the killing involved... ....premeditation and deliberation, or alternatively the killing was caused by child abuse. *If the killing is caused by child abuse, premeditation and deliberation does not need to be proven.*

Without a doubt, these statements were intended to clarify the jury instruction in question and firmly establish in the minds of the grand jurors that it was not necessary for them to find any of the elements of murder to be able to issue an indictment on a charge of *First Degree Murder,* because such would be implied by an act of felony child abuse.

Many other actions and omissions by prosecutors were difficult to understand, such as their failure to attach all evidentiary documents considered (including jury instructions) to the grand jury transcript before filing it with the court for a permanent record as instructed by the Nevada Revised Statutes. It was highly suspicious and unconscionable that this could happen in a Class A felony case. It was prejudicial against Lori's rights to fair and equal treatment under the law as guaranteed by the US Constitution.

Unfortunately, the defense motion documents did not put together very important pieces of the puzzle that could have helped the judge evaluate and succinctly understand the motion; *that is the grand jurors must have assumed (based on doctors' statements) that child abuse (hence Murder by Child Abuse) was committed because they were not shown any evidence* at all that showed or implied that Lori acted with malice aforethought characterized by premeditation or deliberation. Therefore, the indictment was issued solely because of the faulty instructions.

The motion did not question the validity of the Amended Indictment, nor ask why state prosecutors waited until the first day of trial (twenty months after the original indictment), to file an *"Amended Indictment"* upgrading the charge to only *"First Degree Murder by Child Abuse"* without finding any new incriminating evidence of the essential elements needed. This Amended Indictment was a big deal to Lori, especially when considering the mandatory sentencing guidelines. For First Degree Murder she could get a life sentence but for involuntary but for manslaughter the sentence could range from one to four years or probation instead of jail.

In his *"Motion to Dismiss"* Attorney Long raised the same issues that the

Nevada Supreme Court had already agreed were the wrongful application of certain laws and procedures that denied Lori of her constitutional rights as guaranteed under the 5th and 14th Amendments to the US Constitution. Specifically, the "Due Process" provisions require that the established legal procedures and laws cannot be denied a person or circumvented (sidestepped, twisted, or by-passed) by the government. Likewise, the "Equal Protection" provision requires that laws must be applied to all citizens in an unbiased and equal manner. Other constitutional provisions dictate that the prosecution must bear the burden of knowing and alleging the essential elements (components) of how a crime is committed and what law is violated before they charge someone, instead of the other way around. Without these constitutional guarantees, you, or someone you know could be falsely arrested and convicted.

The judge accepted prosecution's arguments, despite the glaring dereliction of the prosecution's statutory duty to preserve the grand jury hearing record and not distort the law. He said he ruled in favor of the prosecution because (1) the original written grand jury instructions could not be found, (2) and without it the defense could not prove their arguments, and (3) the indictment had an alternative theory of Open Murder and not just First Degree Murder by Child Abuse, and the indictment was for Open Murder.

When deciding, the judge also ignored the fact that for all practical purposes, the prosecutor's oral statements functioned as "jury instructions" since they explained what was written in the missing hard-copy of the subject jury instruction. Any thinking person would conclude that because of that wrongful verbal explanation and telling them that the trial jury would later decide (indicating they did not need to decide) what specific degree of murder she should be convicted of, gave an opportunity for grand jurors to issue a murder indictment as previously drafted by prosecutors.

Many experienced attorneys believed the judge should have adhered to the "Best Evidence Rule" when formulating his decision. The strongest and best evidence consisted of the official grand jury hearing transcript of the convoluted and illegal verbal instructions given to them by the prosecution. But the judge overlooked this rule and all requests by the defense were denied, and the prosecutors were given the green light to continue in their manipulative and lawless activities. It also meant that Lori and her defense attorney would continue fighting against insurmountable odds to escape the criminal injustice maze in which they were trapped.

Fight for Justice Continues

Over the next decade, Lori and Defense Attorney Long fought many more courtroom battles including many discovery motions, investigations, exhumation of the deceased, depositions of the Stanford Research Clinic pathologists, status conferences, and trial continuances.

Because the prosecutors and defense attorney could not trust each other to do the right thing, each side played games with the forensic evidence. As the years passed, the case devolved into sessions of *"catch me if you can"* or *"hide and seek"* with each legal team trying to get the upper hand, rather than jointly searching for the truth, and putting an end to the madness. Each step of the court process during the prior twelve years was riddled with arguments between prosecutors and defense about who had possession of the forensic tissue slides at any given moment, which medical experts had reviewed them, and what evidence existed in the slides. It was obvious that neither side trusted the other to be honest and forthcoming with the exchange of evidence.

According to state laws, the police department, the prosecutors, and the coroner were responsible for preserving all evidence, including forensics, and keeping the integrity of evidence by a *"chain of custody"* log. Procedurally, that log should name all items of evidence and where each could always be found. As time went on, the lack of a proper chain of custody log became an immense problem as neither the coroner, police vault, prosecuting attorneys, or defense attorneys knew how many or what specific forensic tissue specimen slides existed, and how many crime scene photographs existed and/or who had possession of them at any specific time. Although there were many other photos taken at various stages of the investigations, some of the photographs taken at Lori's residence disappeared and could not be found and produced despite several requests by Defense Attorney Long.

The state prosecutors went to great expense to obtain a court order to conduct an out-of-state videotaped deposition of the pathologist at the Stanford Research Clinic who originally gave a diagnosis that the deceased child had prior brain injuries that were healing. Ironically, after several sessions of his deposition, prosecutors were unhappy with his testimony and diagnosis, prompting them to file a motion with the court to prevent his sworn testimony from being used during trial on the pretext that they were not privy to the same forensic cytological surgical tissue samples. This was a ludicrous argument and a smoke-screen to keep from having to admit that forensic evidence showed the child had prior head injuries that occurred prior to the toddler's short-distance accidental fall on the day of the tragedy.

Another unusual and expensive step was taken when state prosecutors obtained an order from the court to exhume the body of the toddler (ten and one-half years after her burial) to see if the skull bones showed any scientific evidence of an older healing fracture. Re-autopsy of the child's remains by the county coroner, determined that no additional forensic evidence or help whatsoever was gained from those efforts. Because the child had been buried in a cardboard casket for such a long time, decomposition had accelerated. The destructive nature of the original autopsy and the excavation process further complicated the examination and diagnosis. Ultimately, the coroner decided that no further information could be learned from their efforts.

Strangely, Defense Attorney Long was not allowed to have his own forensic medical specialist examine the body before it was re-buried. Once again, the state set the rules and prevented the defense team from doing their best to defend Lori.

Even at that late date, without exhuming the body the prosecution could have had the proper forensic pathologists examine the preserved microscopic tissue and cell specimens to confirm or debunk the existence of older intracranial injuries; and a DNA analysis could possibly have confirmed whether a pathological condition or disease caused or contributed to the injuries. Prosecutors never hired more highly specialized pathologists but relied solely on those in their rolodex who would vouch for their theories.

Lori and I were extremely distressed to learn that her attorneys remained resolute in not allowing any of the tissue specimens prepared for and/or by the prior Defense ME (with the help of the Coroner in 1997 that were marked with his name) to be examined or discussed during the discovery phase of trial. For various reasons, defense attorneys felt they should keep this information and forensic evidence totally out of the trial process. Although we knew that the prior Defense ME had suffered from his own legal trouble during the first trial, his legal issues had now been resolved and the case against him had been dismissed in large part. We believed he should at least he could be hired as a consultant who would be available to inform Lori's attorneys in real-time while court was in session about technical forensic issues that were being discussed. Contrary to our desires, once again it seemed there was a complete breakdown in the relationship between the prior Defense ME and Defense Attorneys Long that prevented it from happening.

Lori and I suggested that those particular microscopic tissue specimen slides (marked with his initials) be reviewed and analyzed by other pathologists to decide the validity of the Defense ME's diagnoses; and this would build a stronger case for the defense. Instead, the Defense Attorney Long intended to rely primarily on the specimens prepared from one of the two masses removed during surgery that arguable contained macrophages.

Late Decisions Hinder Fair Trial

According to court records, on the day the new trial was to begin, the judge had not yet made a ruling on four important motions made by state prosecutors and one by the defense attorney. Regardless, the judge demanded that trial begin at once after she announced her much-delayed decisions. That delay worked against Lori's best interests as it did not give defense attorney time to consider the impact of her rulings on their trial strategy and to decide which were the most important issues he should focus on.

The prosecution motions included the following; (1) *"Motion to Preclude the Test Results of Defense Experts…"* (concerning the Stanford Research Clinic pathologist who offered evidence of older brain injuries), (2) *"Motion to Preclude Forensic Expert re: Biomechanics"* (to prevent a well-known defense medical pathologist from testifying as an expert about short-distance fall and his research, and (3 and 4) two prosecution Petrocelli Motions to allow testimony concerning two unfounded but alleged *"Uncharged Bad Acts of Child Abuse"* by the defendant.

Also, the fifth motion that the judge had not yet ruled on was the defense motion asking the court to conduct an *"Evidentiary Hearing to Determine the Competency of the State's Expert Witnesses."* This motion was to compel the prosecution to be consistent and only allow germane qualified medical specialist to testify for the state.

Having those five very critical issues left unresolved on the first day of trial put the ball squarely in the prosecution's hands. This was true especially since Lori's defense team had now dwindled down and only consisted of one attorney and his limited time, staff, and resources. After the motion arguments were heard, the judge refused to continue the trial so that another very competent attorney who had previously helped with the case could aid as defense co-counsel. The ruling was a critical set-back for Lori's proper defense.

Among all the pre-trial motions, one of the most disturbing was prosecutors' re-filing of the same two pre-trial motions prosecutors filed twelve years before requesting the court to allow testimony concerning alleged *"Uncharged Bad Acts of Child Abuse"* by the defendant involving her eldest daughter when she was three years old, and an eight-month-old infant who accidentally fell from the high-chair while at daycare. These motions were especially egregious because the prosecutor knew that no evidence of abuse was found during several overlapping investigations by their own department, the police and CPS. Regardless of the facts, prosecutors crafted their motions by citing a mirage of related laws as well as falsehoods and half-truths to paint the worst possible image of Lori as being a habitual child abuser. As usual, the prosecution's motions set in motion the preparation and filing of a sequence of opposing papers, responding, and reply papers. Defense attorneys also hired proper medical experts to testify at the hearings.

One of the other motions filed by the state conflicted with their own history of often hiring medical experts to testify outside the area of their specialty, as they had previously done in this and many other cases. Their motion asked the judge to block the testimony of a defense pathologist who had completed pioneering peer-reviewed research into the consequences of short distance falls that had helped several other defendants win acquittals or dismissal of child abuse charges. His research refuted a long-standing unproven legal and medical theory that short-distance falls of children (under ten feet) can never be dangerous or deadly. The state's objections focused on the pathologist's lack of specific certification as a biomechanical or biomedical engineer, and therefore, claimed he should not be allowed to testify concerning injuries suffered from short-distance falls.

Having the judge's decisions on all five motions delayed until the first day of trial was highly irregular and disturbing. It was common knowledge that this judge had a reputation among attorneys for ignoring applicable laws and proper protocol. Also, Prosecutor Bird was a long-time close friend of this judge, making the defense attorney uncertain about whether this judge was capable of making just and fair decisions.

[Note: A few years later, our prior assessment of the judge's behavior and legal knowledge was proven to be correct when the Nevada Judicial Commission on Judicial Discipline and the Nevada Supreme Court reprimanded her for failure to obey the law by holding a woman in jail for ten days for contempt of court without conducting the required court hearing within seventy-two hours. Consequently, the higher court ordered her to attend several classes to learn about Nevada laws and ethical conduct in the courtroom. However, that reprimand came three years after her illegal actions took place and she was not removed from her position as a judge. It appeared that as a well-connected member of the ruling judicial class, she was shown favoritism and the only reprimand was to attend ethics classes.]

Therefore, Lori's defense attorney was caught in a no-win situation and doomed to defeat except for a super-natural miracle. Not knowing the judge's decisions on those motions in advance of the trial date put Lori's defense in a very precarious position and made it impossible to adequately prepare for trial. The judge insisted that the trial start at once after she made her long-delayed decisions because the case had been lingering in the court for more than a decade.

There were discussions about these motions between prosecutors, defense attorneys and the judge in chambers (privately) that were never transcribed nor placed in the court record, and any decisions made by the judge during those discussions were kept out of the record.

Alford Plea Offered

CHAPTER 14

A few days before re-trial was set to begin, Lori's defense attorney informed her that prosecutors were offering a plea deal. If she would agree to an Alford Plea on Second Degree Murder charges, she could still legally claim her innocence but would voluntarily agree to pay the penalty and serve whatever mandatory sentence the judge imposed, as if she had been found guilty by a jury. The judge would have the choice of ordering a minimum sentence of ten to twenty-five years in state prison or a maximum sentence of ten years to life. The most extreme sentence would mean Lori could remain in prison the rest of her life unless given parole which she would be eligible for after serving a total of ten years.

Her decision of whether to accept the plea bargain offer was a critical once in a life time event, so Lori asked friends and family to meet at her house that evening to pray for Godly wisdom and guidance. About a dozen friends showed up to pray and afterwards they unanimously recommended that she accept the Alford Plea and not engage in any more ligation with the unpredictable and dysfunctional criminal justice system.

The next day directly before a scheduled court hearing, Lori, her sister, her husband, and I met privately with Attorney Robert Long in a conference room at the courthouse to discuss the terms of the offer and make her final decision. The scheduled hearing was for the judge to announce her decision on the various pre-trial motions and then begin the trial process. Lori's attorney explained the consequences of accepting the offer and the possible sentences that could take place if she accepted the plea.

He said that if she accepted the Alford plea, she would have to waive any appellate rights that would otherwise be available to her, as opposed to being convicted by a jury trial. But issues involving a violation of her civil rights guaranteed by the US Constitution could not be waived and would still be available for appeal.

Attorney Robert Long assured us that he was confident Lori would receive a light sentence because he believed the probation and parole department of the Nevada Department of Public Safety would recommended the shortest possible sentence after considering Lori had no prior criminal record, and said the judges rarely go against their recommendation.

After prayerful consultation and consideration of everything she knew about the criminal justice system, such as, the unpredictable behavior, mistaken statements, and theatrics of prosecutors (especially when jurors were present) and the judge's prior behavior and history, Lori nervously agreed to accept the plea bargain. The alternative was for her and her family to endure a re-trial and continue in this maze for the rest of her life with no guarantee of a positive outcome. Of special concern was the fact that another long trial and potential appeal would generate continual publicity, and her growing children would suffer emotional damage from it all. Lori could not to take those risks and informed her attorney she was would accept the offer.

We appeared in court a few minutes later and the judge was informed of her decision. After the judge questioned Lori whether she fully understood the significance of accepting the plea and if it was done under duress, he accepted her plea deal. He then set a sentencing hearing for two months later to allow the Nevada Probation and Parole Department enough time to conduct and update their prior investigation of her character and make sentencing recommendations to the court. Upon a request by her attorney, the judge allowed Lori to go home to get her personal issues in order and appear in court a week later to surrender and start serving her time behind bars even before the sentencing hearing.

Surrendering

Lori had important decisions and arrangements to make before surrendering, such as, how her children would be taken care of, who would handle household financials, upkeep of the home, and who would work the landscaping business. Since her husband was unemployed, and the family had no other source of income, he decided it would be necessary to take on that challenge, although it was not something he was accustomed to doing. It proved to be a wise decision as the business generated enough income for almost six years (during the recession and his unemployment) to meet most of the family's basic needs.

Since Lori's birthday was about five weeks after the date of her scheduled incarceration, her children and I decided to give her an early birthday party. This would provide an opportunity to say thank you and good bye to friends and family as it would be several months before they could visit with each other again. It was a highly emotional birthday party with an outpouring of love and compassion mixed with sadness, but it gave her a measure of strength and courage to help face life behind bars.

The morning that Lori was scheduled to surrender was one I will never forget. While getting dressed, we had a heart-to-heart talk about her decision and what she could be facing. She had slept very little and was crushed in spirit, physically weak, unsteady on her feet, and feeling nauseas and light headed. With a trembling voice and tears in her eyes she told me, *"I do not know if I have the strength to go through with this plea bargain, after all I was in prison before. I don't know what God's purpose is in all this, but I feel this is God's plan for me and I must leave it in his hands."* I responded, *"You can do this with God's help, I know you can. He promises to be with you and will cause some good to come from this tragedy."* Her body trembled as we hugged and cried.

Before Lori surrendered, I asked her, and she agreed to compose a daily journal of her experiences behind bars to keep me and her family informed of how she was coping and what was happening to her. I hoped the journaling would help her keep a sense of connection with us, help pass the time, and help her stay mentally, emotionally, and spiritually balanced.

Along with friends and family, Lori appeared in court at the scheduled time to surrender and begin serving her time at county jail where she would stay until sentencing and space was made available at the women's state prison.

In the interim her attorney was preparing for the upcoming sentencing hearing. In doing so, he asked that we collect letters from family and friends for inclusion in the "Presentencing Investigative Report," to be prepared by Probation and Parole Department for the judge to read prior to sentencing. As a result, more than a dozen of Lori's friends and family members wrote letters of support pleading for the lighter sentence. All of Lori's three children wrote very compelling and heart wrenching letters to the court begging for a light sentence. The following is a beautiful letter written by her nineteen-year-old daughter.

The District Court Judge for Washoe County
Re: Lori Watson – Sentencing

Dear Judge,

   I am Lori's daughter, Tanasha, I've noticed for a long time, that many people find it a challenge to wrap their brains around my mom. Not that she is a difficult person to understand, but that her soul's endurance is unfathomable. And, when thinking about all of the things that my mother has accomplished, or even considered doing, her efforts are of no comparison.
   Yet, my mother is simple. Beyond all of her complexities that seem to wrangle everyone's consciences, my mother strives to serve God by serving other people. That is what she is about, and who she really is.
   Over the duration of this thirteen-year case, my mom has been relentless. Unbelievably, she was able to focus on other things that needed her attention - even while this nightmare stared her straight in the face. God gave her the strength to do more than have selfish pity, or to bury herself in the darkness. Instead, she believes, has faith, and lives.
   With the help of God's love, she has trained herself to fight against the poison designed to kill her spiritually. It is all too ironic that she has achieved so much, with even more force working against her.
   From as far back as I can remember, my mom has always been in constant work mode. Whether the assignment involved household cleaning, keeping the finances afloat, delivering mail, landscaping front and back yards, making phone calls, scheduling appointments, or negotiating with my dad, she was doing it. She was never on her own priority list.
   And even though she was slaving in the sun all day, or working on the computer until dark, she would give us her attention too. When I was in ninth grade, I procrastinated all the time. I procrastinated so badly that, I don't recall having even one page of a ten-page English paper completed, which was to be submitted at noon the next day. Of courses, I complained and groaned about the daunting task and why I waited so long to begin. My mom was concerned my grades would decline and gave me a lecture, like most moms who are adamant about their child's success in school would do. But, when that was over, she decided to also take on the responsibility helping me complete the paper. No, she didn't

write the whole thing herself, but she sat next to the computer all night with me until the next morning. She was my guide. If she chose to sleep to alleviate her own exhaustion instead, then that woman isn't my mom. I would have also received an F.

She did the same for my brother. Granted, I did finish my assignments much more frequently than he did. I vividly remember that her daily routine consisted of working with my brother, reinforcing the knowledge that his teacher had clearly instructed earlier that day, while she tried relentlessly to instill in him the desire be more independent. Helping my brother was the most time consuming and challenging task that she faced, and I'm not sure it ever got easier for her- But she did it anyway.

It is in my mom's nature to constantly pick others up when they are desperate. It's as if she couldn't stand the thought of not being around to assist people when she felt that God had already empowered her to do so.

My mom poured out her heart and energy for my friends as well. A girl who has been my best friend for a while, was going through some family hardships a couple years back. The place where she lived, and the people who she lived with, weren't suitable for her well-being. My mom offered her a room in our house to stay in for a while, until she could somehow mend the issues that divided her family. Although our own family wasn't doing too great financially, my mom put her worries aside to offer stability that someone also needed. It made her happy.

My mom is also a fighter for my friends. After one of my friends and I had taken our placement tests for our college classes, we both disagreed with the results we received in the mail. I had a problem with my math score, and my friend was equally disturbed by her English score. Both scores were contrary to what people had always told us about ourselves and the grades to prove it. The placement testing was a flawed system - especially after we had previously taken these placement tests at another college and had received scores that exceeded our expectations. My mother called the school and objected on both of our behalves. What I consider noteworthy is the fight that she put up for my friend and her talent.

My mom loves to laugh, despite all the things that stressed her out. She didn't laugh a lot. But when she did, it made up for all the times she missed the opportunity. You could hear her from down the street; it was so loud and animated. Today, my long-time friends will come up to me and say, "Your mom has the funniest laugh!" Then they will go ahead to imitate her to the best of their abilities - as if they think they can really copy a laugh like my mom's. It's impossible. Though, they don't ever make fun of it, they simply find joy in reiterating the happiness and enthusiasm that my mom spreads contagiously.

She is also a "people builder," as a famous person would say. Meaning, she encourages people to do the best of their ability. She made them believe that nothing was holding them back from their hearts desires. One day, right after school, I sat down in the living room, eager to finish my homework. However, I began to belt out the song title, "Wasted" by Carrie Underwood. I sat there, singing for at least ten minutes, replacing the lyrics I didn't know with other words, and repeating my favorite versesover and over. Out of nowhere, clapping came from the other end of the house - and the whole time I thought no one was home. I looked up and my mom was standing at the end of the hall with the biggest smile on her face. I was absolutely mortified, as I never sang in front of others. Despite my humiliation, my mom rooted me on and 'wowed' me far too many times. It was the last thing I would expect to hear from anyone after listening to my vocals! But my mom just loves to encourage self-confidence, even when there seems to be no good reason for it.

There is a part of me that yearns to be with my mom. I've always felt it, even when she was already here. When I woke up and discovered that she was too busy to be bothered, I didn't bother her. I merely stayed in the same part of the house with her. It was the same when my mom left to run boring errands. I really didn't like the idea of going to the store for laundry detergent or driving to the post office in the ghetto part of town. However, I just enjoyed being in the presence of her. My dogs feel the same. When my mom stepped out the door, my dogs would stare out the window until she came back. It could have been hours that my dogs refrained from using the bathroom or getting some later. It's as if they were so tense and so focused on my mom's exit that nothing else crossed their little minds.

Although sometimes, it may seem too difficult to focus on anything other than the heart wrenching pain that surrounds us, I do chose to break beyond the pain and see another side. Life is unfair, but there is always a purpose for everything.

In some strange way, I honor God that my mom has to do this. The Bible says that God doesn't give us anything that we cannot handle or overcome. God would not have given her the opportunity to choose this path if he didn't believe in her strength. I also believe that God gives the most difficult tasks to the strongest of people. How amazing it is to approach her situation in that way. Moreover, we are all bigger than our problems. I did hear my mom say once, *"Life is hard, but you just got to get up and kick it in the butt!"*

Thank you for your time, Tanasha Watson

In anticipation of the upcoming sentencing hearing, the deceased child's family requested help from an established anti-child abuse advocacy group. That organization and family members sent the judge fifty emails and letters recommending the maximum sentence for what they believed was a horrible crime committed by Lori. This was no surprise considering the public hysteria that existed because of print and TV media publication of this and other similar cases.

Sentencing Hearing

At the sentencing hearing the deceased child's aunt, mother, father, and grandmother spoke to express their grief and make their recommendations to the judge.

The grandmother spoke first, and it felt strange to see her dressed in a black cocktail dress and high heels as if ready for a night of celebration on the town or making a theatrical presentation. Very proudly, she read a poem about angels and again recited (just as she had done ten years before) what she calculated to be the exact number of seconds, minutes, hours, days, weeks, and months that her grandchild had lived and then asked that Lori be given the greatest sentence allowed by law for her crime.

The deceased child's mother spoke next and told the judge she wanted Lori to spend a year behind bars for each month of the child's life. That calculation and request was puzzling as Lori and I had always considered life as priceless. It sounded like she had a guilty conscious and knew things that caused her to not ask for the maximum sentence of life. Otherwise, how could any mother rationalize that equation?

Of course, Lori gave a brief statement at the hearing saying she had spent every day of the past twelve years grieving over losing that beautiful child whom she loved, and although she did nothing intentionally to cause harm to her, she felt responsible for what happened. Her words were very brief and spoken from her heart.

The father of the deceased child acknowledged Lori's statements and received some consolation from her words and said this was the first time she had expressed grief to them and he also wanted Lori to receive the longest possible prison sentence. Unfortunately, he was not aware that her legal advisors would not allow any such prior conversation and she had truly grieved over the death of the Angie.

I wanted to speak up and say why Lori should not receive the harshest sentence, but was signaled by Attorney Long not to, although he previously said he would arrange for me to do so. Maybe he thought I would say something that would negatively affect the judge's sentencing decision and did not want to take the chance. My emotions were running high and it was all I could do to sit still and obey the attorney's instructions.

As expected, the Nevada Public Safety, Department of Probation and Parole's *"Presentencing Investigation Report"* recommended that Lori receive the least possible sentence. When the judge mentioned their recommendation, Prosecutor Bird went into an emotional tirade and made defamatory statements about them and their incompetence and announced that she was tired of their nonsense. Then, as she had done innumerable times before, she passionately described Lori's heinous crime, and even mentioned the unfounded allegations about her abusing her own and another child. She claimed Lori was a danger to society and should pay the greatest penalty possible.

[Note: During a sentencing hearing, it is considered legal for prosecutors to present hearsay and rumors to persuade the judge (or jury) to give a harsh sentence. Question: Is this not a violation of due process and civil rights as the sentencing affects the life and liberty of the convicted?]

My heart sank into my stomach and my blood pressure increased as I again listened to the prosecutor's dishonest statements. Silently, I wondered when and if this evil woman would ever receive payment that was due her for having such a callous and depraved heart, or did the grace and mercy of God extend to her also?

After hearing the statements of the prosecutor and the victim's family, the judge asked Lori if she understood the terms of the plea bargain and that she was waiving all rights to an appeal. She said she did, and then the judge ordered the maximum sentence (ten years to life) which meant Lori would be eligible for parole after serving a total of ten years.

We learned later that since the greatest term was a life sentence, (instead of a number of years) good behavior while incarcerated could not be counted towards reduction of her time before a parole hearing could take place. Since Lori had previously been incarcerated three years, it would be seven more years before a parole hearing and release could happen. If she had been given the least sentence (10 to 25 years) she would have been eligible for parole within only a few years instead of seven more years. The ten to life sentence was a big deal and not really a bargain because it also meant that she might spend the rest of her life behind bars (same as First Degree Murder.) And even if by the mercy of God, she was released, the rest of her life would be spent on parole.

Much too late, we realized that Lori's attorney could have negotiated with prosecutors that a condition of her acceptance would be that prosecutors recommend the lighter sentence. Instead, Attorney Robert Long told Lori that she must decide on the offer as presented and there was no room to negotiate.

Upon arrival at county jail, Lori was surprised that conditions had improved since she was there twelve years before. It was much cleaner, the food was a lot better, and the guards were more humane and professional. For personal safety reasons, due to the nature of the crime and public hysteria, upon arrival she was put in protective custody in a cell by herself, but five days later was moved to solitary confinement (the hole) which is normally used as punishment for bad behavior, although there was nothing she was being punished for.

The following is a letter she wrote to me a few weeks after arrival at the jail.

Dear Mom,

   If it weren't for you I wouldn't have the strength I do (or the strength that everyone thinks I have.) I've only written three journals and I'm sure they sounded very bad. I'm okay now. I got out of the room for approximately two hours today and it did wonders for me.

   I don't know if we will fully understand the reason or reasons for all this, but I am trying to listen to God and be very grateful for every little

---

thing I can. Even though it's hard to be isolated and think about the next seven years. I have known people who have been in prison 20-30 years. So, I know that we can all do this, if we work together, right? I'm so grateful that I am not in China in prison like those two reporters.

Please be strong and pray with my kids on the phone often because that helps them so much. Please encourage their father because that is what he needs right now. I have told the kids to split the meal responsibilities, so it doesn't all fall on one person.

I'm doing the "Purpose Driven Life" and I'm on day five. It has really given me a lot to think about. It helps me so much to write. I'm trying to find a purpose in all this. I'm trying not to be angry and be open to the life lessons. When I'm done with this, I do not want to be hard like so many others.

Mom, I was speaking with a few of the women and one who has been here for three and one-half years waiting for her case to go forward. Can you imagine that? No sunlight for three and one-half years. Mom, I was in the TV room sitting and listening to the woman in the room telling how their mothers let their husbands or boyfriends sexually molest them and how much they hated their mothers for it. It's so hard to believe that evil is in so many families. Please take care of your health for me. Thank you for always being there for me.

I love you, Lori.

When we realized that parole (early release) was almost *never* granted at the first parole board hearing in cases involving Class A or B felonies, especially those serving a life sentence, our anguish went through the roof. We also learned that unless the prisoner admits to committing the crime, has remorse for it, and has completed recovery classes or therapy, parole will not be granted. It seemed as we were caught in a maze of the criminal justice system with no way of escape. This dilemma became the subject of many passionate conversations between Lori and I over the next several years.

Prison Life
CHAPTER 15

I t was more than six months before Lori could be transported to the same prison she was in ten years before. The delay at first was because she was waiting for sentencing, but it was further delayed because of overcrowding at the prison.

Lori informed me that upon arrival at the state prison, no official or guard greeted them or explained to them what to expect or what the rules were. They were herded off the bus like cattle into a large intake "holding" tank where forty women were kept until their behavior and risk factors could be assessed and assigned to a suitable housing pod. While in the intake holding tank, there seemed to be no rules and chaos ruled the day. It shocked Lori to see several women engaging in outrageous behavior, including using drugs, having sexual relations, and abusing and fighting with each other while the guards did nothing to stop them. She also saw a woman overdose on drugs and be taken away, hopefully to receive medical intervention. While there, the prisoners were brought their meals on paper trays and not allowed to take a shower or change clothing. None of them could have any contact with anyone on the outside until they were risk-evaluated and assigned to a cell.

On the fifth day after arrival, she was allowed to shower and make phone calls. But she was horrified to find the showers were filthy and coated with soap scum and black and orange mold. Also, the toilets, walls, floors, and sinks were beyond dirty, in direct contrast to the cleanliness that existed when a private company ran the prison. Government officials and personnel now in charge had created a chaotic, filthy, and unsafe environment where prisoners were treated like animals in cages with no need for human dignity, respect, and cleanliness.

Once allowed to make phone calls, she called to relay her experiences in the holding tank. Although she had endured shocking experiences she wanted me to know she was alive but had been emotionally and physically ill. Since arrival she had been crying almost continually, suffering from a migraine headache and had been vomiting non-stop for several days before the guards allowed her to receive emergency medical treatment. Previously, the *county jail* medics had prescribed a high dose of Zoloft and the sudden dangerous withdrawal contributed to her misery and headaches. The prison doctors kept her in the medical ward overnight to revive her with intravenous fluid rehydrating and balancing her body chemistry. They also prescribed anti-depressants and medicine to help with the headaches and vomiting. By the time she phoned me she was feeling better.

Upon evaluation, the prison officials decided that Lori needed to be placed in *"protective custody"* and since there was no other place available except the *"hole,"* that was where they housed her. The hole (solitary confinement) is normally used for punishing bad behavior but she had not misbehaved. Regardless, she was kept for several months in an 8 x 8 cell with no exterior windows and one small window in the door. It had a four-inch mattress on a hard surface, no pillow and only one blanket to keep warm at night. She was given new prison clothing which consisted of two blue shirts and pants, underwear, t-shirt, and sandals.

She was only allowed out of her cell twenty minutes each day to make a phone call and hopefully have time left to take a shower. Although this arrangement may have been necessary for her own protection until the public outrage and news coverage subsided, solitary confinement was the most mentally and spiritually exhausting time of her life. To make living conditions worse, the food was scarce and almost inedible, and the guards were aggressive, rude, and unpredictable. She was not given any reading material (except for a newspaper), pen, paper, stamps, tooth brush, toothpaste, comb, shampoo, or decent soap to keep clean. But, she could buy those things from the prison commissary once I deposited funds into in her account.

Lori phoned often to vent her frustrations saying she wondered, among other things, if she would survive being treated like an animal and the inhumane living conditions that made it very difficult for her to sleep or rest. She became more depressed and anxious with each passing day and longed for the time when she would be out of solitary confinement. Lori's despair and misery caused her to question the wisdom of accepting the plea deal and she asked that I call her attorney to ask that he come visit her to discuss options. He visited her but could offer no legal options since she had given up all appeal rights by accepting the plea deal.

True to her natural impulse to make the best of any bad situation, shortly after being placed in *"the hole"* she sent a kite (request) asking the warden for permission to clean the stinky moldy showers and bathrooms when other prisoners were not around. The warden approved her request and the cleaning gave her something to do and more time out of isolation on a somewhat irregular basis. A problem arose when she was given only one small packet of Comet for each bathroom which was insufficient to remove soap scum and eliminate mold permanently. Because of mold spores in the air and dampness, the mold grew back quickly.

One day she phoned and asked me to research into what cleaning chemicals would remove mold permanently. I searched the internet and sent her a printout of what was needed to remove mold and mold spores on surfaces and in the air. Being proactive, she sent the information to the prison warden to try and remedy the mold issues and make safe and sanitary showers available to herself and others. For unknown reasons, the information given was ignored, and the mold continued to grow unchecked. That prompted her to call me a few months later to ask me to report the conditions to the county health department, who sent inspectors to evaluate the mold issues and unsanitary conditions. But the prison administrators only showed the inspectors the front shower stalls and toilets, so they and did not inspect the ones used by inmates. Whether the mold was toxic remained unknown, but it certainly had an odor and was an unsanitary condition the prisoners had to live with. Soon Lori's cleaning expanded to sweeping and mopping the hallways. While cleaning the filth, she contracted a skin rash and infection that itched and tormented her hands for several months even though the doctors tried several different medications.

We were not allowed to apply for visitor status and submit to a background check until after she was transported to state prison. Then, it took another six months for authorities to process and approve the applications which seemed like years to all of us. As you can imagine, Lori had been desperately longing for a hug from her children and husband during the long wait. Once the applications were approved, she was able to have face to face visitation during predetermined hours and days.

Fortunately, the prison was close enough so that her husband and children could regularly visit her and that became their normal weekend routine. The rules for visiting included having a body search, only taking quarters (for vending machine purchases) in a plastic bag into the room, one hug upon arrival and one on departure, no hand holding, no open toe shoes, no clothing colors that resembled blue in any way, no sweats or stretchy material. There were several times when one of the children showed up wearing aqua, or what they thought was green, and were turned away.

Several months later, Lori was moved from protective custody to a general population cell in a section where others convicted of similar crimes were housed. Each cell had a bunk bed with a four-inch mattress, a sheet, one blanket, and a small chest for personal items. Guards would often appear during the middle of the night without a valid reason to conduct a search, throw her and her roommate's belongings in the middle of the floor, search for any unauthorized items, take any items they could not show receipts for, and afterwards leave a mess. The unwarranted searches and harsh treatments were very humiliating and depressing and left her and the other prisoners despondent and angry. The guard's antagonistic attitude made her wonder if they were trying to provoke her to retaliate and be sent to the hole as a result. When she did not "bite the apple," those inspections visits became less frequent and she never was charged with a violation of the rules.

Understandably, there was little peace and quiet as many of Lori's revolving-door roommates were suffering from alcohol or drug withdrawal, physical/emotional abuse, anger, bitterness, Schizophrenia, delusions, and/or lack of impulse control, mental deficiencies, Aids, Cancer, and other illnesses. They were a continual challenge to her personal health and safety, but that did not stop her from helping them whenever she could. Sadly, her help was limited to listening to their painful stories, taking part in group recovery programs such as Celebrate Recovery, giving water to drink, giving free hair-cuts, sharing her food and supplies, painting colorful wall murals for holidays to brighten the atmosphere, and attending memorial services when one of them passed. She walked a tight-rope trying to balance helping other inmates cope with their suffering and her own health and safety.

For many months she worked at minimum wage with a company that repackaged returned merchandise. This was very demanding physical labor and the state took half of her wage as reimbursement for housing costs. Soon the work became too much as sometimes she had to unload several hundred pounds of merchandise on pallets off delivery trucks and the work continued regardless of how extremely cold or hot the weather became. Although she was promoted to a supervisory position, she had to quit working after getting injured a few times and was suffering continual aches and pains.

After that, Lori qualified for a job tutoring and sub-teaching the high school math class. This job paid $50 per month of which she received $35.00. Aside from the low pay, this position presented a unique challenge of keeping a safe and harmonious relationship with other inmates who resented her authority over them. She met each challenge successfully and loved being instrumental in teaching those who were willing to learn.

When younger, Lori had attended a major university studying for a Bachelor Degree in Aeronautical Science but because of financial and health reasons had not earned the degree. Knowing that an Aeronautical Science Degree was off the table, she asked me to find a correspondence course which would make it possible to obtain a *"Bachelor Degree in Business Administration"* while behind bars. After much searching, I discovered that most colleges had switched to online course and did not offer correspondence courses by mail any longer. Since the prisoners were not allowed online access, the online method would not work. But eventually, I found a university that still offered printed courses. With her husband's and my financial and practical aid, Lori enrolled in the correspondence course to finish the remaining classes necessary to obtain that degree.

After Lori completed all other courses and started the accounting and statistical analysis classes, a serious problem arose when the warden would not allow her to have a calculator to perform the complicated math functions, unless the case was transparent and plastic. After searching the internet extensively and making phone calls to several factories, I discovered that no such calculators were being manufactured but the warden would not change her decision. Coincidentally or by divine direction, once Lori started tutoring the high-school math class, the teacher had a calculator and secretly allowed her to use it to complete her homework assignments.

Another problem we faced was finding the required text books in a format that was acceptable to the prison, since prisoners were not allowed to own or have any hard-cover books which most textbooks are. Finding soft-backed textbooks which was a continual challenge. At first, the prison allowed the college to copy the hardcover onto paper and glue it on as the cover (replacing the hardcopy). Then later the new warden decided they that was not acceptable and only original textbooks could be sent.

Despite those difficulties and a few years of effort and determination, Lori completed all the required courses and obtained her BBA. Few prisoners have been able to achieve that goal while behind bars and this was made possible only by God's grace and mercy as He honored Lori's determination, intelligence, and hard work.

By federal law, the meals at the prison were supposed to meet the same nutritional standards as meals fed to the military. However, that was not the case and the inmates had to buy added food from the commissary to be nourished sufficiently. The portions served by the prison were much smaller, an example would be a teaspoon full of peanut butter spread thinly on white bread or small celery stalk. When they occasionally had salads or fresh fruit, they were served in miniature servings. Over time, this disturbed Lori and she learned about the legal menu requirements and sent a kite to the warden asking for an improvement in the menus and larger portion sizes. Although the warden told Lori that she instructed the kitchen to change, nothing improved, and the prisoners continued to be undernourished. The prison was dealing with limited financial resources during a time of economic recession. Regardless, several inmates were very clever and learned to cook tasty meals and deserts by combining unusual ingredients bought at the commissary and cooking them in the microwave to share with each other, especially on birthdays and holidays.

Fortunately, we could usually deposit enough funds into her account to buy canned or packaged food from the commissary on a regular basis. Additionally, once each quarter she could place an order, not to exceed $125.00, from a designated outside supplier for necessities such as soft-packaged food, clothing, shoes, and personal items. Sadly, the items were grossly overpriced as the state received a part of the sales price at the expense of prisoners or their families who could barely afford the purchases.

Lori experienced some very unfortunate frightful events at the prison. The first happened shortly after arrival when she saw an OB/GYN doctor because of continuing pain in her side. While examining her, the doctor rammed his speculum with such force it injured her cervix causing her to jump and scream out in pain. The doctor did not act surprised or concerned about her response. Lori was in excruciating pain for several days, especially when urinating. She wrote me about the pain she was still having because of the abuse. When she mentioned it to another inmate, she said the same thing also happened to her. In all, she learned there were a dozen women who had been assaulted by this same doctor. Complaints had already been made over several months to the authorities and attorneys, and the ACLU was already involved. Sadly, the doctor was not charged with any crimes but was simply transferred to another prison.

On another occasion, Lori's roommate confided in her that she had been raped by a prison guard and later learned he had raped three other women. Thankfully, Lori was not one of them, and she encouraged the victims to file complaints to the Prison Rape Elimination Commission (PREA) office that investigates and tries to prevent rape in women's prisons. Despite many complaints, the guard was still there many months afterwards, while the women trembled in fear of what might happen to them next. Eventually, the guard was also transferred to another prison and no criminal charges were filed against him.

Another of Lori's efforts to improve her and fellow inmates' lives was to revive the Girl Scout program that she had helped set up ten years before when she was at the same prison but had since been pushed aside. But, she did not want to be the face of the efforts and avoided any recognition or notoriety. This program allowed Lori and her youngest daughter, and all other mothers and daughters, the opportunity to come together one evening every other week to enjoy arts and crafts, learn new skills, and play games.

In addition to earning her BBA degree, Lori completed several courses such as word processing and many self-improvement courses to help her recover from hurts, hang-ups, and habits that she experienced.

As it came closer to the time for the parole board hearing, her heightened anxiety became more obvious. Starting more than six months prior to the expected hearing date, she and I began searching for the right way to approach it. I printed and sent to her online guidelines and attorney websites. It was widely known that parole is almost never granted to lifers at the first parole hearing and that parole is automatically tabled for another hearing two to three years later, and even then, an admission of guilt would be necessary before parole could be granted.

Family Life

CHAPTER 16

L ori's children were badly affected by her absence, especially the two younger ones because they no longer had their mom's daily guidance and emotional support. They could not understand why and what had happened. Many nights they cried themselves to sleep.

Lori's teenage son struggled with a lack of confidence, an inability to do his homework, poor attendance and below grade level performance. It became necessary to enroll him in continuation courses online provided by the school district. With the aid of his older sister, myself, and a great aunt, he completed all courses and graduated from high school. I was amazed at how smart he was and how quickly he completed his homework and testing online, proving that all he needed was encouragement and personal attention from those who loved him.

Lori's twelve-year-old daughter who was a six-week-old infant when these tragedies began, seemed to suffer the most from her mother being absent for the second time. Consequently, I tried to always be available to love her and talk to her. After receiving a desperate phone call from her saying she was going to run away or commit suicide, I convinced her father to get Christian counseling to help her make sense of life. Although she was very intelligent and always excelled in school, she was angry and unable to process or accept what had happened to her mom. Over time, her older sister became a reliable support system and role model who gave her the daily conversations and emotional support she needed.

Lori's older daughter was the most resilient and steady one since she was grounded in her faith and was very smart, level headed, and compassionate. She became someone her two siblings admired and looked up to for advice and emotional support.

During all this tiresome indescribable journey, by God's grace and mercy, and good training of their parents and the church, none of the three children took on bad habits such as drinking, drugs, partying, or acting out sexually. This was my constant prayer that they would survive in good shape physically, emotionally, and spiritually, and not be destroyed or incapacitated like so many other children have become in similar circumstances.

Many years of separation and financial stresses brought added strain to a marriage already struggling to keep an equilibrium. Although the criminal and civil cases brought new unsolvable problems, anguish, tears, anger, resentment, and indescribable turmoil for both Lori and her husband, they remained committed to their marriage vows. To help Lori's husband cope with life, the local church provided free counseling for several years to him as a "single" dad of three kids with his wife behind bars. That counseling was extremely beneficial in keeping the marriage and family together.

Within a year of Lori being incarcerated, the family home went into foreclosure while at the same time her husband was trying to get a loan modification. The foreclosure was a major disturbing event that needed the help and coordination of family and friends. Two days before the move-out deadline, with help from a friend and myself, an affordable condo was rented, and the family was able to move on time

During most of the next seven years, several friends and family members continued helping Lori and her family financially. They also contributed money to pay for an attorney to represent her at the upcoming parole board hearing.

Parole Hearing

CHAPTER 17

As it got closer to the time when a parole board hearing would be scheduled, the phone calls from Lori became more frequent and emotional. She was in a quandary about how to handle the hearing because of advice she received from many directions that she must confess to murder before parole would be approved. She was also confused about whether she needed to invest in an attorney to represent her at the hearing. I told her she should have an attorney guide her because of the issues involved with the Alford plea (maintaining her innocence) and the statistical likelihood that she would *not* be released since anyone serving a term of life for a violent "Class A Felony" almost never gets paroled, especially at the first parole hearing.

As the time for the hearing approached, Lori was filled with anguish and fear that she would spend the rest of life behind bars and told me she would rather be dead if that was the outcome of the parole hearing. She had reached the limit of her ability to cope with the hostile and unhealthy existence and was gravitating toward making up a story, so the commissioners would grant her parole. I told her that lying was not in her character, and it would boomerang and cause unexpected problems. Especially, if what was said did not totally comport with the record, and parole was not granted on the first try. I reminded her of a story about another hearing wherein the inmate made up a story, and at the next parole board hearing contradicted details of his first story. Being aware of his first statements the board denied parole for the second and third time. I warned

Lori that this could happen to her, and that the first parole hearing normally just lays the foundation for the next hearing, so it was extremely important not to mess it up.

During several frantic phone conversations, she informed me she was having full-blown anxiety attacks affecting her breathing, heart rate, and thinking and was in constant physical pain because she felt trapped. I felt inept with my responses, but I reminded her to simply trust God and He would protect her. I told her that church friends and family, in addition to Christians in several states, were praying that she would be paroled. But my words did not penetrate her weary mind and stormy soul. Perhaps, I needed to just listen, and my silence would be more eloquent and effective than my speech.

Lori and I made several attempts to contact her criminal attorney for advice but strangely he would not accept either of our many phone calls. Frustrated and perplexed, about six months prior to the expected hearing, she asked me to call Attorney Arial who for or a short time helped with her defense. She was widely known and respected for standing for inmates at parole board hearings with successful results. Attorney Arial said she would represent my daughter for $2800 and accept payment in three installments and instructed her assistant to accept collect calls from Lori. It was heartening to hear Attorney Arial say that Lori should have never been coerced into accepting a plea bargain that sent her to a maximum term of life in prison, and she would do her best to get her released. She agreed to supervise the whole process including preparing the *"Parole Package"* of information that is typically given to the commissioners several days prior to the hearing.

Finally, forty-five days prior to the set day the parole board website announced the date of the hearing as September 22, 2015 at 2:30 in the afternoon. With a firm date set, Attorney Arial visited Lori at the prison to discuss the issues involved and give advice. When Lori mentioned the possibility of concocting a confession in order to get paroled, the attorney said if she was going to do that she would *not* represent her, and her only choice was to trust her and to tell the truth.

Attorney Arial wanted as many supporters as possible attend the hearing and she asked us to collect letters addressed to the board recommending the granting of parole and a pledge to help Lori during her adjustment to life as a parolee. We were successful in collecting a couple dozen letters and sent them to the attorney for the commissioners to read. The letters, especially ones from her three children and husband, were heartfelt, emotional, and revealed how Lori's life and had affected and inspired them.

I concluded my letter with this statement:

> Since none of us can change yesterday, each of us only have today-this moment in the great expanse of eternity to do what is right, to act justly, to love mercy and to walk humbly before our God. For all these reasons and many more, I plead with you to show mercy and grace at a time when it is so desperately needed and deserved and grant her release on parole at this time. We will be eternally grateful.

Lori's long journey through this maze challenged Lori's natural "Type A" personality to always have the answer and her inclination to be the leader. Yet, Lori was encouraged by the strength and intelligence of Attorney Arial and allowed her to take the lead in directing the next course of events.

And on that basis, Attorney Arial put together a comprehensive "*Parole Package.*" It included a copy of dozens of certificates of self-improvement courses and educational classes that Lori earned while serving ten years behind bars, including her High School Diploma and a copy of her BBA degree, a copy of letters of support from her children, husband, family members and friends, and a plan addressing where she would be living with her goals and plans for future success as a parolee. Since only one person besides Lori and her attorney would be allowed to speak at the hearing, Lori's daughter volunteered to do so.

Several family members and I made plans to attend the hearing to show our undying love and support. My plans were suddenly interrupted two days before the scheduled hearing when doctors diagnosed that the fast-growing lesion on one of my legs was an aggressive form of cancer and needed to be removed at once before it spread. The day before the hearing, surgery was performed, and I was instructed to keep my leg elevated. Another hinderance to my attendance arose when forest fires swept across the hills, valleys, and roads, that same day blocking traffic into Reno. Once again, my plans were interrupted by forces beyond my control. Was God trying to tell me something?

Being very distressed by the circumstances, I did not sleep well and contemplated the unbelievable events of the prior nineteen years. I prayed for a successful hearing, that Lori would be calm and make proper statements, and a solution would enable me to attend the hearing. Very early the next morning I felt compelled to write a letter and fax it to the chairperson and members of the parole board, explaining the reason why I was not in attendance, and other things. For months, my heart had been burdened by knowledge that the board needed information brought to their attention that could make a huge difference in their decision, especially since Lori was not guilty of any criminal act. My letter faxed to the chairperson and board members early that morning, said in part:

> I do not want to leave this earth with regrets that I did not provide you with information that could have assisted you in making a just decision. Over the past nineteen years since this case began, I have become intimately familiar with the related facts. As a paralegal aiding with the civil case, I spent innumerable hours studying the various documents and transcripts of numerous hearings and trial testimony.
>
> Although I realize that the purpose of your hearing is not to retry the case, I feel it is important to provide you with several documents and pathology reports (see items 1 through 6 attached) that offer mitigating evidence of prior intracranial injuries contradicting claims of prosecutors and clarifying some of the circumstances involved.

I prayed that my letter and attachments of forensic material would be more impactful than my physical appearance since I would not be allowed to speak even if I was there.

At the scheduled day and time, all fifteen seats in the room were filled with friends and family members and more were standing in the hallway leading into the video-conferencing venue. Plus, a few others were allowed to sit with Lori at the prison during the hearing. There was a three-way video conferencing system connecting the venue to the parole board and the prison where Lori was waiting.

For unknown reasons, none of Angie's family or friends showed up for the hearing although they were notified of it. I believe that was an answer to prayer as it could have affected the outcome.

It was a hallowed and somber event molded by prayers and well wishes. The air was filled with electrified anticipation as the chairperson announced the hearing was in order and recognized the video appearances of Lori and Attorney Arial. She mentioned the fax received from me that morning and explained why I could not be there. After the board members asked Lori a few questions, her attorney reminded them that the purpose of the hearing was only to decide whether she would be a danger to the community and could transition successfully to being free and it was not about her guilt or innocence. Her attorney said that Lori had already paid that price and met all requirements for release on parole and emphasized Lori's completion of many self-improvement and academic courses, including earning her high-school diploma and a Bachelor of Science Degree in Business Administration.

Then Lori's daughter, Tanasha, gave a very heart-felt and inspiring speech describing how proud she was of her mother's character, and her desire to always model her mom's courage, strength, undying faith, and her habit of helping others less fortunate. She explained how she deeply missed her mom's nurturing and guidance through the years, except when visiting across a table and sharing a hug upon arrival and departure at the prison. Her mom's actions and life taught her that even when terrible things happen, to always be her best self, make the most of what God has given her, to work hard, and always do what was right. Tanasha declared that no matter what happens she would always be there for her mom and pleaded with them to send her mom home where she should be. Her well-spoken affectionate speech pierced every heart and tears flowed freely.

Next, the chairperson asked if Lori wanted to say something. She responded by saying that she had grieved for more than nineteen years over the death of Angie and regretted the heartache and suffering it brought to both families and wished it had not happened. She explained that little Angie was very special, so full of life and beautiful with big blue eyes and blond hair and knew she could have become even more special-like her own daughters were-if this horrible thing had not happened. Lori said that life is precious and priceless, and reminded the board that even a thousand years behind bars would not bring Angie back. She then asked to be released so she could go home with her husband and family. Her monologue and sincere demeanor silenced the room. When she finished speaking everyone wept with sadness and compassion.

Then the chairperson thanked everyone and announced the board's decision would be posted on their website in about six weeks and dismissed the hearing.

After the hearing, Lori called me to say all went well, she and others were very encouraged by the commissioners' kind attitude and felt there was a real chance of parole being granted, but that decision would need to be approved by the governor. She informed me that her attorney told her the former lead prosecutor (now-retired) on her case wrote a letter to the board recommending against parole. Strangely, the letter was signed by her and written on letterhead showing she was still a representative of the Washoe District Attorney's office. Knowing she had retired, Attorney Arial called the district attorney who said the letter was unauthorized and, conversely, he would have recommended that parole be granted and would correct the record.

Family members and friends commented about the overwhelming optimism they felt when the hearing was over and how the board members were not antagonistic nor accusatory toward Lori as expected. Having an excellent attorney there was a big step in the right direction, but there were many other things that made it a good event. Too many to count.

Home Coming
CHAPTER 18

Lori's husband and children were extremely anxious to find out if she would be coming home and called a designated person at the Nevada Department of Corrections often to ask about the board's decision, so they knew before the website posted the news that parole had been granted. We were thrilled and grateful to learn that prayers had been answered and she would be released in late November.

On the designated date, her family and I met at the facility to greet and hug Lori the moment she was released. Since it was early morning, we then met other family members at a local gourmet breakfast café where we enjoyed a delicious assortment of epicurean delights. Lori was amazed at how good the food tasted and could not stop talking about it.

The whole day was filled with lots of laughter, smiles and gratitude as she arrived home. Her family and I surprised her with a huge WELCOME HOME HERO poster and colorful balloons that decorated the small condo living room and we had bought fresh fruit and vegetables especially for her. Later in the day, a hair stylist she knew gave her a free haircut and style, and that evening her husband treated more than thirty friends and family members to dinner at a pizza parlor to celebrate her homecoming.

It was a busy joy filled day, God had answered our prayers in a variety of ways that culminated in a wonderful day of blessings. Although many people believe the devil is in the details, I realized that many times God works in the small details, instead of lightning bolts or burning bushes. He had shown us this by causing a variety of details, events, and people to work together to make Lori's parole possible.

Since she had spent the prior seven years looking at gray walls and floors, Lori was amazed at the beauty of trees, plants, flowers, blue skies, and mountains. Once she learned how to use the iPhone her daughter gave her, she would often send me pictures of what she saw in keeping with her natural love and interest in nature, especially plants and animals.

It is understandable that Lori responded to her new-found freedom with a phobia about being in confined and crowded places like stores, theatres, or any gatherings with lots of people. While shopping for groceries she would make a bee-line to the exact aisle holding the item she needed and leave as quickly as possible to avoid having a full-blown panic attack that she could not control. Leaving was the only solution.

For many months, she seemed to be suffering from a stress disorder because nightmares interrupted her sleep causing her to relive terrifying and traumatic events of the past. Additionally, she reacted strongly to stimulus such as loud noises, cruelty to animals or children, suffering of others, and any unfair or uncomfortable situations.

Since Lori's diet in prison had been very limited and consisted mostly of highly processed carbohydrates and very little fresh or cooked vegetables and fruit, her health had declined. She had continual swelling, stiffness, and pains in her joints and muscles. Once home, she had several physical exams with blood tests and x-rays. The doctor prescribed mega doses of Vitamin D because blood test showed none in her blood, and the deficiency would cause pain and weaken her immune system. He also found that Osteoarthritis had eroded the cartilage in her joints and ligaments, causing the stiffness, extensive swelling, and painful joints and muscles she was experiencing. He prescribed pain and anti-anxiety medication to help her adjust to her new life and react better to difficult circumstances and sleep better at night.

Despite her poor health, Lori worked diligently to put what she learned in prison and elsewhere to good use by restarting her landscaping business to support herself and supplement the family income.

Several months later, her female parole officer insisted she confirm the status of her efforts and income by bringing her business license, monthly bank statements, and profit and loss statements to her for review. When she asked me whether she should do that as it seemed "over the top," I replied that although it may not be a proper request, it seemed harmless and told her to black out the account numbers and give the documents to the parole officer to stay in their good graces. Besides, the terms of parole included "*Mandatory Supervision*" for the rest of her life and she would need to get prior authorization to visit anyone or any place outside of Nevada. This was a burdensome process but one that Lori did not complain about and much better than life behind bars.

As time passed, Lori became more settled into a normal routine; enjoying the beauty of nature, healthy food, and re-adjusting to living with her husband and three adult children, while taking care of the home and working diligently at her landscaping and lawn care business.

For years I prayed that the inexplicable events she suffered during the past twenty-years would not cause her to be mentally unbalanced, bitter and have a hard heart. It is clear that did not happen, but it would take time and effort, and relying on God to heal her body and purify her mind and spirit. In the interim, we allowed her the time and freedom to do so, while praying it would happen quickly. It is still a work in progress.

Life Lessons
CHAPTER 19

One of the most profound lessons I learned more deeply by this long treacherous journey was that each time I leaned on God and sought His presence, the Holy Spirit brought inexplicable peace, comfort, and strength to my soul. This happened consistently during the many unfair, fearful, unexplainable, and life-threatening battles we fought against the unpredictable and powerful state of Nevada and Lori's incarceration. Having the knowledge that He would never leave or forsake us, that all things works out for good to those who love Him, and that evil doers would be punished according to God's will and timing (either in this life or eternity) freed us from the natural human desire to be angry, seek revenge, and feel hopeless. Knowing that God is all-powerful, and a consuming fire lifted our spirits. Many scriptures I memorized when a young child came to my mind, including;

> Romans 12:19 (RCV):
> My friends, do not try to punish others when they wrong you, but wait for God to punish them with his anger. It is written: "I will punish those who do wrong; I will repay them," says the Lord.

During moments of reflection, I often thought of the prophet Job in the Bible and the mystery of why he was afflicted and suffered so badly. I realized that sometimes suffering is necessary to prove our true character and the true nature of our faith to ourselves and others. Other times it is to improve our character and spirit by developing humility, trust, patience, and perseverance, that we may become more like Christ while still in our imperfect human bodies. Frequently, we suffer because we act like children or sheep who have lost our way and are disciplined by our Heavenly Father to prevent us from suffering a greater harm. More often, I believe a combination of those dynamics is why we suffer because we all have short-comings, failures, weakness, biases, and hang-ups that need to be brought to our conscious mind and healed so we can live a more abundant and joyful life.

At various times, Lori (while in prison) and I (separately) were involved in and uplifted by the Celebrate Recovery ministry that modeled and encouraged praying the *"Serenity Prayer"* which says:

> *God, give me grace to accept with serenity*
> *the things that cannot be changed,*
> *courage to change the things which should be changed,*
> *and the wisdom to know the difference.*
> *Living one day at a time,*
> *Enjoying one moment at a time,*
> *Accepting hardship as a pathway to peace,*
> *Taking, as Jesus did, This sinful world as it is,*
> *Not as I would have it,...*

By Reinhold Niebuhr (1892-1971)

Each time we prayed this prayer, we were reminded that although we are justified (vindicated or pardoned) by faith in Christ when we accepted the gifts of eternal life and the Holy Spirit, our mortal lives are being sanctified (made holy) by how we live each day, the decisions we make, and how we respond to adversity. 1Thessalonians 4:3 (NIV) says, *"It is God's will that you should be sanctified..."* Surrendering to God's will in each situation is the key to being reasonably happy in this life and supremely happy with Him in the life to come.

In a very real way it was obvious that God was working according to His own time clock, when and where He chose. We live on Earth with designated finite time zones that set the times we should or should not do things as mentioned in Ecclesiastes 3:1 (NIV), which says: *"There is a time for everything, and a season for every activity under the heavens..."*

However, the master of the universe (galaxies and stars) would have a heavenly or universal eternal clock (if he has one) that does not measure time according to our earthly time zones. The apostle Peter explains it in 2 Peter 3:8 (NASV) by saying:

> But do not let this one fact escape your notice, beloved, that with the Lord one day is like a thousand years, and a thousand years like one day.

God's plan for each of us and His reasons will be revealed on His schedule, whether today, in a week, years down the road, or maybe not until we are in Heaven where He is preparing a place for us free from injustices, fear, and suffering.

In the interim, scripture also tells us to take care of and rule over the earth.

> Genesis 1:26 (RCV):
> Then God said, "Let us make human beings in our image and likeness. And let them rule over the fish in the sea and the birds in the sky, over the tame animals, over all the earth, and over all the small crawling animals on the earth."

Several scriptures challenge us to make the Earth a more loving and just place to live, such as;

> Micah 6:8 (NIV):
> He has shown you, O mortal, what is good.
> And what does the Lord require of you?
> To act justly and to love mercy and to walk humbly with your God.

> Also, Deuteronomy 16: 20 (NIV):
> Follow justice and justice alone, so that you may live and possess the land the Lord your God is giving you.

In keeping with those instructions, serious defects in our criminal justice systems need to be corrected to make it more efficient and just, while not violating constitutionally guaranteed and God given civil rights and freedoms.

The postscripts to this story names several issues and defects in the criminal justice system that must be addressed and rectified. There is also a summary of modern research that disputes the myths associated with SBS and SDF and the need for modernization of the forensic investigative procedures by the criminal justice system.

Criminal Justice Reforms
POSTSCRIPT 1

Fallen Baby, Fallen Justice serves to show that our criminal justice system is broken and plagued with many dangerous defects. These defects include relying on invalid, antiquated, or improper forensic science, using improper and obsolete investigative procedures and techniques, and the absence of laws that hold prosecutors and police officers and their departments personally responsible for distorting, withholding, or ignoring of evidence, as well as participating in other types of professional misconduct. Too often, these defects send innocent people to prison, allow criminals to go unpunished, devastate families and individuals, violate civil rights, and squander untold millions of private and tax payor dollars.

Many state and federal laws make it is almost impossible to punish government agencies or their employees, such as coroners, judges, police, and prosecutors accountable for misconduct, ignorance, gross professional negligence, or incompetence regardless of whether such conduct violates civil rights or causes extreme human suffering. Currently, these wrongdoers most often only receive a reprimand from their respective departments or their bar association which does not alleviate the damage done to defendants and their families.

New criminal statutes are needed in most states to offer more immediate relief to victims of prosecutorial misconduct and negligence that rips families apart, throws them into emotional and financial shambles and forces them to rely on public aid or on the generosity of charities and others to survive, often while the accused languishes in prison. Currently, those prosecutorial wrongdoings can be addressed during an expensive and time-consuming appeal for relief from a higher court which does nothing to compensate the defendant for losses. Moreover, the appeal can only be filed after all local trial court remedies have been exhausted and typically stretches over many years with more attorney fees and costs.

Neither legal experts nor legislatures have evaluated the following suggested reforms. Therefore, it is recognized that each suggestion needs to be evaluated thoroughly and structured in a manner that comports with the Bill of Rights, and proper federal and state laws.

Broken Moral Compasses

Many injustices have arisen because many criminal justice systems (police, prosecutors, defense attorneys, judges, jails, and prisons) work on the theory of *"Moral Relativism"* that teaches that reality, truth, right, and wrong are subjective and relative to, and/or decided, by their own goals, feelings, and thinking and that there is no absolute truth. Moral relativism has come into prominence in this country because of a lack of understanding of basic Judeo-Christian values and standards as outlined in the Ten Commandments, the guidelines upon which our criminal laws are based. These values and standards are given by God as a yardstick to measure right and wrong conduct and to act as a compass in guiding us to truth, justice, and a more abundant life. When obeyed, these commandments preserve life, liberty, justice, the pursuit of happiness, and property rights. Conversely, when disregarded, ethical dizziness, injustice, civil disorder, confusion, greed, and chaos becomes the norm in society and in our court rooms.

The problem of moral relativism is difficult to resolve, but it would help if police, prosecutors, and judges were trained and compelled by law to only rely on fact-based objective evidence before filing charges and prosecuting a suspect. New laws are needed to impose punitive damages for violating that principle.

Proposed Solution No. 1:

In cases where there is only circumstantial evidence, (no witnesses, objective facts, documents, or forensics) guilt must be proven after objectively evaluating all (and providing it to the defense) contradictory circumstances and evidence. If law enforcement personnel are found to be acting contrary to these requirements, (regardless of whether it is considered as prejudicial to the defendant) then either a dismissal, misstrial, or a reversal of a guilty verdict should be declared pursuant to a motion by the defendant and order of the court assessing punitive damages as mentioned below in the next paragraph.

Proposed Solution No. 2:

Prosecutors and police or their bosses sometimes withhold and ignore information that does not support their case or arguments. When this happens, they should be ordered to pay punitive damages, defendant's lost wages, attorney fees and costs when found by a court to have willfully or negligently ignored or withheld evidence, witnesses, or circumstance from the defense, *regardless of whether the withheld information is thought to prove or disprove guilt or innocence.*

The punitive damages should be imposed by a motion filed in the trial court by defense attorneys at any time after a guilty verdict or false confession is entered. *These remedies are extremely important because it is impossible to predict where the withheld information may lead defense investigators and where it may enhance their ability to discover more relevant or exculpatory evidence.*

Relying on Unqualified Experts and Faulty Forensic Science

In moments of crises, unqualified emergency room doctors habitually give diagnoses that police investigators and prosecutors rely upon as gospel to file criminal charges before proper forensic medical specialists have secured and evaluated all reported events and medical evidence. Moreover, most criminal investigators, prosecuting attorneys, coroners, and emergency room doctors do not have the medical training or the ability to sufficiently investigate and analyze complex medical issues. This is especially troublesome when knowledge of the latest discoveries and technologies are necessary for a proper defense and fair trial. This problem demands that drastic changes be made in how investigations are conducted. The following are suggestions that would help immensely.

Proposed Solution No. 1:

Laws should be changed to require that before criminal charges can be filed in cases where abuse or intentional injury is suspected where there is only circumstantial evidence, the diagnosis of emergency room doctors should be insufficient to file criminal charges. Based upon the emergency room doctors' opinions of abuse being the possible cause, a panel of at least three court approved board-certified medical specialists (germane to the victim's specific symptoms and physical injuries) should complete a thorough forensic examination. Each panel member would independently prepare a written medical diagnosis and then engage in a joint *"Discovery Conference"* to share their individual findings and then issue a majority consensus report of the cause of injuries or death. Only upon a majority vote of the panel could criminal charges be filed against an individual. In the interim proper protective custody arrangements must protect all victims.

The expense of conducting a forensic investigation at the beginning phase of the case is significantly less than spending millions of dollars on a lengthy trial, drawn out appeals, and incarcerating innocent individuals for decades or life. Also, the devastating emotional and financial damage done to an innocent person's family and children would be minimized.

Proposed Solution No. 2:

After the results of the forensic investigation outlined above have resulted in a majority opinion that there was child abuse and charges are filed, new statutes should stipulate that the case should be tried by a *"Complex Criminal/Medical Issues Court."* This special court would be staffed by at least three other board-certified medical specialists (consistent with the injuries) who would serve as judges to examine all the medical evidence and legal issues before reaching a unanimous verdict. A professional jury, such as this, would be more likely to discover the truth and make a just verdict. These new laws are necessary because most prosecutors, judges, and juries of our peers do not usually understand legalese, medical science, medical terminology, nor can they decipher medical expert witness testimony accurately.

[Note: The suggested *"Complex Criminal/Medical Issues Court"* could be structured in a similar manner as the California "Complex Civil Litigation Court" that handles cases involving complicated legal and evidentiary issues involved in antitrust claims, construction defects, securities claims, or investment losses, environmental, mass tort claims and class actions when only specialist take part in reaching a verdict.]

Withholding and Distorting Evidence

The withholding and distorting of evidence collected during an investigation by prosecutors from the defense is illegal but there are inadequate criminal and civil laws to impose punitive damages on government personal or their departments when it occurs. Prosecutors and police currently tend to reveal to the defense only evidence they think is relevant or they intend to use at trial rather than all the evidence collected during their investigation. Since it is almost impossible to hold them responsible for this misconduct, it continues to go unchecked and too often results in wrongful convictions and incarcerations at an enormous cost of human suffering and taxpayer dollars.

Currently, defense attorneys can make a motion requesting either a dismissal or mistrial on the premise that the misconduct was sufficiently prejudicial against a defendant to have made a difference in the jury verdict. But the motion may not be successful for various reasons, including the mood of the judge at the time and whether the judge thinks the withheld information is sufficiently prejudicial against the defendant to have made a difference in the outcome. If this defense motion is unsuccessful, then the defense can file an appeal or petition with a higher court requesting relief. Sadly, these remedies are very expensive and often take many years to process and complete. In the meantime, prosecutors and their departments have no fear of serious repercussions or monetary punitive damages levied against them for their unlawful acts which may include playing "hide-and-seek" with evidence, making false and unsupported allegations, violating civil rights, withholding, ignoring, or distorting evidence, and making false arrests.

Specifically, during trial closing (summarization of evidence presented) arguments, false and unsupported statements made to the judge and jury are especially egregious because the defendant no longer has an opportunity to defend against the new unfounded allegations. These statements by prosecutors violate the "due process" and "equal treatment" requirements of the Fifth and Fourteenth Amendment which demand that individuals are not subjected to the arbitrary exercise of governmental power. These actions also violate an individual's right to confront witnesses as guaranteed by the Sixth Amendment to the US Constitution.

Overzealous prosecutors ignore, or are unaware of, guidelines published by The American Bar Association about how to conduct closing arguments and currently there is no easy or practical way to ensure the guidelines are followed. The guidelines can be read at:

http://www.americanbar.org/groups/public_eduCTion/resources/law_related_eduCTion_network/how_Courts_work/closingarguments. html (Accessed 3/15/2016)

Proposed Solution No. 1:

Since it is impossible to predict what adverse consequences or affect any false and misleading statement, and/or the withholding or distorting of evidence may have in proving the innocence or guilt of a defendant, new laws are needed to prevent such behavior. Also, the ability of defense attorneys to adequately conduct their own comprehensive investigation is stifled by withheld or misleading information. Therefore, new laws are needed to demand that the court dismiss the charges or reverse a guilty verdict when it is found by the court that either of the above-mentioned prosecutorial misconduct has happened, *regardless of whether the offending actions are prejudicial against the defendant.*

Proposed Solution No. 2:

In addition to the above suggested dismissal, the offending police investigator, prosecutor or their department should be personally fined a mandatory minimum penalty of $10,000, plus attorney fees and costs, and lost wages be paid to the defendant. This fine would be subject to an evidentiary hearing following a motion in the criminal case filed by the defense at any time after discovering proof of prosecutor or police misconduct. Although these recommendations may seem extreme, it is time that the scales of justice become equally balanced.

Charging of More Serious Crimes Than Warranted

Many times, police and prosecutors knowingly charge a suspect with a more serious crime than the evidence supports or will distort or ignore circumstantial evidence not in their favor. Prosecutors use this as a "bait and switch" tactic to pressure an accused suspect to accept a *plea bargain* to a less serious offense. Alternatively, this technique is used by prosecutors in hopes that evidence will surface later to justify the more severe charge. This technique is especially successful when it is known that a defendant is of a lower educational, social, and/or economic status in life and cannot afford to pay for adequate legal representation. Consequentially, whether guilty or not, many such defendants plead guilty to a less serious offense rather than endure a more life-altering, lengthy, expensive, and humiliating trial.

Ironically, it is beyond dispute that this unsavory strategy by prosecutors leaves those who are guilty of violent crimes such as assault, battery, burglary, theft, rape, sexual assault, murder, and kidnapping to go unpunished and free to victimize other citizens.

Proposed Solution No. 1:

When this type of prosecutorial misconduct occurs, the accused defendant should be allowed to file a petition or a motion with the trial court, *at any time* after finding evidence of misconduct, asking that all charges be dismissed, and/or related arrest and guilty plea be invalidated and expunged (erased permanently) from the public record.

Proposed Solution No. 2:

In addition to the above possible dismissal, following a successful motion or petition by the defense at any time after discovery of misconduct, prosecutors and/or their department should reimburse the accused (or public defender's office) for all legal expenses, personal incidental monetary losses, and pay personal punitive damages of no less than $10,000, upon the successful granting of the petition or motion. If prosecutorial misconduct has led to imprisonment or jail time; the prosecutor (working for the state and county) should pay the accused added damages equivalent to lost income according to proof or no less than $200 per day (whichever is greater) for each day the defendant was illegally incarcerated.

These new statutes imposing penalties, damages, and restitution on public servants in criminal cases would be like current statutes in some states that makes it possible for restitution be paid when private citizens make a false police report that results in a search and rescue, swat team, or first responder efforts, or who files a frivolous lawsuit in a civil case.

CPS Laws Contribute to Neglect and Abuse of Children

Currently, mandatory reporting laws in many states unintentionally contribute to further child abuse, public hysteria, unrest, and insecurity because the reporting laws demand not only the reporting of incidents where there is actual evidence or witnessing of abuse, but also require the reporting of suspected past or future possible abuse or neglect based on a "reasonable" assumption of the party making the report to CPS. [Cite: Nevada Revised Statute 200.50925, et. seq.] Although the statutes try to define the word "reasonable," it is clear that what is "reasonable" to one person may not be to another, based on the same set of facts and circumstances. Too often these "reasonable assumptions" are based on personal biases, circumstances, motives, mental illness, or the intelligence of the reporting person. Further, sometimes during times of marital distress or divorce a disgruntled party complains to CPS to seek revenge or create an unfair advantage against an opposing party during a child custody family court hearing.

Presently, these "reasonable" reports to CPS stay on most state databases **permanently,** with no ability of the accused party to have the report and its index removed. Keeping unfounded and unsubstantiated records of reports to CPS for long periods of time is detrimental to the accused person and their children as it adversely affects their relationships, reputation, and ability to obtain certain types of employment. More importantly, the CPS record "poisons the well" of evidence during future investigations and litigations by creating an unfair cloud of guilt that deprives the individual of equal protection and due process rights that are guaranteed by the US Constitution.

Current statutes in many states place professionals, doctors, teachers, child care providers, counselors and therapists in a very vulnerable spot and motivates them, (even when unwarranted) to over report to protect themselves from being charged later with a misdemeanor if something should go wrong which would cause them to be subjected to disciplinary actions by state licensing boards, (Cite: NRS 432B.220) such as revocation of a professional license.

In addition to wasting public resources, harming innocent individuals, and causing unintentional neglect and abuse of children, current laws make it possible for mentally disturbed individuals, disgruntled divorcees, and others to misuse the system to seek revenge for any real or imagined wrong done to them based upon their own misguided "reasonable" assumptions. Consequently, thousands of families have been destroyed, children damaged, and freedoms lost because of those unsubstantiated "reasonable" reports that are permanently enshrined in CPS records.

Equally important is the fact that because of current reporting laws, CPS systems across the nature are overwhelmed with chasing down unfounded allegations when available resources should and could be more wisely spent in protecting children who really need help. This dichotomy is a waste of resources that results in many cases of extreme child abuse falling through the cracks causing children to be subjected to more abuse and sometimes death because they are without proper intervention and protection by CPS. Many of the above problems are supported by a report published online by Clark County Department of Family Services, Nevada. The 2014 Statistical Report says that Clark County CPS received a total of 38,728 phone reports, and of them 21,262 were referred and logged as reports of child abuse or neglect. After investigations, only 2,234 (10.5%) of them were substantiated.

In 2017, Clark County Family Services, received 29,717 referrals for child abuse investigations, 11,650 (39%) were investigated, and after investigations only 20% of them, or 2,392 (8%) of referrals were substantiated as child abuse. This means that the permanent CPS index added 27,325 people as potential child abusers in 2017 alone. These statistics are gleaned from public records published on line by the agency.

Obviously, needless time and money was spent taking reports and investigating allegations from disgruntled people who "reasonably" believe that (1) child abuse is likely to take place in the future, or (2) believe it has taken place in the past. Many times, these calls are made without valid evidence to support the allegations.

Proposed Solution No. 1:

Legislative reforms could eliminate more waste of CPS financial and personnel resources and focus more directly on protecting children who really have been abused, neglected, or are in imminent danger. To accomplish this goal, the mandatory reporting laws should be corrected to only compel reporting of child abuse or neglect when there is either (1) unexplained physical injuries on the child, (2) abuse or neglect was witnessed by the reporting party (not 2nd hand info), (3) admitted by someone, (4) claim of abuse by a child of at least five years old, or (5) where there is evidence that the child is in imminent and continuing danger of physical or emotional abuse and neglect, such as from homelessness, unsafe living conditions, mental illness, hunger, or uncontrollable fits of anger, drug or alcohol addiction or intoxication by a parent, custodian or caregiver.

Proposed Solution No. 2:

In circumstantial cases, the investigation and prosecution of allegations of physical or emotional abuse should be handled as suggested above in the section entitled *"Relying on Unqualified Doctors and Faulty Forensic Science"* that recommends better ways to investigate and prosecute child abuse and child murder cases.

Proposed Solution No. 3:

New state laws should be passed to require that all CPS data, records, and reports of suspected child abuse that are unsubstantiated be expunged (erased completely from the database) automatically at the end of twenty-four months after the report was made to CPS. This time limit could only be extended by (1) filing of a criminal charge during that time against the perpetrator, or (2) CPS obtaining an order from the court to extend the record keeping by CPS upon giving proof to the court of a compelling reason to keep the record active. Otherwise, all digital and paper records, and indices of unsubstantiated child abuse referrals should be removed in their entirety, since keeping them indefinitely violates the right to due process, to confront witnesses, and to equal legal treatment and protection as guaranteed by the US Constitution.

Civil Rights Violations

Violations of civil rights by police and prosecutors too often deprive citizens of their personal freedoms, and equal protections under the law that is due them. Further, all citizens deserve access to an unbiased law enforcement and a criminal justice system that actively and habitually recognizes those rights.

Unfortunately, violations of Lori's civil rights occurred many times during almost thirteen years that the state of Nevada spent millions of taxpayer dollars prosecuting her. There were specific violations of her rights to due process (fair trial, equal protection, the right to confront witnesses, and proof beyond a reasonable doubt) that are guaranteed by either the 5th, 6th, and 14th Amendments to the US Constitution. The local court refused to recognize these rights and apply them to the case, but her rights were ultimately confirmed by the Nevada Supreme Court's ruling after her first trial. But that did not stop the abusive behavior of prosecutors.

You may remember that during closing arguments Prosecutors Snuffelpaw and Bird brought up new unfounded allegations (not presented at trial) in the presence of jurors that procedurally precluded Lori's attorneys from disproving those allegations. The untimely allegations violated the 6th Amendment to the US Constitution (the right to confront witnesses) in addition to violating her right to due process, equal protection, and fair trial provisions of the 5th and 14th Amendment.

Further, in the first trial, the judge's decision (regarding opening the door) in response to the prosecution motions to allow them to introduce evidence of prior uncharged bad acts violated and/or infringed on her fundamental right to testify on her own behalf concerning the events of the day in question as guaranteed by the 5th, 6th, and 14th Amendments. This right has been confirmed many times by US Supreme Court rulings. Sadly, the judge ruled that if defense attorneys "opened the door" by bringing up or discussing Lori's good reputation or prior conduct, the state could also bring up the uncharged and unproven allegations of child abuse in front of the jury which she would also then must defend against. Therefore, his order prevented Lori from testifying concerning what happened on the day in question without the threat of immediate and severe adverse consequences. These adverse consequences could be interpreted as a violation of her civil rights.

Proposed Solution No. 1:

New state civil rights and criminal laws must be changed to impose severe monetary punitive damages against the offending party and/or department at the trial court level, and a dismissal of all criminal charges when the prosecution violates a civil right of a defendant. These damages should be assessed regardless of whether the related trial verdict or court decision favors a defendant. This change would help level the playing field between the all-powerful government law enforcement agencies and accused defendants. The proposed new laws would specify that a defense motion can be filed instantly by defense attorneys in the trial court, seeking punitive damages to be paid to the defendant from the budget of each offending agency, or each responsible individual(s), equivalent to three times the defendant's attorney fees, miscellaneous cost, and a minimum of $200 per day for lost wages. The award of punitive damages should be paid within sixty days of the trial or appellate court's decision regarding same. These damages would be available instead of any monetary compensation or reimbursements that may be available from a civil or criminal complaint filed with the Civil Rights Division of the US Justice Department, or any other government agency.

As it is now, civil right violations are more often understood and addressed by an appellate (upon appeal of a guilty verdict) or federal court, during which time most defendants languish for many years behind bars and their loved ones and families are physically, emotionally, and financially suffering.

Proposed Solution No. 2:

All criminal defense attorneys, prosecutors, police, and trial judges should be better educated about how to recognize and evaluate violations of civil rights. This problem could be addressed by the ABA and each state bar association by demanding the completion of at least sixteen hours of continuing education classes per reporting period addressing how to recognize and avoid violating civil rights of defendants.

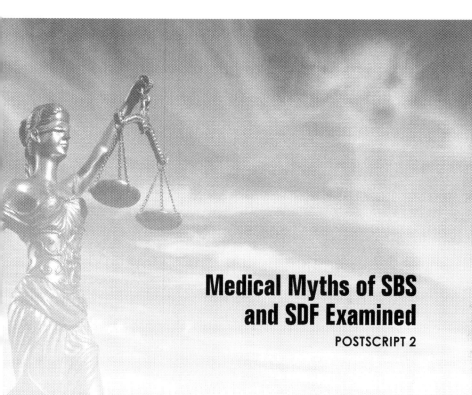

Medical Myths of SBS and SDF Examined

POSTSCRIPT 2

Modern medical and forensic research refutes or cast serious doubt on two theories that have been the cornerstone for prosecuting and convicting thousands of individuals for child abuse or murder by child abuse for more than forty years. The first theory is that a triad of symptoms, bleeding on the brain, swelling, and bleeding behind eyes are always irrefutable evidence of child abuse by Shaken Baby Syndrome (SBS) when there are no other physical symptoms, or readily available explanation for those injuries. The second theory is that a child's short distance fall of ten feet or less (SDF) can never be dangerous nor deadly to infants or young children. Both theories have repeatedly been relied upon by prosecutors and so-called child abuse experts to prove child abuse (by intentional abusive head trauma) and have contributed a conviction rate of 89% (higher than for any other crime) of those charged and tried for committing child abuse or child murder by abuse.

My research into the validity of those two theories began vigorously during the related civil case while helping my daughter defend herself while she was serving a life sentence for First Degree Murder by Child Abuse. It was necessary for me, as her mother and a paralegal, to take the lead in preparing and processing all the legal court papers and handling the discovery (investigative) phase of that litigation on her behalf. Thus, learning as much as possible about the legal and forensic issues involved became

LEE WALLACE

my passion. I resolved to find and accept the truth no matter where the facts took me.

During the criminal case trial, a dozen medical experts could not agree as to how, when, and where the child's intracranial injuries happened and whether they were intentionally inflicted. Several prosecution medical experts (but not all) claimed that the child's head injuries were exclusively and incontrovertibly "hallmarks of child abuse" and that all of them happened the same afternoon that doctors examined her in the emergency room. Medical experts for the prosecution testified that the child's head injuries were intentionally inflicted, but upon cross-examination they said the same injuries could have been inflicted by an accidental fall, but disagreed as to the necessary falling height, ranging from eight feet to falling off a two-story building or at least twenty feet.

Conversely, defense medical experts believed the reported short-distance fall of about four feet along with an unknown earlier traumatic event, shown by forensic tissue specimens, caused the skull fracture, head injuries and death. Three different pathological reports discussed during trial, showed there was healing of intracranial injuries sustained no less than twenty-four to forty-eight before the child was unintentionally re-injured by the reported short-distance fall and taken to the emergency room.

Ironically, during the discovery phase of the subject civil case, two other forensic pathologists who did not have a chance to testify in court confirmed there was evidence of several older injuries with indications of pathological anomalies that could have caused them. But those issues were not fully explored before Lori's business liability insurance carrier decided to settle the Rison civil case and pay an enormous sum of money to the deceased child's family. Since Lori was without financial resources to continue further litigation or conduct forensic investigation, she agreed to a global settlement between all individual parties to the two civil suits for negligence, et al., without admitting any wrong doing.

Even after the conclusion of both the criminal and civil litigations, my search for answers continued as I studied the grand jury transcript, autopsy report, witness statements, police reports, medical records, and reviewed several pediatric and forensic medical journals online, as well as consulting with various forensic and pediatric specialists. My online search found many recent scientific research efforts published in peer-reviewed medical journals as well as US Government statistics that illuminate the issues and theories of SBS, SDF, and physical anomalies and diseases that mimic abusive head trauma. The following is a summary of that research.

SBS and SDF History

During the 1990s, most of the peer-reviewed medical and forensic journals insisted that SDF (short distance falls) could not produce skull fractures or TBI (traumatic brain injuries) and, therefore should not be of urgent concern to parents, investigators or examining doctors; and that a CT scan was unnecessary. Those medical journals set the standards used by many emergency room doctors and prosecutors as the basis for deciding that non-accidental trauma (child abuse) had occurred. Consequently, many professionals and prosecutors ruled out the possibility that a short-distance fall, or some other accidental event, had caused a child's intracranial injuries and skull fractures in the absence of immediate tell-tail symptoms. In fact, many emergency room doctors, pediatricians, criminal justice professionals and others in their spheres of influence (hired medical experts) erroneously believed that a child could not suffer TBI unless falling from the height of a two-story building. [Strangely, this "two-story fall" theory originated during the World War II era when Hitler's anatomical research goons would drop cadaver skulls and live subjects from differing heights to figure out what the skull would look like after impact.]

During that same period, the Shaken Baby Syndrome (SBS) myth evolved which promoted the belief that the existence of a certain triad of physical injuries (bleeding in the retinas of the eyes, bleeding under the dura matter of the brain aka subdural hematoma, and brain tissue swelling) were always proof of SBS, even when there was no evidence of other physical injuries or abuse.

These two theories were relied upon by doctors and prosecutors to send untold number of innocent people to prison. However, over the past several decades, medical science and forensic technologies have advanced and expanded with lightning speed into previously unknown territories. As a result, pathologists, neuropathologists, hematopathologist, histologists, pediatric radiologists, biomechanical engineers, and other specialists have now provided clinical doctors, pediatricians, medical examiners, coroners, and parents with a better understanding of the complex dynamics of traumatic brain injuries, shaken baby syndrome, and short-distance falls.

More importantly, medical researchers have also discovered several previously unknown physical attributes, rare pathological conditions, and congenital anomalies with symptoms that mimic abusive head trauma and

SBS and have published their findings in many peer-reviewed medical journals and newspapers.

However, the courts and the entire justice system have been slow to acknowledge and accept the latest knowledge and research as valid and have continued prosecuting and convicting innocent caretakers based on unfounded medical theories, especially in circumstantial cases with no corroborating witness of an accidental fall or other readily available conflicting evidence.

SBS and SBS Theories Challenged by Specialists

Many US newspapers such as the *NY Times*, Chicago Tribune, *Washington Post*, and others, reported that challenges to these two medical urban legends (the SBS and SDF) have come from doctors and scientists worldwide, including forensic neuro-pathologists, neuro-ophthalmologists, radiologists, physicists, forensic pathologists, biomedical engineers, and neurosurgeons from the USA, Britain, Sweden, Hong Kong, and Argentina.

Recently, Northwestern University's Medill Justice Project in collaboration with the *Washington Post* completed the first known systematic analysis of child abuse and SBS criminal cases since 2001. The results were published in a comprehensive three part, multiple sectioned, Washington Post article written by Debbie Cenziper on March 20, 2015, entitled, *"A disputed diagnosis imprisons parents."* It can be found online at https://www.washingtonpost.com/graphics/investigations/shaken-baby-syndrome/ (Accessed 05/29/18). The researchers completed a comprehensive overview of both sides of the main issues and history of how the SBS theory came about as well as the stories of several innocent victims who were caught by it and other misconceptions that are now proven by science to be wrong. They discovered and analyzed nearly 2000 cases from 2001 to 2015 by searching newspaper articles and court records where caregivers were accused and convicted of abuse by SBS. The study was conducted over a one-year period and found that more than 10% of those cases in 47 states were either dismissed, dropped, or the defendants found not guilty, or convictions were overturned primarily because *of the latest scientific discoveries and medical science.* The researchers found that shaking *alone could not produce the triad of symptoms that were once considered the gold standard for diagnosing SBS,* and scientists have discovered many pathological conditions and/or genetic defects confirmed to cause those same injuries. It was notable that hundreds of the victims also suffered extensive bruises and broken bones with prosecutors alleging that along with shaking, the infants and children had also been slammed, thrown, or beaten. Others were without visible injuries, in which cases doctors and prosecutors focused only on the SBS triad of internal injuries without any other corroborating evidence of being slammed, thrown, or beaten.

The article reported that many indigent prisoners received help from lawyers affiliated with a variety of non-profit organization and received free legal services. Those non-profits included the Medill Justice Project, or another member of The Innocence Network, which is a worldwide network of sixty-eight independent organizations, consisting of fifty-six US based and twelve non-US based affiliates, who volunteer pro-bono to exonerate defendants who are wrongly convicted. The network's affiliates consist of volunteers, attorneys, and law school students who were working on at least a hundred SBS criminal cases in 2016.

Numerous courts in several countries on two continents have successfully challenged the shaken baby diagnosis. Last year the Supreme Court in Sweden ruled that scientific support for the diagnosis turned out to be uncertain; and in 2005, Britain's Court of Appeal found that the triad of head and eye injuries alone were not absolute proof of abuse based upon newly discovered scientific evidence.

There are hundreds of doctors who now dispute the theory that the three mentioned head injuries are caused by shaking. The Washington Post article only mentioned nine of the many prominent doctors who were once believers in the SBS theory but have recently changed their thinking based on recent scientific discoveries and medical knowledge.

Among the nine doctors mentioned was pediatric neurosurgeon, Dr. Norman Guthkelch, who originally played a key role in developing the SBS theory. Many years before, Dr. Guthkelch studied twenty-three cases and discovered that *five of them* had bleeding on the surface of the brain but no external signs of injury causing him to propose that shaking could have caused the bleeding. He made those statement when he was a young doctor after a social worker told him it was a common practice for parents in Britain to discipline their children by giving them a good shaking and he could think of no other thing that could have caused the three symptoms. His hypothesis was published in a two-page paper in the British Medical Journal in May 1971 and was then promoted by other doctors who coined the phrase of "shaken baby syndrome." Dr. Guthkelch proposed that shaking could tear the veins in the cranial cavity, triggering the triad of brain injuries. However, he has since then come to believe the science is faulty and there should be an independent review of cases where defendants were convicted because of an SBS diagnosis and believes innocent people should not be in prison. He believes the diagnosis has been overused and misapplied and innocent people are being falsely convicted. Since his retirement, he reviews circumstantial criminal cases where charges of SBS have been alleged and works to find the truth in each case.

In an attempt to settle the disputed theory of SBS, the US government got into the action in 2009 when the US National Institutes of Health funded a research study by using anesthetized baby pigs to figure out whether shaking can cause the severe brain and eye injuries linked to the diagnosis. After spending considerable time and money, government-sponsored testing was unable to show that violent shaking could produce the bleeding, swelling and eye hemorrhages attributed to the syndrome.

In addition to that government sponsored research, very comprehensive research was conducted by two doctors who reviewed original research papers (citing fifty-three of them) in the National Library of Medicine 1968 through 2010, involving case histories and statistics of short distance falls of young children of varying age groups who were admitted to hospital or received medical attention. The results of their research were published in a six-page article entitled, *"Fatal acute intracranial injury, subdural hematoma, and retinal hemorrhages caused by stairway fall"* in the *Journal of Forensic Science*, October 24, 2011, by researchers Patrick E. Lantz, M.D. and Daniel E. Couture, M.D. at the Department of Pathology and Department of Neurosurgery at Wake Forest University School of Medicine. It is published online at: https://onlinelibrary.wiley.com/doi/abs/10.1111/j.1556-4029.2011.01892.x (Accessed 05/29/18).

After reviewing the work and statistics of others, these doctors concluded that:

> These published reports of original data are discordant and controversial, making the correct classification of a young child's death following a reported short fall a diagnostic challenge. Most childhood stairway and low-level falls do not cause serious head injuries. Nevertheless, not all seemingly minor falls are minor.

This case report refutes a pervasive belief that childhood low-height falls are invariably trivial events and cannot cause subdural bleeding, fatal intracranial injuries, and extensive multilayered RHs (Retinal Hemorrhages). The harmful and potentially devastating consequences for a caregiver or family facing a false allegation of child abuse obligate physicians to thoroughly investigate and accurately classify pediatric accidental head injuries.

In summary, cumulative research shows that not all seemingly minor falls are truly minor and refutes a pervasive belief of many "hired guns" by prosecutors in criminal cases, that all low-height falls are always trivial events and cannot have deadly consequences.

On September 13, 2015, the *New York Times* published an article entitled *"Shaken baby syndrome; A diagnosis that divides the medical world."* The online version is at http://www.nytimes.com/2015/09/14/ us/shaken-baby-syndrome-a-diagnosis-that-divides-the-medical-world.html?ref=topics& r=0b This article also gave an account of the Northwestern University, Medill Project research and compiled an online video of several cases in their Retro section of many defendants who were wrongly incarcerated based on the disputed theory of SBS. It starts with the British nanny case, Louise Woodward and includes an interview with Dr. Barnes who testified against her. Since reviewing the science in depth, Dr. Barnes has regretted his testimony and has changed his thinking.

On December 1, 2011, the *ABA* (American Bar Association) *Journal* published a report addressed to its members that explored cases of several wrongful convictions in several countries that were overturned because of the latest medical discoveries and forensic science. It was written by Mark Hansen and entitled *"Unsettling Science: Experts are still debating whether shaken baby syndrome exists."* This and related online articles can be found at http://www.abajournal.com/search/results/ search&keywords=Unsettling+science/ (Accessed 7/1/2016) Although several cases are reported, the first case highlighted was the case of Audrey Edmunds whose conviction was overturned by the Wisconsin Appeals Court. This was the first case that an appeals court questioned the scientific basis for a shaken baby theory, ruling for the defendant. It was hoped that the Wisconsin ruling will lead to a systematic court review of the evidence in other shaken baby cases or even an independent examination of the underlying science by a neutral third party like the National Academy of

Sciences. Audrey was aided and represented by members of the Wisconsin Innocence Project in her search for justice.

This ABA article points out that several scientific studies have been conducted attempting to prove the theory, but none have been successful and says in part:

> A growing chorus of critics says the entire theory rests on uncertain scientific footings that continues to erode under the weight of scientific scrutiny raising the specter that hundreds if not thousands of innocent people-parents, grandparents, babysitters, nannies, or boyfriends have faced criminal charges and imprisoned in the past several decades for crimes they have not committed.

It is hoped that the criminal justice system and police investigators will become better informed about the precise forensic issues concerning SDF and SBS, and traumatic head injuries and their sequela. This will enable them to properly investigate a child's injuries before destroying the lives of innocent caregivers and parents.

Fragility of Infant Sculls Revealed

Professor of Bioengineering, Susan S. Margulies, PhD., and graduate student Kirk Thibault, PhD., conducted extensive research at the University of Pennsylvania, Bioengineering Department into the fragility of infant skulls. The eight-page technical paper of their research appeared in the Journal of Biomechanical Engineering in August 2000; 122(4); 364-371. The article entitled *"Infant Skull and Suture Properties: Measurements and Implications for Mechanisms of Pediatric Brain Injury,"* can be found at https://www.ncbi.nlm.nih.gov/pubmed/11036559 (Accessed 5/17/18). Their research revealed that an infant skull is only one-eighth as strong as an adult brain and can undergo six-fold larger deformations before fracturing, making blows to infant's malleable skulls far more likely to intrude into the cranial cavity and deform and distort the infant brain beneath. These researchers also found that:

> ... a child's skull is incompletely fused at birth and the sutures joining the bony skull plates have less than

half the strength of the bone, allowing the skull to deform and distort the infant brain beneath. The skull and sutures reach adult thickness and strength only during early adolescence.

Several other researchers have shown that although an actual skull fracture may not happen upon impact, the intrusion into the cranial cavity many times distorts the brain underneath causing TBI that may later become symptomatic and deadly, hours, days, weeks, or months later. This includes research conducted by Drs. David Greenes and Sara Schutzman, Pediatricians at Children's Hospital in Boston who collected and analyzed the medical records of 101 children under the age of two who were admitted to the hospital over a three-year period. The doctors reported that head trauma in children cause more than 500,000 emergency department visits, 95,000 hospital admissions, 7,000 deaths, and 29,000 permanent disabilities each year in the USA with hospital costs of more than $1 Billion.

Their nine-page report was published in the Annals of Emergency Medicine, 2001 (Volume 7, Issue 1, Pages 65-74) and can be found online at: https://www.sciencedirect.com/science/article/pii/S0196064401524282 (Accessed August 11, 2018). These researchers found that:

> The majority of patients have minor head trauma, and, although most of these injuries are insignificant, minor head trauma causes a large number of intracranial injuries. The largest *reduction in head trauma mortality rates results from preventing deterioration and secondary brain injury in patients with minor or moderate head injuries who initially appear to be at low risk.*

Among other things, the doctors further explained that (1) infant skulls, especially in the posterior regions, lack the thickness found in the skulls of older children and adults, and (2) knocks to the forehead pose less of a danger than an injury to the back of the head.

For several decades most of the data in medical research literature and government statistics about SDF, SBS, intracranial injuries, and skull fractures in children have not been age-specific enough to be clinically meaningful. That makes it more difficult, if not impossible, to predict the severity of head injuries from a specific fall because essential elements of age and fall dynamics have been unrecorded or uncollected. This has resulted in several conflicting and confusing opinions in peer-reviewed medical journals about the ramifications of SDF and SBS, especially concerning children younger than five.

Moreover, many recent medical journals have published results of research concerning various conditions that cause thin, weak, and brittle bones that can contribute to the severity of skull fractures and severe brain injuries that mimic SBS and abusive head trauma. Therefore, proper forensic investigative procedures by our criminal justice system (including police and coroner offices) must be implemented to determine more accurately what causes each specific head injury and prevent wrongful conviction of innocent caregivers.

Fall Dynamics Must Be Considered

Aside from pathological conditions, recent medical journals shed light on various dynamic elements to consider when evaluating a fall or allegations of child abuse. Notably, biomedical engineers have proven and documented that there are many elements besides the distance fallen which contribute to the nature and severity of skull fractures and head injuries. Those factors include the shock absorbency and shape of the landing surface, the brittleness or fragility and form of the falling object, the internal pressure under the skull, the speed of the fall (whether the falling object was propelled such as in a "slip and fall" accident), and the amount of air resistance which can also be caused by the shape of the falling object.

Numerous relevant peer-reviewed research articles support the fact that it is possible, although rare, for fatal injuries to be inflicted on infants and children who fall only a short-distance. The dangers increase when there is an underlying (many times undiagnosed) prior head injury, pathological disease, a genetic defect, neurological conditions, and if a child's head is the point of impact.

One peer-reviewed publication entitled, *"Fractures from Short Falls: Implications in Children Under Age 5"* can be found at: https://www.consultant360.com/articles/fractures-short-falls-implications-children-under-age-5 (Accessed May 15, 2018). The ten-page (with tables) research article was composed by Authors Linda S. Nield, MD, Melissa R. Larzo, MD, Deepak M Kamat, MD, Ph. D., and published in *Pediatric Consultants,* Vol.

5, May 1, 2006. After reviewing twenty-six research papers on the subject, among other findings, the doctors concluded:

> If the child's head is the first point of impact... a skull fracture may result. Although several cases of linear skull fractures following falls from short distances have been reported, it is highly unusual for a child to sustain a complex skull fracture in this manner.
>
> ...An accidental fall onto an object or against an edged surface from less than 5 feet can result in a depressed skull fracture in a young child. Unfortunately, every day falls .... have led to severe head injury--some accompanied by skull fractures-- that in some cases have proved fatal.

Another enlightening article disputing claims that a force equivalent to falling from a two-story building (or 15 to 20 feet) onto concrete must occur before catastrophic brain damage and skull fractures can result was published December 2013, Vol. 35, No. 4, in the *J. Indian Acad Forensic Med Journal*, at http://www.indianjournals.com/ijor. aspx?target=ijor:jiafm&volume=35&issue=4&article=001. (Accessed 5/17/18)

This study focused on a community where housing existed with flat rooftops that had no barriers to keep children from falling off them. The goal was to analyze the pattern of head injuries in victims aged 0-10 years and the pattern's correlation with different heights and their relationship, if any, to age and gender.

Most of the subjects were school-age children, not toddlers or infants. This study was done at JNMCH, AMU, Aligarh, India on 173 children who came to the hospital during a 12-month period (January 1, 2011, to December 31, 2011) who had fallen from heights ranging from 0-9 feet. Excluded from the study were those who died as a result of falling and that number was not given.

This research revealed that skull fractures sometimes happened from a fall of three to four feet in infants who have thinner and weaker skull bones and that the primary impact is usually the site of the most severe injury. If the head is the first body part to impact a hard surface, there is more likely to be a massive skull fracture, but the height of the fall alone does not determine the severity of the injuries. An accidental fall onto an object or against an edged surface from less than five feet can result in a depressed skull fracture. This report also showed that most minor head injuries will heal on their own without any complications. However, statistics also show that days, weeks or months later, others become symptomatic and can result in catastrophic CITBI (Clinically Important Traumatic Brain Injury) and even death. Those are more likely to happen if the child had prior bumps on the head or suffers from a pathological conditions or genetic disorders.

In the US medical community, the lack of detailed information of falls of young children, including complications arising after short-distance falls (SDF), has caused assumptions and conclusions that were based on faulty data. Few medical journals recognized the discrepancy between the number of real-life TBI in children (and their repercussions) and the statistics reported by one hundred emergency rooms that make reports to the US National Electronic Injury Surveillance System (NEISS).

Other medical journals also report that severe brain injuries to young children are caused by SDF, such as the following seven page article found online at http://europepmc.org/abstract/MED/6720110, published by Europe PubMed Central, by Weber W Festschrift fur Rechtsmedizin. *Journal of Legal Medicine, 1984, 92*(2):87-94]. (Accessed 05/17/18) According to the journal, falls from a standing position can cause skull fractures in infants without specific symptoms. The article states:

> ... Experimental test series concerned with the stumbling height (82 cm (3 ft.) in free fall) and three various types of floor-stone, carpet, and foam-backed linoleum-were carried out. In each case, skull fractures were seen. In three cases the fractures crossed the sutures. CONCLUSIONS: (1) Each fall of an infant from the height of a table may cause a skull fracture, which may lead to death; (2) when child mishandling is suspected, all circumstances must be taken into consideration

Numerous other publications over the past several decades have given specific accounts where short distance falls have resulted in complex skull fractures, brain injuries and death to infants and children under five years of age.

As previously mentioned, the medical experts hired to testify in the subject murder trial each had a different idea about what distance was necessary to cause the toddler's specific skull fractures and intracranial injuries. Their testimony ranged from defense experts who said that the short distance fall (from approximately four feet) could have caused life-threatening injuries (because of the prior injuries) to the state's experts giving conflicting opinions; one prosecution expert claimed that a ten-foot fall was necessary, while another claimed that a fall from a two-story building (15 to 25 feet) was needed. Both opinions were in direct conflict with the Washoe County Chief Medical Examiner who opined that a fall from a minimum of eight feet was needed to inflict the same skull fracture and brain injuries as the deceased toddler. Although the state's experts could not agree on the exact distance needed, they believed that an SDF could not be life threatening and therefore, the toddler's injuries were intentionally inflicted.

An unspoken message conveyed repeatedly in the subject criminal case (by prosecuting attorneys and the state's paid medical experts) was that intentional injuries are always more forceful and deadlier than accidental ones. That supposition is neither logical nor supported by scientific scrutiny and analysis. Accident reconstructionist have calculated that falling off a 3.3 feet high desk results in speed at impact of 10 m.p.h. Similarly, a 15-mph speed at impact is equivalent to falling 7.5 feet - off a step ladder. A 20-mph impact speed is equivalent to falling 13.4 feet from the roof of a one-story building. A 25-m.p.h. impact speed is equivalent to falling 20.5 feet -from the top of a two-story building. This is interesting because if prosecutors and their hired experts were correct, that means the 22-pound toddler (in the subject case) would have been shaken or slammed onto something at a speed of twenty-five m.p.h., by a non-athletic mother. This analysis poses the questions of whether the young mother was physically strong enough to swing her arm at that speed while holding the toddler, and if so, would there not have been other physical injuries on the child such as hand-prints and torn ligaments? The resulting injuries would depend upon not only the distance, but the hardness and shape on the landing surface and the part of the body struck first, among other things.

Short-Distance Falls More Dangerous Than Shaking

While medical researchers were challenging the diagnosis of SBS, biomechanical and biomedical engineers began asking whether accidental falls from sofas, beds, changing tables and playground equipment could trigger the same deadly injuries. Their research raised more questions about the science behind the theory of SBS and possible causes of TBI. As a result, The Washington Post commissioned its own SBS and short-distance falling tests late in 2014 at an engineering lab outside Detroit by consulting with Biomechanical Engineer Chris Van Ee, an accident reconstruction specialist who conducted the study. The engineer tested the science behind SBS by comparing the acceleration generated by shaking and falling a short distance. Crash-test dummies used in the experimentation showed that "short falls" produced far more acceleration to the head than shaking. In the tests, a 195-pound man vigorously shook a twenty-two-pound crash-test dummy and compared the results against falling from a couch. Astonishingly, the engineers found that shaking generated a peak between 6 to 8 Gs, compared to a peak of 112 Gs when there was a direct impact to the head during a fall resulted in force that was at least 14 times (112/8) greater than shaking could produce.

Through accident reconstruction, biomechanical modeling, cadaver studies and scaling from animals and adults, engineers have estimated that the threshold for serious injuries in babies is about 50 to 90 Gs. But since researchers cannot conduct test on live infants, the exact threshold still is unknown. Regardless, their calculations strongly disprove the belief by expert witnesses, some medical doctors, and prosecutors that a more significant force is experienced by shaking a baby than when one falls a short distance.

CDC, CPSC & NEISS Reports of Short Distance Falls

Additionally, I discovered several existing and readily available US government statistics reporting traumatic injuries and deaths to small children who suffered from short-distance falls when using various baby accessories or appliances. It is important to remember that specific details of each of the reported statistics, skull fractures and deaths mentioned here are not known, and this postscript is only a cursory overview and not a scientific analysis of all relevant details. To my knowledge, most of the statistical reports mentioned below have never been scientifically analyzed and beg for further biomedical and forensic study. Regardless, the following paragraphs are brief statistical summaries of many short-distance falls (less than ten feet) that have had catastrophic and deadly consequences.

Fatalities from Using Carriers, Car/Bumper Seats

In my quest for information about the consequences of short-distance falls, I ordered statistics from the CDC (Center for Disease Control and Prevention) concerning injuries to children caused by defective and recalled baby carriers. I received reports in 2001 that from 1998 to 2001 there were 830 reported injuries sustained by children by falling from their baby carriers and car seats. Of those, 103 of the children (or 12.4%) had skull fractures while the number of deaths is not reported in those statistics for unknown reasons. It is safe to assume that since the falls happened while using baby carriers, the children were under three years old, and the skull fractures were from a height of much less than four feet.

More to the point, the CDC and the US Consumer Product Safety Commission (CPSC) compiled and published a report entitled *"Deaths Associated with Infant Carriers-United States, 1986-1991,"* It is found at https://www.ncbi.nlm.nih.gov/pubmed/?term=Deaths+Associated+with+Infant+Carriers-United+States%2C+1986-1991 (Accessed 6/27/2017)

It warned the public and healthcare providers about injuries caused by using these appliances. Since we know that only a small number of all children's accidents, injuries and deaths were reported to the CPSC, the actual numbers were much higher. The report stated:

> In the United States, injuries are the leading cause of death and disability among children aged 1- 4 years and the sixth leading cause of death and disability among infants less than one year. Often such injuries and deaths are associated with the use of consumer products, including products designed for children less than one year (i.e., strollers, walkers, car seats, infant seats, and infant carriers). From January 1986 through October 1991, the CPSC received reports of 26 fatalities associated with infant carrier related injuries.

Additionally, the CPSC received reports of a minimum of 285 deaths for fiscal years 1992 through 1996 of children under five years of age, associated with the use of baby appliances and twenty-two (4.4%) of deaths were from using baby carriers or car seats (excluding auto-related accidents). According to government estimates, only 10% of incidents are routinely conveyed to them. Therefore, the total of deaths during that five-year period would be roughly (10x285) 2850, and of those, 4 to 5% (142.5) of those deaths resulted using car seats or baby carriers. These statistics collected by the US government resulted in the recall of various baby appliances and inspired new regulations that set guidelines for manufacturing of safer equipment and appliances for children, which has since reduced the number of injuries and deaths.

While details and distances of the reported falls, injuries and deaths may not have been scientifically evaluated, it is safe to assume that baby carriers, and car seats are customarily used within proximity (1 to 4 feet) to the floor or ground and would undoubtedly qualify as short-distance (under 10 feet) falls.

These and other related statistics about injuries and deaths associated with the use of baby products are found at https://www.cpsc.gov/Research--Statistics/Toys-and-Childrens-Products (Accessed 6/28/2017).

Shopping Cart Falls Can Be Deadly

Shopping carts have not been classified by the government as "*Children Products*" and not included in the above statistics. However, many mothers of small children are concerned about the danger of their children falling from grocery carts while shopping. In response to consumer interests, the CPSC compiled and published a report dated September 2013, entitled "*Shopping Cart Injuries to Children Younger than Five Years Old, 2008-2012.*" It is found online at: https (Accessed June 5, 2016). This report, compiled from data received from NEISS (National Electronic Injury Surveillance System), estimates the number of visits to emergency rooms involving grocery cart accidents averaged 21,600 per year between 2008 and 2012. The majority of those accidents (84%) were from children falling from grocery carts or a total of 18,144 each year. Internal head injuries were estimated to be 44% of all them with an average of 7983 per year. Skull fractures were not tallied separately but were included in the classification of internal head injuries.

Furthermore, the same article revealed that the CPSC staff received a report of 37 other accidents (from other sources) involving shopping carts and children younger than five years. That report showed that 5% of those children had internal head injuries, and 5% died because of falling from the grocery carts. These reported statistics were from other US government agencies, the Injury and Potential Injury Incident (IPII) database, the In-Depth Investigation (INDP) database, and the Death Certificate (DTHS) database. Hypothetically speaking, if this same 5% death rate is applied to the above mentioned NEISS report to CPSC (which estimates there is a yearly average of 7983 internal organ/head injuries), there would be at least 399 deaths each year (5% of 7,983) in the USA from shopping cart-related falls. For the sake of arguments, if we assume there is a 50% margin of error in those numbers, then there would still be approximately 200 children dying annually during those five years because of short-distance (3 to 5 feet) falls from grocery carts.

A critical CPSC Safety Alert published in 2010 warned the public about shopping cart dangers:

> Falls can be fatal. A 3-month-old infant died in 2011 after his car seat fell out of a shopping cart when the shopping cart rolled over a speed bump in a grocery store parking lot. In 1994, a 3-year-old boy died after he stood up in the cart and fell over backward and hit his head.

In 1996 it was widely reported that sixty-two children during a fifteen-month period (from March 1993 through May 1994) were treated in the emergency department of a large hospital after falling from grocery carts. Of the eleven who had x-rays taken, skull fractures were found in five of them (or 8% of the total sixty-two victims), and 79% of the children suffered head injuries of various kinds. Follow-up information about rate of death and permanent impairment of the victims was not shown.

That same year a study from Great Britain reported that ten children were seen at an emergency department after falling from grocery carts. All children had head injuries, 30% needed hospitalization, one died from the fall, and one died after being thrown to the ground when the shopping cart overturned. Although this is a small sample, the total death rate was 20%, (10% from SDF and 10% died after being thrown from the cart a short distance.)

Based on the above available statistics the rate of death from falling from grocery carts is between 5 to 10% and goes a long way toward disputing the two-story fall diagnosis. Obviously, an SDF can be dangerous and deadly as there are many instances where (with the right dynamics) they have caused complex skull fractures, intracranial injuries, and untimely deaths.

Unsafe Highchairs and Booster Seats

Over the past several decades, the US Consumer Product Safety Commission has recalled thousands of highchairs for not meeting safety standards and causing traumatic head injuries and deaths of children. Since highchair and booster seats are usually from 20 to 40 inches from the ground (many times with the child's head being the point of impact) a fall from one would be considered a dangerous short-distance fall.

To substantiate the possibility of closed head (no skull fracturing) injuries of children under three who fell short-distances (from sitting in chairs), please refer to government sponsored research entitled *"Pediatric injuries associated with high chairs and chairs in the United States, 2003-2010,"* Kurinsky RM, Rochette ELM, Smith GA. The Research Institute at Nationwide Children's Hospital, Columbus, Ohio, analyzed data from NEISS and published the results online at http://www.ncbi.nlm.nih.gov/pubmed/24322954 (Accessed 5/26/16). Their analysis found the following:

> Falling was the most common injury mechanism associated with high chairs (92.8%) and chairs (87.3%). Closed head injury was the most common diagnosis associated with high chairs (37.3%) and increased in number (P = .005) and rate (P = .006) from 2003 to 2010. Child caregivers should adequately engage high chair safety restraint systems and encourage proper behaviors by young children when using chairs.

Additionally, the US Consumer Product Safety Commission reported that short-distance falls have resulted in clinically significant brain injuries and skull fractures when children fell from raised baby seats which are typically designed to allow toddlers to sit at the dining table with adults and other children. One such product is Bumbo Baby Seats. At the time of their recall by the CPSC in 2007, they were only aware of twenty-eight babies falling while using the seat and three of them (11%) suffered skull fractures, while other intracranial injuries (whether diagnosed or not) were not reported separately.

By the time of the second recall of Bumbo baby seats, on August 15, 2012, there was reported to the CPSC a total of fifty injuries caused by using them on an elevated surface. Nineteen of them, (38%) suffered skull fractures from SDF when they maneuvered out of the seats. Although the actual height of each fall was not recorded, it is logical that they were from tabletops, countertops, or chairs. Again, the number of the reported accidents only are a small fraction of the total number of accidents and injuries sustained. Unfortunately, these statistics were not designed to reflect any lucid interval, later complications, or sequelae that sometimes occurs within days, weeks or months after the skull fractures first happened, nor the number of deaths that resulted.

Further forensic medical and scientific analysis of data relating to infant and children's short-distance falls needs to be conducted that focuses on children under three years of age, separated explicitly by age, and the relevant dynamics of each fall. This research is crucial because many children under three are unable to describe what happened, are uncoordinated, and top heavy with the head more likely being the point of impact. Furthermore, because the infant's or toddler's long-term memory and verbal abilities have not yet matured, the child often cannot verbalize the details of what happened during and after a traumatic event, nor the pain or discomfort experienced.

Playground Equipment Falls

In 2000, Pathologist Dr. John Plunkett completed research into injuries suffered from short-distance falls (under 10 feet) while using playground equipment. He analyzed the dynamics and consequences of eighteen fatal pediatric injuries sustained by children who had fallen a short distance while using playground equipment to see if the accidents were witnessed, or investigated, whether there were lucid intervals, skull fractures, traumatic brain injuries, and the specificity of retinal hemorrhages.

When his work was completed, his seventeen-page peer-reviewed research entitled *"Fatal pediatric head injuries caused by short-distance falls,"* was published in the American Journal of Forensic Medicine and Pathology, 2001 Mar;22(1):1-12. It can be found online at http://www.ncbi.nlm.nih.gov/pubmed/11444653. (Accessed 05/28/18) After exhaustive review and scientific analysis of hospital and emergency medical service records, law enforcement reports and coroner or medical examiner reports for all eighteen fatalities resulting from falls less than ten feet while using playground equipment, Dr. Plunkett reached the following conclusions:

Every fall is a complex event. There must be a biomechanical analysis for any incident in which the severity of the injury appears to be inconsistent with the history. The question is not "Can an infant or child be seriously injured or killed from a short-distance fall?" but rather "If a child falls (x) meters and strikes his or her head on a non-yielding surface, what will happen?"

Retinal hemorrhage may occur whenever intracranial pressure exceeds venous pressure or whenever there is venous obstruction. The characteristic of the bleeding cannot be used to determine the ultimate cause.

Axonal damage is unlikely to be the mechanism for lethal injury in a low-velocity impact such as from a fall.

Cerebrovascular thrombosis or dissection must be considered in any injury with delayed deterioration, and especially in one with a cerebral infarct or an unusual distribution for cerebral edema.

A fall from less than 3 meters (10 feet) in an infant or child may cause fatal head injury and may not result in immediately visible symptoms. The injury may be associated with bilateral retinal hemorrhage, and an associated subdural hematoma may extend into the interhemispheric fissure. A history by the caretaker that the child may have fallen cannot be dismissed.

Dr. Plunkett's historical research and peer-reviewed article became a poke in the eye of many doctors and prosecutors who had unthinkingly bought into the ideas that a short-distance fall (SDF) is never catastrophic, and that the specified triad of injuries are always attributable to shaken baby syndrome (SBS). For more than forty years, emergency room doctors, medical experts and prosecutors built their cases upon those two theories that became "medical urban legends." Those two medical urban legends were used in convicting many innocent caregivers in cases when they reported only minor accidents or SDFs but had no eye-witnesses or readily available supporting evidence available to confirm their account.

Beginning about 1990, more pediatricians, forensic pathologist, biomechanical and biomedical engineers, independently of each other, began investigating the theory and science of SBS and the false belief that SDF cannot cause intracranial injuries, skull fractures or death. Many peer-reviewed articles began to appear in various medical journals that seriously questioned or refuted those theories, some of which were referenced by Dr. Plunkett in his research article. Because of Dr. Plunkett's research and pathological expertise, he became an expert witness for the defense in many criminal cases involving child abuse and murder cases. Because his testimony helped win acquittals for many defendants, prosecutors and others took retaliatory actions to discredit him and prevent him from testifying as a criminal defense expert witness. The retaliatory measures included complaining to his medical licensing board and the filing of a criminal complaint against him by the disgruntled Deschutes County District Attorney in Oregon, alleging he lied about his opinions during his testimony in a criminal case involving "Shaken Baby Syndrome." After great expense and trouble, Dr. Plunkett was acquitted of those charges. This incident shows how strongly the criminal justice establishments object to being challenged and reveals their unwillingness to learn and accept the latest discoveries in forensic science.

Many other peer-reviewed research publications allude to the possibility of traumatic brain injuries (TBI) and skull fractures resulting from short-distance falls. One such article published online at http://www.ncbi.nlm.nih.gov/pubmed/20375838 (Accessed 05/28/18) was titled, "*The role of epidemiology in determining if a simple short fall can cause fatal head injury in an infant, a subject review and reflection.*" It was written by Johnathon P. Ehsani, MPH, Joseph E. Ibrahim, PhD, Lyndal Bugeja, BA(Hons), and Stephen Cordner, FRCPA. The nine-page research report was written from an epidemiological perspective and points out the complexity and difficulty of predicting the result of a short-distance fall based on statistics because the dynamics of each fall are complex and interdependent upon the unique elements of each fall. It was an extensive compilation and analysis of existing medical journal publications and statistics about SDF, and critique of Dr. Plunkett's research. It begins by saying:

> This article is a subject review summarizing and interpreting the existing knowledge on the question "Can a simple short fall cause fatal head injury in an infant?" It also reflects on the challenges of undertaking a review in the contentious area of pediatric forensic pathology. The authors found and considered 1055 publications for inclusion using explicit selection criteria, 27 publications were included in the subject review, the literature

suggests that it is rare but possible, for fatal head injury to occur from a simple short fall. Large population studies of childhood injuries show that severe head injury from a short fall is extremely rare.

Once again, the research did not consider the fact that pediatricians and parents during that period were advised against brain scans or further investigation when there were no immediate symptoms. This resulted in skewed data, since many such falls were not reported or examined. Regardless, the researchers arrived at similar conclusions as Dr. Plunkett by saying such severe head injuries are possible, although rare.

Pediatric Radiological Misdiagnosis

Another issue contributing to wrongful convictions is the frequent misdiagnosis of traumatic brain injuries, child abuse, and SBS caused by the lack of specialized radiological training and experience in performing and diagnosing CT brain scans of infants and children. Highly skilled pediatric radiologists and neuroradiologists indicate that less specialized radiologists unfamiliar with the ever-changing infant brain anatomy do not accurately recognize the natural cranial sutures (separation lines between skull plates), accessory sutures, wormian bones, and fontanels (soft tissue spots) that are normal and ever-changing in a growing child or infant. Unless trained in this specialty, radiologists do not recognize the need for further ultrasound or magnetic resonance scanning to diagnoses intracranial neurological conditions, diseases, or defects that mimic child abuse. These issues are addressed by Alok A. Bhatt, MD, Jon Hunsaker, MD, and Peter Kalina, MD, in an article entitled "Pearls and pitfalls of pediatric head trauma imaging," dated June 5, 2014, published online by Applied Radiology, Pediatric Community, at http://appliedradiology.com/articles/pearls-and-pitfalls-of-pediatric-head-trauma-imaging (Accessed 5/23/18). The lack of proper radiological training in infant brain anatomies has caused radiologists, expert witnesses, and prosecutors to exaggerate and/or misdiagnose the nature of skull fractures.

Also, a pediatric defense neurologist in the subject criminal case reported it is common for small children who suffer an SDF to have unnoticed hairline fractures along the suture lines when they are without complications or further traumatic events. Research shows that a small percentage of those same children sometimes, days, weeks or months later suffer significant intracranial injuries or growing fractures that become life-threatening and need emergency medical intervention.

Medical journals explain that in the US, even when children who suffered a short-distance fall were examined in an emergency room, often doctors did not order a CT scan because of concerns about radiation exposure on young brains. This recommendation was promoted by much peer-reviewed medical literature in the 1990s which instructed doctors that a CT scan of a child's head was necessary only if one or more of the following symptoms was visible:

- Loss of consciousness for more than a few minutes
- Vomiting, change in appetite, eating, or nursing habits
- Unusual crying and inability to be consoled, headache
- Irritability, unusual sensitivity to noise or light
- Change in ability to pay attention, bad moods
- Change in sleep habits, more than usual, or only lying on one side
- One or both eyes dilate or appear unequal in size
- Loss of interest in playing with favorite toys or activities

Consequently, it is safe to assume that in the past, most children in the US who accidentally suffered varying degrees of TBI from an SDF were not given a CT scan shortly after falling. Because of that prevailing advice more detailed statistics could not be collected. The missing or rare data includes the age of each child, total number of falls, the height of each fall, the nature of the surface fallen onto, prior health condition of the patient, number that resulted in skull fractures and/or TBI, the number of lucid intervals before becoming symptomatic or critically ill, and the number of deaths experienced.

Moreover, the above advice previously given to medical doctors and parents has been corrected based on recent discoveries. Online pediatric medical journals and the American Academy of Pediatrics have updated their instructions to doctors and parents to recommend performing a CT on a child who falls from a height of three (3) feet or more above the landing surface or ground. Additionally, the following dynamics are more likely to cause serious head injuries and when present the examining doctor should recommend a CT scan to rule out intracranial injuries and skull fractures and may need further medical intervention.

- A motor vehicle accident
- Falling from three or more feet off the ground
- Falling five or more stairs
- Falling off a bicycle without a helmet

Medical doctors are aware that continual advancements in medical imaging modalities, including Computed Tomography (CT) Technology, Magnetic Resonance Imaging (MRI), Positron Emission Tomography (PET), and PET-CT (combining PET and CT), and Ultrasound, enhance the ability to properly (at a higher resolution) and safely diagnose (using less radiation) and treat brain injuries and conditions that mimic abusive head trauma when done by qualified technicians and doctors.

Vaccine Complications Mimic SBS and Child Abuse

Measles, Mumps & Rubella (MMR) Vaccination Dangers: During the time the subject criminal and civil cases were being litigated, information was readily available from the Center for Disease Control, Merck, and Kaiser Permanente warning about dangers of MMR vaccinations. Their disclosures said a severe but rare reaction to immunizations might include one or more of the following symptoms; fever, permanent brain damage, coma, fainting, vomiting, brain swelling, and seizures. Any of those conditions alone could, if left untreated, lead to complications that could result in death or mental disability.

In 1997, and continuing to the present, the CDC and manufacturers recommended against getting the MMR shots if one has low blood platelet count, cancer, or any brain injury.

Further, the manufacturer Merck's disclosures specifically warned about preexisting cerebral injuries when it said:

> ...caution should be employed in administration of M-M-R II to persons with a history of cerebral injury, individual or family histories of convulsions, or any other condition in which stress due to fever should be avoided.

Also, the CDC publications warned about the dangers of receiving multiple immunizations at one time and that doing so has caused hydrocephalus, swelling, hemorrhage and sometimes that can result in brain damage and death.

Diphtheria, Pertussis, and Tetanus (DPT and DTaP) Dangers: The disclosures for these immunizations prepared for the consumer warns against giving them under certain circumstances. It says that rare but severe complications could occur, such as permanent seizures, coma, and permanent brain damage, although the dangers of death or permanent brain damage were minimal.

Astonishingly, the government reports that over half of more than $3,300,000,000 ($3.3 Billion) paid in damages to thousands of claimants, under the US National Childhood Vaccine Injury Act (funded by US Government instead of manufacturers) was because of the administration of DPT or DTaP. The claims involved brain inflammation and encephalopathy resulting in permanent brain damage and deaths caused by the immunizations. Although the number of deaths is not reported on the CDC website, more information and the updated amount of damages paid out for each vaccine is available on their website at https://vaers.hhs.gov/index. The government estimates that only about 1 in 100 doctors report adverse reactions caused by immunizations to the CDC. Therefore, the actual number and severity of adverse reactions and deaths are much more than the numbers recorded.

There are many accounts of criminal cases where defendants were accused of child abuse and/or child murder but later freed when it was decided that immunizations could have caused the deaths. A few of those cases and related issues are discussed in an article published by *Redbook Magazine* in September 2000, page 158, entitled, *"Was it murder, or a bad vaccine?"* written by Jan Goodwin. It is found at http://www.whale.to/m/sbs21.html (Accessed 5/23/18). The article also mentions several well-respected doctors who understand the nature of the injuries and symptoms associated with vaccinations that mimic child abuse, and/or SBS. One of those doctors declared:

> There is a sudden groundswell of these cases, agrees John Menkes, M.D., a pediatric neurologist at Cedars-Sinai Hospital in Los Angeles who is regarded by many as the 'father' of his specialty. Even when there are other, more likely medical explanations for a baby's injuries, Menkes says, prosecutors rush to judgment-and he is cynical about the reasons. Ambitious prosecutors get their names in the paper. It's a career boost for them.

One of many criminal cases that involved an infant's adverse reactions to immunizations was the Alan Yurko case. After his 10-week old son died, in 1999, he was prosecuted and found guilty under the SBS theory and sentenced to life in prison. Upon appeal, his case was overturned by a judge ruling that a botched autopsy had contributed to his conviction and that new evidence concerning vaccines called for a new trial. After that a plea deal was reached with prosecutors, when he pleaded no contest to manslaughter and was sentenced to time already served.

Valuable information and reference material about the consequences and symptoms of adverse reactions to immunizations (once attributed only to the triad of symptoms germane to SBS, and/or abusive head traumas) is contained in the STATEMENT OF AMICI CURIAE IN SUPPORT OF APPELLANT YURKO APPEAL AND STATEMENT OF AMICI CURIAE -VACCINE BRIEF, written by Joseph L. Hammons, Esq. and Ron Fujino, Esq., which resulted in the reversal of Yurko's conviction. The brief is found at HTTP:// www. aapsonline.org/judicial/yurko1.pdf (Accessed 5/23/18).

The brief filed with the court concluded with the following statement:

> While research on vaccines and allegations of non-accidental trauma to children is in its genesis, preliminary studies suggest that vaccines can produce conditions that worsen prior subdural hematomas and cause retinal hemorrhages. Research also shows that recently vaccinated children may be more vulnerable to injuries when falling a short distance or experiencing a minor accident. It is clear that some children should not be vaccinated. Children should be screened for contraindications before inoculations and children should be watched closely after shots. Finally, more research needs to be conducted on the cumulative effects of vaccines, their contents, and production processes.

Adverse reactions to vaccines have played a part in many criminal cases involving child deaths but have mostly been ignored and overlooked by medical examiners and expert witnesses. Conversely, statistics from the CDC report that over $3.7000,000,000 was paid to claimants in damages since the start of the National Vaccine Injury Compensation (NVIC) program began in 1988 until June 2, 2017. The latest data is published by the US government at: https://www.hrsa.gov/vaccinecompensation/data/ (Accessed 6/28/2017)

Logic tells us that if there were no basis for these claims, there would be no need for the program or payment of damages to the victims and their families. Eighty percent of those claims were paid after settlement negotiations in favor of the claimants.

Conditions That Mimic SBS and Child Abuse.

Many, if not most, medical examiners, police, prosecutors, and CPS investigators do not consider that there are pathologic conditions that can cause skull fractures and intracranial (brain) injuries that should be thoroughly explored and ruled out before concluding non-accidental injury occurred. Some of those conditions are listed in an article published by the University of British Columbia by researcher Teresa Liang, entitled *"Common pediatric bone diseases- approach to pathological fractures."* It can be found http://learn.pediatrics.ubc.ca/body-systems/musculoskeletal-system/common-pediatric-bone-diseases-approach-to-pathological-fractures/ (Accessed 05/24/18)
It reads in part:

> Background: It is common for children to present with fractures after experiencing trauma. However, children may also present with pathological fractures, which are fractures that occur in abnormal bones and typically occur during routine activity or after minor trauma. It is important to be able to distinguish between traumatic fractures and pathological fractures as the prognosis and treatment can vary quite considerably....
> Pathophysiology: Although there are many potential etiologies for weakened bone manifesting as pathological fractures, it is simple to divide it into three categories with common etiologies:
> * Metabolic bone disease - e.g., Rickets
> * Bone tumors – e.g., Benign tumors (non-ossifying fibroma and osteochondroma) and malignant tumors (osteosarcoma and Ewing's sarcoma)
> * Connective tissue bone diseases - e.g., Osteogenesis imperfect.

The research showed that tumors, regardless of whether they are benign or malignant, can cause pathological fractures by growing and replacing normal bone tissue. This results in an abnormal, weakened bone more prone to fractures.

Several medical publications and pediatric journals reveal many other conditions and events that cause intracranial injuries (mimicking child abuse and SBS) that can eventually lead to skull fractures and death, such as:

- Injury at birth
- Vaccine reactions (MMR, DPT, DTaP, HIB)
- Vitamin and mineral deficiencies
- Genetic cranial defects, enlarged or enlarging head - macrocephaly.
- Congenital vascular defects – such as Arteriovenous Malformations etc.
- Blood or bleeding disorders
- High bilirubin levels
- Short-distance falls
- Growing skull fractures
- Brain or bone tumors and/or malignancies
- Infections
- Poisons
- Brittle bone diseases, i.e., Osteogenesis Imperfecta
- Autoimmune conditions
- Metabolic disorders – of various kinds

As previously mentioned, many medical specialists have uncovered alternative explanations for the triad of injuries that were once attributed exclusively to SBS and intentional abuse by the caregiver. Several of those examples are reported in an article entitled, *"The significance of macrocephaly or enlarging head circumference in infants with the triad: Further evidence of mimics of shaken baby syndrome,"* written by researchers David Miller, Patrick Barnes, Marvin E. Miller, Medical Examiners, published June 2015 by Wright State University, Pediatric Faculty Publications, online at: http://corescholar.libraries.wright.edu/pediatrics/1. (Accessed 05/24/18). It discusses six (6) cases where child abuse charges were filed against caregivers, but after careful forensic examination of the evidence by specialists, various pathological conditions were diagnosed as the culprits. Researchers reported the following:

Infants with the triad (neurologic dysfunction, subdural hematoma [SDH], and retinal hemorrhage) are often diagnosed as victims of shaken baby syndrome. Medical conditions/predisposing factors to developing the triad are often dismissed: short falls, birth-related SDH that enlarges, macrocephaly, sinus/cortical vein thrombosis, and others. Six infants with the triad are described in which child abuse was diagnosed, but parents denied wrongdoing. All 6 had either macrocephaly or enlarging head circumference, which suggested medical explanations. Three infants incurred short falls, 1 had a difficult delivery in which there was likely a rebleed of a birth-related SDH, 1 had a spontaneous SDH associated with increased extra-axial fluid spaces, and 1 had a sinus thrombosis. Following legal proceedings, all 6 infants were returned to their parents, and there has been no child maltreatment in follow-up, suggesting child abuse never happened. The results show that alternative medical explanations for causing the triad should be considered and that macrocephaly or an enlarging head circumference raises the possibility of a medical explanation.

Mimics of (SBS) Shaken Baby Syndrome and (AHT) Abusive Head Trauma: The alternative medical explanations of the 6 infants include the following;

3 infants with short fall(s) associated with macrocephaly, 1 infant with spontaneous (SDH) subdural hematoma, and IEAFS (increased extra-axial fluid spaces), 1 infant with a birth-related SDH that enlarged, and 1 infant with a transverse sinus thrombosis.

Researchers at the same university composed an *"Open Letter on Shaken Baby Syndrome and Courts; a Flawed and False Premise"* which was authored by thirty-seven medical professionals. (Cite: Wrenna ll, L. Bache, B. Pragnell, C. et al 2015 *Open Letter on Shaken Baby Syndrome and Courts: A False and Flawed Premise, Argument & Critique,* Received Jan. Published Feb. http://www.argumentcritique.com/special-edition .htm) Accessed 05/24/18.

The open letter addresses the flawed expert witness system, and states in part:

> Parents and caregivers in many countries have been falsely accused of injuring or killing a child and face allegations of child abuse, manslaughter, or murder. SBS and its variants have been conceptualized in several ways. Generally speaking, the ' Triad ' of symptoms involves retinal hemorrhages, subdural hemorrhages and ischemic encephalopathy being interpreted as signs of child abuse. Many such accused parents and caregivers are given long prison sentences and their children are permanently removed from their families. In some jurisdictions, they can even be sentenced to death.
>
> ...It can be shown in many such instances that the evidence of the prosecution experts alleging death or serious injury from SBS is demonstrably flawed. The scientific basis for the assertion that these injuries are the consequence of deliberately inflicted violent shaking is highly contentious. Biomechanical evidence has shown that shaking without contact would only produce the triad of injuries in association with other injuries to the neck and spinal column that are typically not found in alleged SBS cases. Over the past decade it has been found that many of the accused parents /caregivers do not fit the conventional profile of those who commit child abuse and the pattern of injuries has been found to result from alternative etiologies than shaking.

Many times, prosecutors are too quick to file criminal charges before completing a thorough forensic investigation. They prematurely rush to avenge the death of an infant or small child in response to the victim's family, public outrage, and media hysteria before exploring other possibilities. Once an arrest appeases the fire of societal revenge, any possible precipitating medical conditions are overlooked or deliberately ignored by police investigators, coroners, medical examiners, and expert witnesses. This dichotomy is especially common in circumstantial cases where the accused does not have the financial or political clout to demand a thorough forensic investigation.

Statistics show that once criminal charges are filed with the courts before a thorough forensic examination of all the evidence is conducted, the conviction and imprisonment of innocent individuals is most often the result, as research shows that about 90% of child abuse and/or child murder cases end with a guilty verdict. These needless convictions are an enormous unwarranted depletion of millions of dollars from private and public resources and deprive citizens of their life, liberty, and pursuit of happiness. This prevailing phenomenon has fostered discontent and mistrust of police and our criminal justice systems.

Wrongful Convictions Demand Reforms

The rapid increase in scientific research and medical knowledge and easy access to that information by the public, medical, and legal professionals is creating a revolution in the manner that serious crimes are investigated and prosecuted. As a result, several non-profits, such as the Innocence Project, the Innocence Network, and others, working in conjunction with many law schools across the country are pushing for criminal justice reforms and implementation of federal standards in forensic investigative standards and laboratories. Those organizations have also helped set up *"Conviction Integrity Units"* (CIU) in twenty-four prosecutorial offices (in eleven different states) across the country to prevent, find, and correct false convictions. In addition to other exonerations, these CIUs have resulted in 151 exonerations from 2003 through 2015. Numerous non-profit organizations are overwhelmed with requests from prisoners asking for help in proving their innocence.

Many of convictions have been overturned because they were based on unproven or improper forensic science and investigative techniques, in addition to various forms of misconduct or mistakes by law enforcement and prosecuting officials that often also included one or more of the following:

- Employing suggestion when conducting identification procedures
- Coercing false confessions
- Lying or intentionally misleading jurors about their observations
- Not turning over exculpatory evidence to prosecutors
- Giving incentives to secure unreliable evidence from informants
- Withholding exculpatory evidence from defense

LEE WALLACE

- Deliberately mishandling, mistreating, or destroying evidence
- Allowing witnesses who they know or should know are not truthful to testify
- Pressuring defense witnesses not to testify
- Relying on fraudulent forensic experts
- Making misleading arguments that overstate the probative value of testimony

Other valuable and insightful information can be found at http://www.innocenceproject.org/causes/government-misconduct/ (Accessed 6/2/16)

Also, the Northern California Innocence Project mentioned different specific reasons contributing to wrongful convictions on their webpage at http://law.scu.edu/ncip/why-we-act/ (Accessed 6/2/16), such as eyewitness error, false confessions, faulty forensic science, ineffective assistance of counsel, informants, and official misconduct.

In June 2005, the Social Science Research Network (SSRN) published a thirty-two-page research paper authored by Peter A. Joy, called "*The Relationship between Prosecutorial Misconduct and Wrongful Convictions: Shaping Remedies for a Broken System*," (Wisconsin Law Review, Vol. 2006, p. 399, 2006; Washington U. School of Law Working Paper No. 06-11-05.) Available at SSRN: https://ssrn.com/abstract=948307) (Accessed 5/24/18)

After reviewing thousands of court rulings, the researchers found:

> Prosecutorial misconduct is one of the leading causes, or contributing causes, of wrongful convictions. This paper contends that prosecutorial misconduct is not chiefly the result of isolated instances of unprincipled choices or the failure of character on the part of some prosecutors. Rather, prosecutorial misconduct is largely the result of three **institutional conditions: vague ethics rules that provide ambiguous guidance to prosecutors, vast discretionary authority with little or no transparency; and inadequate remedies for prosecutor misconduct**. These three conditions create perverse incentives for prosecutors to engage in, rather than refrain from, prosecutorial misconduct.

Other statistics showing the wide-spread problem of prosecutorial misconduct and wrongful convictions were posted in a recent video on YouTube by The Innocence Project (only one of many non-profits working on exonerations). The Innocence Project received over 51,000 letters from 1993 through 2015 from individuals asking for help in getting their convictions overturned. (Go to: https://www.youtube.com/watch?v=t4LIxQIP_IY) (Accessed 05/24/18). However, because of the lack of funding and personnel, only a small fraction of the requests is accepted for review by their attorneys. Regardless, The Innocence Project alone has facilitated the reversal of more than 356 convictions as of May 2018, in the United States.

For the first time in history, a National Registry of Exonerations was launched in 2012 as a joint effort of the University of Michigan Law School and the Northwestern University School of Law to keep track of exonerations and related causes of false convictions. They have documented more than 1810 exonerations dating back to convictions as early as 1989. Currently, an average of three exonerations are added each week to their database, and the frequency is steadily increasing. They found that a record 58 CIU (Conviction Integrity Units) exonerations took place in 2015. Overall, CIUs have helped secure 151 exonerations from 2003 through 2015, but the number of CIUs and exonerations has accelerated in the past few years. Three-quarters of all CIU exonerations occurred in 2014 and 2015. Their newsletter can be found at https://www.law.umich.edu/special/exoneration/Documents/2.2016_Newsletter_Art2.pdf (Accessed 6/2/16).

What Can We Do Now?

Although many of the issues mentioned above are specific to our family's struggles, they also apply to many other US citizens who are caught, (or in the future may be caught) in a maze of the criminal justice system with no way to escape. Without question, thousands of innocent people have been wrongly charged, convicted, and sentenced to long prison terms.

At the very least, the information and statistics referenced above should compel emergency room doctors, investigators, medical examiners, and prosecutors to not be so quick to conclude that the only possible explanation for a child's mysterious skull fracture and intracranial brain injury is child abuse. In the interest of justice, why not investigate whether a short-distance fall, a pathological condition, genetic defect, or prior injury may have been a primary precipitating event to cause a child's injuries or death? The cost of first conducting a forensic investigation is significantly less than the cost of prosecuting, lengthy appeals, and incarcerating an innocent person for a felony for many years, or life in prison.

Fortunately, a newly formed coalition is at work across the country to promote and support efforts for the creation of federal forensic standards that will address major deficiencies in the criminal justice forensic arena. The Innocence Project convened the *Just Science Coalition* to launch the *Campaign for Forensic Standards* and the formation of a national outreach network of state leaders who are promoting the adoption of federal forensic standards to prevent wrongful convictions and help apprehend the true perpetrators of crime.

The Innocence Project alone recently reported that invalidated or improper forensic science played a role in the wrongful conviction in more than half of 244 wrongful convictions overturned as a result of modern DNA testing. These cases involve a wide range of issues from blatant prosecutorial misconduct to reliance on practices that have not been confirmed through empirical study. Information about this was published October 10, 2014 in an article entitled *"The Need for Forensic Reform"* at: https://www.innocenceproject.org/the-need-for-forensic-reform/ (Accessed April 2018).

Sadly, many government officials, public servants, and legislators need to be reminded that the purpose and primary goal of our legal systems and government agencies must be to protect and serve within the framework of the US Constitution.

Until our broken criminal justice system is transformed to assure that the guilty are convicted and the innocent are fully protected, individual freedoms are at risk and you or someone you know could be unjustly arrested and convicted. Therefore, it is hoped this writing compels you to support state and federal legislation that will make the justice system more efficient and just for the benefit of rich and poor alike, regardless of race, color, or creed.

The following Biblical passages are challenges to each of us:

> Leviticus 19:15 (NASB)
> You shall do no injustice in judgment;
> you shall not be partial to the poor nor defer to the great,
> but you are to judge your neighbor fairly.

FALLEN JUSTICE

Micah 6:8 (NCV)
The Lord has told you, human, what is good;
he has told you what he wants from you:
to do what is right to other people,
love being kind to others,
and live humbly, obeying your God.

Desmond Tutu said, *"If you are neutral in situations of injustice, you have chosen the side of the oppressor."*

About the Author

Author, **Lee Wallace, was born at the dawn of the atomic age in** 1942 near Oak Ridge, Tennessee, one of thirteen children. She professed faith in Christ and was baptized as a seven-year old. Today, Lee is a mother, grandmother, and a great-grandmother. She lives in Riverside County, California and attends church in the area.

Lee has more than twenty-five years of experience writing as a paralegal. Lee's goal in writing this fictionalized account of her real-life experiences is to inspire, educate, and encourage those facing similar circumstances. For privacy reasons, the identities of all individuals, professionals, public and private entities, dates, and places have been changed.

Co-author/editor, Dr. Pam Pryfogle, EdD, is an Early Childhood and Education Professor at California Baptist University, Riverside, California, and an experienced editor. Pam served in the region of Lira, Uganda as a Purpose Driven Practitioner and PEACE Ambassador through Saddleback Church of Lake Forest, California. Pam has most recently traveled with her filmmaker son to Northern Uganda to work with village wives. She also facilitates two support groups and provides counseling to individuals seeking purpose and direction through the crises in their lives.

Pam is an author and researcher. As an Early Childhood Content Expert, Pam journals her life's experiences and incorporates her writing in her blog https://travelinggrace.wordpress.com/. Her most recent published work is Adversity Influencing Regard for Education in Northern Uganda: A Phenomenological Study of Langi Mothers' Value of Learning.

Pam lives in St. Maries, Idaho. She is a Court Appointed Special Advocate (CASA) working with children taken by the court from their homes and placed in Foster Care. Pam is blessed to be the mother of five and the grandmother of nine. Care of her three youngest grandchildren occupies much of her time.

Printed in the United States
By Bookmasters